P9-DYZ-335

JAPANESE FOR BUSY PEOPLE

I

JAPANESE FOR BUSY PEOPLE

Revised Edition

BUSY

PEOPLE

Association for Japanese-Language Teaching

KODANSHA INTERNATIONAL
Tokyo • New York • London

Publication of this textbook has been assisted by a grant from the Japan Foundation.

Distributed in the United States by Kodansha America, Inc., 114 Fifth Avenue, New York, N.Y. 10011, and in the United Kingdom and continental Europe by Kodansha Europe Ltd., 95 Aldwych, London WC2B 4JF.

Published by Kodansha International Ltd., 17-14 Otowa 1-chome, Bunkyo-ku, Tokyo 112, and Kodansha America, Inc. Copyright © 1994 by the Association for Japanese-Language Teaching. All rights reserved. Printed in Japan.
ISBN 4-7700-1882-7

First edition, 1984
Revised edition, 1994
94 95 96 10 9 8 7 6 5 4 3 2

CONTENTS

change the order for the syllabus

Appendices

PREFACE TO THE REVISED EDITION

When *Japanese for Busy People I* was first published in 1984, followed by *Japanese for Busy People II* in 1990, we little expected the overwhelming success that these books have enjoyed, not only within Japan but among students and teachers the world over. In preparing this revised edition, we have taken into account the responses and comments of both students and teachers who have used the course.

The revisions to Book I are minor in nature, and mainly consist of small amendments to make the grammatical explanations easier to understand, to add further explanations of points that we discovered students had difficulty with, and to increase the naturalness of practice sentences and dialogues. In addition, some new appendices have been included, listing particles, interrogatives, sentence patterns, and the *kanji* introduced in the volume.

More fundamental revisions have been made to Book II, which has been expanded and divided into two volumes, Book II and Book III. This has allowed a larger typeface to be used throughout, making it easier to read. Various other changes have been made in order to make the transition from Book I to Book II smoother, to render the introduction of new grammatical elements clearer, and to present more natural practice dialogues and sentences.

Association for Japanese-Language Teaching (AJALT)

INTRODUCTION

Japanese for Busy People is for people who want to learn essential Japanese as quickly and as effectively as possible.

Preparation of this textbook is based on more than twenty years' experience of AJALT's specially trained staff in teaching beginning through advanced Japanese to students from approximately forty countries. Prior to publication, the material was reviewed and tested in the classroom with about 200 students, and revisions were made as necessary.

This course might be described as "survival Japanese," for the language learned can be put to immediate use in conversational situations. The simplistic or childish ways of expression found in most beginning texts do not occur. While vocabulary and grammar patterns have been limited to about one-third of those in the ordinary beginning text, the selection has been made after a careful study of the situations in which foreigners may have to speak Japanese. The objective is to enable the student to obtain the information he needs and to communicate what he or she wants to say in uncomplicated but *adult* language. The stress is not simply on grammatical accuracy. Careful consideration has been given to the actual linguistic patterns in Japanese communication.

To make the course effective, concise reference is made in the Notes to the linguistic customs underlying these communication patterns. The Grammar sections explain the structure and grammatical principles of Japanese whenever it is thought that such explanations would be helpful in understanding and applying the conversational patterns presented. Grammar and vocabulary are made available to the student as necessary, but he is not overburdened by having to learn excessive amounts of either for some undefined future contingency.

Although this is an introductory text, it does provide a solid foundation for the study of Japanese at a higher level. Every student should be able to obtain a good grasp of just what *kind of language* Japanese is while learning the basic conversational patterns. Because of this, it should be of value not only to people who are approaching Japanese for the first time but also a good review for people who already know a little Japanese but wish to confirm whether they are using the phrases they know in the right situations.

The amount of time needed to complete this course will naturally vary, depending on the individual. In AJALT classes, which meet for two and a half hours a day, five days a week, the course takes four weeks, or a total of about fifty hours. In addition, two to three hours a day are needed for preparation and review.

Arrangement of the Book

Basic guides to writing, pronunciation and grammar are presented in the immediately following sections, after which come Useful Daily Expressions and Signs in

Daily Life. The main text is divided into thirty lessons. At the end of the book are the Appendices, Quiz Answers, Glossaries and Index. Nearly all of the lessons deal with conversational situations. These are supplemented by four reading and review lessons.

The two modes of communication, oral and written, are different. In a conversational situation, speaker and listener share a good deal of information. In a natural conversation, much of this information is omitted and the speakers are able to communicate in a rather elliptical fashion. In a story, a report or a letter, however, it is necessary to write an organized, well-structured composition in order to communicate all the information needed in a logical fashion. In our experience, the student can learn Japanese most effectively if he studies both conversation and written Japanese from the very beginning.

This is one reason for the short review lessons. From Lesson 3, Summary Sentences (marked by ·) in Japanese and English follow the Opening Dialogue or Text. These sentences also show the differences between the oral and written languages. In addition, besides a title for ready reference, most lessons have at the beginning a Topic Sentence in English to orient the student to the main situation in the lesson. These should be of special value when teaching students for whom English is a second language.

Lessons are generally based on a particular conversational situation, such as shopping, talking on the telephone, and so on. Strategically placed throughout the book are ten Grammar sections to cover the most important grammar patterns. With the exception of the review lessons, each lesson has Notes, a Practice section consisting of Key Sentences, Exercises and Short Dialogue(s), and a Quiz. This arrangement will be especially helpful to people who want to study on their own.

To the Teacher

To understand the overall plan adopted in this book, it is best to first read it from beginning to end.

Work on pronunciation is especially important at the introductory level. The sounds represented by double consonants in romanization, long vowels and the nasalized **n** sound are especially difficult for foreigners, but it is also important to help the student learn how to pronounce the five vowels correctly. Even though he has a Japanese teacher, the student should be encouraged to listen to the accompanying tapes both for basic pronunciation and for the flow of speech.

In teaching *kana*, you should consider using charts or a *kana* workbook. You should make it clear to the student that mastering *kana* will help him with pronunciation, and pronunciation should be emphasized whenever you are helping the student with *hiragana* or *katakana*. You may want to have the student learn *kana* before you begin the text. However, the text is designed so that it is quite possible to have the student work on both at the same time. He should be able to master *hiragana* by the time he reaches Lesson 10. As much as possible, class time should be devoted to actually using Japanese. The student should study the Notes and Grammar sections before class.

The Dialogues are very short and, while the practice sections are designed to reinforce the patterns introduced, the Exercises give relatively few examples. You should select additional vocabulary—for example, from the appendices—that will be of interest to the student and have him practice each pattern using these new words in order to increase the amount of oral practice. But it is best not to try for too much at one time. It is better to proceed at a steady pace, increase vocabulary gradually, and work on improving weak points after several lessons, than to introduce a lot of new vocabulary and try for perfection in each lesson. Do not allow the class to get bogged down in one lesson.

Since each lesson is based on a particular conversational situation and emphasizes specific points of grammar, the time required for each lesson is not the same. One lesson may require only one hour while another requires three hours. Adjectives, for example, are introduced in Lessons 13 and 14, and these lessons will require more time simply because of the quantity of material to be covered.

The following suggestions concern the student's preparation. Before class, he should listen to the tape of the Opening Dialogue to get a feeling for the flow of conversation between native speakers. Then he should listen to the vocabulary for each lesson while memorizing the English meanings. These two points should be the main emphasis of his preparation.

Encourage the student to review each lesson after each class meeting. At this time, it is important to insist that the student diligently memorize the Dialogues, Summary Sentences and Key Sentences.

The Quizzes may be done either in class or as homework. In either case, the teacher should check them carefully, not only to correct mistakes but also to identify individual problems and find ways to correct them.

Self-study

The main parts of each lesson are printed in both *hiragana* and *katakana* and romanized Japanese (*rōmaji*). Learning will be more effective if you try to master *hiragana* by the time you are halfway through the book.

We strongly recommend that you devote sufficient time to pronunciation, accent and intonation, either by taking advantage of the tapes or by having your Japanese friends help you.

It is essential that you read the Japanese portions of the text out loud. First, take a look at the Dialogue at the beginning of the lesson. Then carefully study the Notes and the Grammar, where applicable, until you understand them completely. The Practice section gives more examples of the important patterns in the Dialogue. You should spend plenty of time repeating these patterns in a clear voice. Frequent repetition is essential. Using the appendices, you can try substituting words in each pattern while imagining situations in which you might find yourself. Remember, these patterns will only be useful if you can use them in actual situations. When you feel that you have mastered the patterns in the lesson, do the Quiz at the end. Finally, after you have completed all these steps, go back to the beginning of the lesson and thoroughly memorize the Opening Dialogue, Summary Sentences and Key Sentences.

ACKNOWLEDGMENTS for Book I
Compilation of this textbook has been a cooperative endeavor, and we deeply appreciate the collective efforts and individual contributions of Mss. Sachiko Adachi, Nori Andō, Haruko Matsui, Shigeko Miyazaki, Sachiko Okaniwa, Terumi Sawada and Yuriko Yobuko. For English translations and editorial assistance, we wish to thank Ms. Dorothy Britton.

ACKNOWLEDGMENTS for the Revised Edition of Book I
We would like to express our gratitude to the following people: Mss. Haruko Matsui, Junko Shinada, Keiko Ito, Mikiko Ochiai and Satoko Mizoguchi.

WRITING AND PRONUNCIATION

There are three kinds of Japanese writing:

1. *Kanji*: Chinese characters or ideographs, each conveying an idea, most of which have at least two readings.

2. *Hiragana*: A phonetic syllabary. The symbols are curvalinear in style.

3. *Katakana*: The second syllabary used primarily for foreign names and place names and words of foreign origin. The symbols are made up of straight lines.

Written Japanese normally makes use of all three, as in the following example:

"I am going to Canada." 私はカナダに行きます。

kanji	**Watashi** 私		**i-** 行	
hiragana	**wa** は	**に**	**kimasu** きます	
katakana	**Kanada** カナダ			

Besides these three forms of writing, Japanese is sometimes written in *rōmaji* (Roman letters), particularly for the convenience of foreigners. This is generally used in teaching conversational Japanese to foreigners when time is limited. There are various systems for transliterating Japanese in the Roman alphabet. In this book we use the modified Hepburn system.

HIRAGANA, KATAKANA AND RŌMAJI

The *kana* to the left are *hiragana*; *katakana* are in parentheses.

I Basic Syllables: Vowel, Consonant plus vowel and **n**

c \ v	a あ（ア）	i い（イ）	u う（ウ）	e え（エ）	o お（オ）
k	ka か（カ）	ki き（キ）	ku く（ク）	ke け（ケ）	ko こ（コ）
s	sa さ（サ）	shi し（シ）	su す（ス）	se せ（セ）	so そ（ソ）
t	ta た（タ）	chi ち（チ）	tsu つ（ツ）	te て（テ）	to と（ト）
n	na な（ナ）	ni に（ニ）	nu ぬ（ヌ）	ne ね（ネ）	no の（ノ）
h	ha は（ハ）	hi ひ（ヒ）	fu ふ（フ）	he へ（ヘ）	ho ほ（ホ）
m	ma ま（マ）	mi み（ミ）	mu む（ム）	me め（メ）	mo も（モ）
y	ya や（ヤ）	[i い（イ）]	yu ゆ（ユ）	[e え（エ）]	yo よ（ヨ）
r	ra ら（ラ）	ri り（リ）	ru る（ル）	re れ（レ）	ro ろ（ロ）
w	wa わ（ワ）	[i い（イ）]	[u う（ウ）]	[e え（エ）]	o を（ヲ）
n, m	— ん（ン）				

Note: The syllables **yi**, **ye**, **wi**, **wu** and **we** do not occur in modern Japanese.

II Modified Syllables: Consonant plus basic vowel

g	ga が (ガ)	gi ぎ (ギ)	gu ぐ (グ)	ge げ (ゲ)	go ご (ゴ)
z	za ざ (ザ)	ji じ (ジ)	zu ず (ズ)	ze ぜ (ゼ)	zo ぞ (ソ)
d	da だ (ダ)	ji ぢ (チ)	zu づ (ツ)	de で (デ)	do ど (ド)
b	ba ば (バ)	bi び (ビ)	bu ぶ (ブ)	be べ (ベ)	bo ぼ (ボ)
p	pa ぱ (パ)	pi ぴ (ピ)	pu ぷ (プ)	pe ぺ (ペ)	po ぽ (ポ)

III Modified Syllables: Consonant plus **ya, yu, yo**

kya きゃ (キャ)	kyu きゅ (キュ)	kyo きょ (キョ)
sha しゃ (シャ)	shu しゅ (シュ)	sho しょ (ショ)
cha ちゃ (チャ)	chu ちゅ (チュ)	cho ちょ (チョ)
nya にゃ (ニャ)	nyu にゅ (ニュ)	nyo にょ (ニョ)
hya ひゃ (ヒャ)	hyu ひゅ (ヒュ)	hyo ひょ (ヒョ)
mya みゃ (ミャ)	myu みゅ (ミュ)	myo みょ (ミョ)
rya りゃ (リャ)	ryu りゅ (リュ)	ryo りょ (リョ)
gya ぎゃ (ギャ)	gyu ぎゅ (ギュ)	gyo ぎょ (ギョ)
ja じゃ (ジャ)	ju じゅ (ジュ)	jo じょ (ジョ)
bya びゃ (ビャ)	byu びゅ (ビュ)	byo びょ (ビョ)
pya ぴゃ (ピャ)	pyu ぴゅ (ピュ)	pyo ぴょ (ピョ)

IV Double Consonants

kk, pp, ss, tt	っ (ッ)

(See Note 6.)

V Long Vowels

ā	ああ	(アー)
ii, ī	いい	(イー)
ū	うう	(ウー)
ē, ei	ええ、えい	(エー)
ō	おう、おお	(オー)

POINTS TO NOTE

1. The top line of the Japanese syllabary consists of the five vowels: **a, i, u, e, o**. They are short vowels, pronounced clearly and crisply. If you pronounce the vowels in the following English sentence, making them all short, you will have

their approximate sounds. The **u** is pronounced with no movement forward of the lips.

Ah, we soon get old.

   a   **i** **u** **e o**

2. Long vowels are written as shown in Chart V. **Ē** or **ei** is most often written えい but ええ is also sometimes encountered.
   おう is the general rule for **ō** but in some words it is traditionally written おお. Long vowels are a doubling of the single vowel and care should be taken to pronounce them as a continuous sound, equal in value to two identical short vowels.

3. The rest of the syllabary from the second line down in Chart I are syllables formed by a consonant and a vowel.

4. Japanese consonants more or less resemble English. Listen to the cassette tape or a native speaker for the exact sounds. Especially note the following: *t* in the **ta** row, *f* in the syllable **fu** and *r* in the **ra** row. The *g* in the syllables **ga, gi, gu, ge** and **go** at the beginning of a word is hard (like the [g] in garden), but when it occurs in the middle or in the last syllable of a word, it often becomes nasal, as in **eiga** ("movie"). The particle **ga**, too, is usually pronounced in this way. However, many Japanese today use a *g* sound which is not nasal.
   N is the only independent consonant not combined with a vowel. When it is at the end of a word it is pronounced somewhat nasally. Otherwise it is usually pronounced like the English [n]. But if it is followed by syllables beginning with *b*, *m* or *p*, it is pronounced more like [m] and accordingly spelled with an *m* in this textbook. Special care is necessary when syllabic **n** is followed by a vowel as in the word **kin'en**. (**ki-n-en**, "no smoking"). Note that this is different in syllable division from **kinen** (**ki-ne-n**, "anniversary").

5. As explained above, *hiragana* and *katakana* are phonetic symbols and each is one syllable in length. The syllables in Chart III which consist of two symbols—the second written smaller—are also only one syllable in length if the vowel is short, longer if the vowel is long.

6. What are written in Roman letters as the double consonants **kk**, **pp**, **ss** and **tt** in Chart IV are expressed in *kana* (*hiragana* and *katakana*) with a small **tsu** in place of the first consonant. I.e., けっこん **kekkon** ("marriage"), きっぷ **kip-pu** ("ticket"), まっすぐ **massugu** ("straight") and きって **kitte**, ("stamp"). This small っ is one syllable in length, and there is the slightest pause after it is pronounced (as in the English word *book'keeping*). In the case of the **chi** syllable, the **tsu** is represented by a *t* in Roman letters, i.e., マッチ **matchi** (" match").

7. In *hiragana*, the syllables **ji** and **zu** are written じ and ず as a general rule. In a few rare cases, they are traditionally written ぢ and づ

8. *Hiragana* follows a tradition in which the following three particles are written a special way:
      o when used as a particle is written を, not お.
      e when used as a particle is written へ, not え.
      wa when used as a particle is written は, not わ.

CHARACTERISTICS OF JAPANESE GRAMMAR

The grammar in this text is derived from a natural analysis of the Japanese language, rather than being an interpretation adapted to the syntax of Western languages. We have given as few technical terms as possible, choosing ones that will make for a smooth transition from the basic level to more advanced study.

The following points are basic and in most cases reflect differences between the grammar of Japanese and that of English, or other European languages. Specific explanations and examples are given in Grammar I through Grammar X, the notes and the appendices.

1. Japanese nouns have neither gender nor number. But plurals of certain words can be expressed by the use of a suffix.

2. The verb generally comes at the end of the sentence or clause.
   ex. **Watashi wa Nihon-jin desu**. I am a Japanese.
   Watashi wa Kyōtō ni ikimasu. I go to Kyoto.

3. Verb conjugation is not affected by the gender, number or person of the subject.

4. Verb conjugation shows only two tenses, the present form and the past form. Whether use of the present form refers to habitual action or the future, and whether the past form is equivalent to the English past tense, present perfect or past perfect can be determined from the context.

5. Japanese adjectives, unlike English ones, are inflected to show present and past, affirmative and negative.

6. The grammatical function of nouns is indicated by particles. Their role is similar to English prepositions, but since they always come after the word, they are sometimes referred to as postpositions.
   ex. **Tōkyō de**, at Tokyo
   15-nichi ni, on the 15 (of the month)

7. Many degrees of politeness are expressable in Japanese. In this book the style is one which anyone may use without being rude.

Note: The following abbreviations are used in this book:

aff.	affirmative
neg.	negative
A*a*:	Answer, affirmative
A*n*:	Answer, negative
ex.	example
-i adj.	**-i** adjective
-na adj.	**-na** adjective

USEFUL DAILY EXPRESSIONS

1. おはようございます。**Ohayōgozaimasu**. Good morning! Used until about 10 A.M.

2. こんにちは。**Konnichiwa**. Hello. A rather informal greeting used from about 10 A.M. until sundown.

3. こんばんは。**Kombanwa**. Good evening.

4. さようなら。**Sayōnara**. Good-bye. On more formal occasions one uses **Shitsurei shimasu**.

5. おやすみなさい。**Oyasumi nasai**. Good night. Said at night before going to bed. When parting at night outside the home, **Sayōnara** is more usual.

6. では また。／じゃ また。 **Dewa mata./Ja mata**. Well then . . . Said informally when parting from relatives or friends.

7. いってらっしゃい。**Itte rasshai**. So long. (*lit.* "Go and come back.") Said to members of a household as they leave the house.

8. いってまいります。**Itte mairimasu**. So long. (*lit.* "[I'm] going and coming back.") This is the reply to **Itte rasshai**.

9. ただいま。**Tadaima**. I'm back. (*lit.* "[I have returned] Just now.") Said by a person on returning home.

10. おかえりなさい。 **Okaeri nasai**. Welcome home. This is the reply to **Tadaima**.

Home use

11. おげんきですか。 **O-genki desu ka**. How are you? (*lit.* "Are you well?")

12. ありがとうございます。げんきです。 **Arigatō gozaimasu. Genki desu**. Fine, thank you.

13. おめでとうございます。 **Omedetō gozaimasu**. Congratulations!

14. おだいじに。**O-daijini**. Take care of yourself.

15. どうも ありがとうございます。**Dōmo arigatō gozaimasu**. Thank you very much.

16. どういたしまして。**Dō itashimashite**. You're welcome.

17. すみません。**Sumimasen**. Excuse me. I'm sorry.

18. ちょっと まってください。**Chotto matte kudasai**. Wait just a moment, please.

19. もう いちどおねがいします。 **Mō ichido onegaishimasu**. Once more, please.

20. おさきに。**Osakini**. Pardon my going first (before you). Said when leaving the office or a meeting ahead of other people.

21. どうぞ おさきに。 **Dōzo osakini**. Please, go ahead.

22. きをつけて。 **Ki o tsukete**. Take care!/Be careful!

23. あぶない。 **Abunai**. Look out! (*lit.* "It's dangerous.")

24. だめです。 **Dame desu**. Out of the question./Impossible./No good.

25. がんばってください。 **Gambatte kudasai**. Keep your chin up! Said to encourage someone.

案 内

annai
Information

chikatetsu
Subway, Underground

takushī-noriba
Taxi Stand

eki
(railway) Station

eigyōchū
Open

jumbichū
Getting ready to open.
(May also indicate
"Closed for the day.")

kippu-uriba
Ticket Office

改 札 口

kaisatsuguchi
Ticket Gate

精算所

seisanjo
(fare) Adjustment Office

休
業
中

kyūgyōchū
Closed

16

hijōguchi
Emergency Exit

iriguchi
Entrance

deguchi
Exit

osu
Push

hiku
Pull

erebētā
Elevator

uketsuke
Reception

esukarētā
Escalator

o-tearai
Toilet

otoko
Men, Gentlemen

keshō-shitsu
Powder Room

onna
Women, Ladies

右折禁止

usetsu kinshi
No right turn

左折禁止

sasetsu kinshi
No left turn

駐車禁止
NO PARKING

chūsha kinshi
No Parking

Te o furenaide kudasai.
Do not touch.

一方通行路

ippōtsūkōro
One Way Street

Gomi o sutenaide kudasai.
Please don't litter.

Shibafu no naka ni hairanaide kudasai.
Please keep off the grass.

駐車場

chūshajō
Parking lot

禁　煙
NO SMOKING

kin'en
No Smoking

立入
禁止

tachiiri kinshi
No Admittance

注意

chūi
Caution!

工事中

kōjichū
Under Construction

危　険
DANGER

kiken
Danger!

18　SIGNS IN DAILY LIFE

LESSON **1** INTRODUCTIONS

Mr. Hayashi introduces Mr. Smith to Mr. Tanaka.

はやし：たなかさん、こちらは　スミスさんです。

スミス：はじめまして。スミスです。どうぞ　よろしく。

たなか：はじめまして。とうきょうでんきの　たなかです。
　　　　どうぞ　よろしく。

はやし：スミスさんは　ABCの　べんごしです。

Hayashi: Tanaka-san, kochira wa Sumisu-san desu.
Sumisu: Hajimemashite. Sumisu desu. Dōzo yoroshiku.
Tanaka: Hajimemashite. Tōkyō Denki no Tanaka desu. Dōzo yoroshiku.
Hayashi: Sumisu-san wa ABC no bengoshi desu.

Hayashi: Mr. Tanaka, this is Mr. Smith.
Smith: How do you do. My name's Smith. I'm very glad to meet you.
Tanaka: How do you do. I'm Tanaka from Tokyo Electric. I'm very glad to meet you.
Hayashi: Mr. Smith is ABC's lawyer.

Vocabulary		
はやし	**Hayashi**	a surname
たなかさん	**Tanaka-san**	a surname with honorific
～さん	**-san**	Mr., Mrs., Ms., Miss (suffix)
こちら	**kochira**	this one (implies this person)
は	**wa**	as for (topic marker, particle)
スミス	**Sumisu**	Smith
です	**desu**	is
はじめまして	**hajimemashite**	How do you do.
わたし	**watashi**	I
どうぞ　よろしく	**dōzo yoroshiku**	*lit.* Please favor me.
とうきょうでんき	**Tōkyō Denki**	Tokyo Electric (company name)
の	**no**	= 's (possessive particle)
ABC	**ĒBĪSHĪ**	ABC (company name)
べんごし	**bengoshi**	lawyer

19

GRAMMAR I

Lessons 1–5   Identifying People and Things

1. noun 1 **WA** noun 2 **DESU**
2. noun 1 **WA** noun 2 **DESU KA**
   Hai, (noun 1 **wa**) noun 2 **desu.**
   Iie, (noun 1 **wa**) noun 2 **dewa/ja arimasen.**

Present Form		Past Form	
aff.	*neg.*	*aff.*	*neg.*
desu	**dewa arimasen**	**deshita**	**dewa arimasendeshita**
is	is not	was	was not

- Particle **wa**. Topic marker.
  Wa follows noun 1 indicating that it is the topic under discussion. Noun 2 is then identified and the phrase is concluded with **desu**. The topic is often the same as the subject, but not necessarily. It is also possible for the object to be the topic. (See Note 2, p. 54; Grammar III, p. 66; Note 3, p. 183.) The . . . **wa** . . . **desu** structure is not affected by person or number.
  ex. **A-san wa bengoshi desu.** "Mr. A is a lawyer."
  A-san to B-san wa bengoshi desu. "Mr. A and Mrs. B are lawyers."

- Particle **ka**. Question marker.
  The formation of questions in Japanese is easy. Put **ka** at the end of a sentence and it becomes a question. No change in word order is required even when the question contains interrogative words such as who, what, when, etc. Intonation normally rises on the particle **ka** only, i.e., . . . **desu ka.** ↗

- **Hai** and **Iie**
  Hai is virtually the same as "yes." **Iie** is virtually the same as "no." It is better, however, to think of **hai** as meaning, "That's right," and **iie** as meaning, "That's wrong." Otherwise negative questions can be a problem. I.e., to the question, **Ja, banana ga arimasen ka**, "So you have no bananas?" the reply is **Hai, arimasen**, "That's right, we have none." Or **Iie, arimasu**, "That's wrong, we have some."

- Omission of topic (noun 1)
  When it is obvious to the other person what the topic is, it is generally omitted.
  ex. **[Watashi wa] Sumisu desu.** "(As for me) I'm Smith."
  But when it is necessary to make the topic clear, it is not omitted.
  ex. **Kochira wa Sumisu-san desu.** "This is Mr. Smith."

• **Dewa arimasen./Ja arimasen**.
Negative form of **desu. Ja** is more informal than **dewa**.

NOTES

1. **Tanaka-san**
   San is a title of respect added to a name, so it cannot be used after one's own name. **San** may be used with both male and female names, and with either surname or given name. It may even be suffixed to the name of an occupation.
   ex. **Bengoshi-san**, "Mr. Lawyer."

2. **Kochira wa Sumisu-san desu.**
   Kochira, "this one," implies "this person here" and is a polite way of saying "this person."

3. **Hajimemashite.**
   Salutation used on meeting a person for the first time. It is a form of the verb **hajimeru**, "to begin."

4. **[Watashi wa] Sumisu desu**.
   "My name's Smith." (*lit.* "I'm Smith.")
   Especially in conversational Japanese, **watashi**, "I," is hardly ever used. **Anata**, "you," is similarly avoided, especially when addressing superiors, in which case the person's surname, title or occupation is used when necessary.

5. **Dōzo yoroshiku.**
   A phrase used when being introduced, it is usually combined with **hajimemashite**. It is also used when taking one's leave after having asked a favor. **Yoroshiku** means "good" and is a request for the other person's favorable consideration in the future. It can also be used as follows: **Tanaka-san ni yoroshiku**. "Please give my regards to Mr. Tanaka."

6. **Tōkyō Denki no (Tanaka desu).**
   The possessive particle **no** indicates ownership or attribution and comes after the noun it modifies, like " 's" in English. Here it shows that Mr. Tanaka belongs to, in the sense that he works for, Tokyo Electric. Japanese customarily give their company and position when being introduced.

7. **Dare/donata**, "who?"
   The basic word for "who" is **dare**, but **donata** is more polite.
   ex. **Kochira wa dare desu ka**. "Who is this?"
   Kochira wa donata desu ka. "Might I ask who this is?"

PRACTICE

KEY SENTENCES

1. **[Watashi wa] Sumisu desu.**
2. **[Watashi wa] ABC no Sumisu desu.**

3. **Kochira wa Tanaka-san desu.**

4. **Tanaka-san wa bengoshi dewa arimasen.**

1. My name's Smith.
2. I'm Smith from ABC.
3. This is Mr. Tanaka.
4. Mr. Tanaka is not a lawyer.

EXERCISES

I Practice the following pattern by changing the underlined part as in the example given.

    ex. **[Watashi wa] Sumisu desu.**

       1. **Amerika Taishikan no Sumisu**

       2. **Amerika-jin**

       3. **bengoshi**

II Make dialogues by changing the underlined parts as in the examples given.

    A. *ex.* **Q: [Anata wa] Sumisu-san desu ka.**

        A: Hai, Sumisu desu.

        1. **Tanaka**

    B. *ex.* **Q: [Anata wa] Nihon-jin desu ka.**

        A*a*: Hai, Nihon-jin desu.

        A*n*: Iie, Nihon-jin dewa arimasen.

        1. **bengoshi**

        2. **hisho**

    C. *ex.* **Q: [Anata wa] Nihon-jin desu ka, Chūgoku-jin desu ka.**

        A: Nihon-jin desu.

        1. **Amerika-jin, Doitsu-jin**

        2. **gakusei, kaishain**

        3. **bengoshi, hisho**

    D. *ex.* **Q: [Anata wa] Donata desu ka.**

        A: Sumisu desu.

        1. **Tanaka**

        2. **Amerika Taishikan no Tanaka**

        3. **Nihon Ginkō no Tanaka**

    E. *ex.* **Q: Kochira wa donata desu ka.**

        A: Sumisu-san desu.

        1. **Tanaka-san**

        2. **Nihon Ginkō no Tanaka-san**

Amerika Taishikan	American Embassy	**iie**	no
Amerika	America	**hisho**	secretary
taishikan	embassy	**Chūgoku-jin**	a Chinese
Amerika-jin	an American	**Chūgoku**	China
-jin	person (suffix)	**Doitsu-jin**	a German
anata	you	**Doitsu**	Germany
ka	=? (question marker, particle)	**gakusei**	student
		kaishain	company employee
hai	yes, certainly	**donata**	who
Nihon-jin	a Japanese	**Nihon Ginkō**	Bank of Japan
Nihon	Japan	**ginkō**	bank

SHORT DIALOGUES

1. **Sumisu:** **Tanaka-san desu ka.**
   Tanaka: **Hai, Tanaka desu.**
   Sumisu: **Tanaka-san wa gakusei desu ka.**
   Tanaka: **Iie, gakusei dewa arimasen. Kaishain desu.**

   Smith: Are you Mr. Tanaka?
   Tanaka: Yes, I am.
   Smith: Are you a student.
   Tanaka: No, I'm not a student. I'm a company employee.

2. Mr. Hayashi introduces Miss Yamada to Mr. Tanaka.
   Hayashi: **Go-shōkai shimasu. Kochira wa Yamada-san desu. Sumisu-san no hisho desu. Kochira wa Tanaka-san desu.**
   Yamada: **Hajimemashite. Yamada desu. Dōzo yoroshiku.**
   Tanaka: **Hajimemashite. Tanaka desu. Dōzo yoroshiku.**

   Hayashi: Let me introduce you. This is Miss Yamada. She is Mr. Smith's secretary. This is Mr. Tanaka.
   Yamada: How do you do. My name's Yamada. I'm very glad to meet you.
   Tanaka: How do you do. My name's Tanaka. I'm very glad to meet you.

Vocabulary

go-shōkai shimasu	Let me introduce you.
Yamada	a surname

QUIZ

I Supposing you are Mr. Smith in the opening dialogue, answer the following questions.

1. **Donata desu ka.**
   A.

2. **Nihon-jin desu ka.**
   A.

3. **Kaishain desu ka, bengoshi desu ka.**
   A.

II Complete the questions so that they fit the answers.

1. **(   ) desu ka.**
   Hai, Sumisu desu.
2. **Sumisu-san wa (   ) desu ka.**
   Iie, Doitsu-jin dewa arimasen.
3. **Sumisu-san wa (   ) desu ka, kaishain desu ka.**
   Bengoshi desu.
4. **Kochira wa (   ) desu ka.**
   Tanaka-san desu.

III Put the appropriate particles in the parentheses.

1. **Kochira (   ) Yamada-san desu.**
2. **Hayashi-san wa bengoshi desu (   ), kaishain desu (   ).**
   Kaishain desu.
3. **Sumisu-san wa ABC (   ) bengoshi desu.**

IV Translate into Japanese.

1. I'm Smith.
2. How do you do. I'm glad to meet you.
3. Miss Yamada, this is Mr. Tanaka of Tokyo Electric.
4. Is Mr. Smith American or German?

LESSON 2 ADDRESS AND TELEPHONE NUMBER

Mr. Tanaka gives Mr. Smith his business card. Mr. Smith cannot read *kanji*.

たなか : わたしの　めいしです。どうぞ。

スミス : どうも　ありがとうございます。これは　たなかさんの
　　　　　なまえですか。

たなか : ええ、そうです。たなかです。

スミス : これは？

たなか : かいしゃの　なまえです。とうきょうでんきです。

スミス : これは　かいしゃの　でんわばんごうですか。

たなか : はい、かいしゃのです。03–3400–9031です。うちの　でんわ
　　　　　ばんごうは　045–326–8871です。

Tanaka:	Watashi no meishi desu. Dōzo.
Sumisu:	Dōmo arigatō gozaimasu. Kore wa Tanaka-san no namae desu ka.
Tanaka:	Ee, sō desu. TA-NA-KA desu.
Sumisu:	Kore wa?
Tanaka:	Kaisha no namae desu. TŌ-KYŌ DEN-KI desu.
Sumisu:	Kore wa kaisha no denwa-bangō desu ka.
Tanaka:	Hai, kaisha no desu. Zero-san no san-yon-zero-zero no kyū-zero-san-ichi desu. Uchi no denwa-bangō wa zero-yon-go no san-ni-roku no hachi-hachi-nana-ichi desu.

Tanaka:	This is my busness card. Please . . .
Smith:	Thank you very much. Is this (your) name?
Tanaka:	Yes. That's right. Tanaka.
Smith:	And this?
Tanaka:	(That's) the name of my company, Tokyo Electric.
Smith:	Is this the company's telephone number?
Tanaka:	Yes, it's the company's. (03) 3400–9031. (My) home telephone number is (045) 326–8871.

わたしの	**watashi no**	my
めいし	**meishi**	business card (*lit.* "name card")
どうぞ	**dōzo**	please (accept)
どうも ありがとう ございます	**dōmo arigatō gozaimasu**	Thank you very much.
どうも	**dōmo**	very much
ありがとう ございます	**arigatō gozaimasu**	(I am) grateful
これ	**kore**	this
なまえ	**namae**	name
ええ	**ee**	yes
そうです	**sō desu**	that's right
これは?	**kore wa?**	as for this?
かいしゃ	**kaisha**	company
でんわばんごう	**denwa-bangō**	telephone number
でんわ	**denwa**	telephone
ばんごう	**bangō**	number
かいしゃのです	**kaisha no desu**	It is the company's.
うち	**uchi**	home

NOTES

1. Meishi

Japanese, particularly those in business, carry business cards which they exchange during introductions. A few hand-written words on a business card can serve as a convenient introduction.

2. Kore wa Tanaka-san no namae desu ka.

Note that although addressing Mr. Tanaka, Mr. Smith uses his name rather than saying **anata no**, "your." (See Note 4, p. 21.)

3. Ee.

"Yes." Less formal than **hai**.

4. Sō desu.

When replying to questions that end with **desu ka, sō** can be used instead of repeating the noun.

5. Kore wa?

A rising intonation on the particle **wa** makes this informal phrase a question without using the question marker **ka**.

6. Kaisha no desu.

Short for **kaisha no denwa-bangō desu**. This sort of abbreviated expression is often used in Japanese.

7. **(03) 3400–9031**

   Spoken as **zero-san no san-yon-zero-zero no kyū-zero-san-ichi**. The area code (Tokyo's is 03), the exchange and the number are joined by the particle **no**. In telephone numbers 0 is often pronounced **zero** in Japanese.

8. **Nani/nan,** ''what''

   ''What'' is **nani**, but it often becomes **nan**, as in **Kore wa nan desu ka**. ''What is this?''

9. **Nan-ban,** ''What number?''

   ex. **Tanaka-san no denwa-bangō wa nan-ban desu ka.** ''What is Mr. Tanaka's telephone number?''

PRACTICE

KEY SENTENCES

1. **Kore wa meishi desu.**
2. **Kore wa meishi dewa arimasen.**
3. **Kore wa Tanaka-san no tokei desu. Kore wa Tanaka-san no desu.**
4. **Kaisha no denwa-bangō wa (03) 3400–9031 desu.**

1. This is a business card. (These are business cards.)
2. This is not a business card.
3. This is Mr. Tanaka's watch. This is Mr. Tanaka's.
4. The company's telephone number is (03) 3400–9031.

> **Vocabulary**

tokei   clock, watch

EXERCISES

I Look at the pictures and practice the following pattern by changing the underlined part as in the example given.

   ex. **Kore wa meishi desu.**

   1. **hon**   4. **kagi**
   2. **shimbun**   5. **denwa**
   3. **tokei**   6. **kuruma**

II Make dialogues by changing the underlined parts as in the examples given.

    A. *ex.* **Q: Kore wa <u>meishi</u> desu ka.**

          A*a*: Hai, <u>meishi</u> desu.

          A*n*: Iie, <u>meishi</u> dewa arimasen. <u>Hon</u> desu.

        1. **hon, shimbun**

        2. **jūsho, denwa-bangō**

    B. *ex.* **Q: Kore wa nan desu ka.**

          A: <u>Namae</u> desu.

        1. **tokei**

        2. **kagi**

        3. **denwa**

    C. *ex.* **Q: Kore wa <u>Tanaka-san</u> no kuruma desu ka.**

          A*a*: Hai, <u>Tanaka-san</u> no kuruma desu. <u>Tanaka-san</u> no desu.

          A*n*: Iie, <u>Tanaka-san</u> no kuruma dewa arimasen. <u>Tanaka-san</u> no dewa arimasen.

        1. **Sumisu-san**

        2. **kaisha**

    D. *ex.* **Q: Kore wa dare no hon desu ka.**

          A: <u>Tanaka-san</u> no desu.

        1. **Sumisu-san**

        2. **kaisha**

        3. **watashi**

preferred
*- for phone numbers

III Numbers: Memorize the numbers from 0 to 20.

0, zero/rei	7, shichi/nana*	14, jūshi/jūyon
1, ichi	8, hachi	15, jūgo
2, ni	9, *kyū/ku	16, jūroku
3, san	10, jū	17, jūshichi/jūnana
4, shi/yon*	11, jūichi	18, jūhachi
5, go	12, jūni	19, jūkyū/jūku
6, roku	13, jūsan	20, nijū

100 hyaku

IV Telephone numbers: Practice saying the following telephone numbers.

    (03) 3742–8955. **Zero-san no san-nana-yon-ni no hachi-kyū-go-go.**

    3401–5634. **San-yon-zero-ichi no go-roku-san-yon.**

    Zero, yon, nana and **kyū** are used for 0, 4, 7 and 9 in telephone numbers.

V Make dialogues by changing the underlined parts as in the example given.

    ex. **Q: <u>Kaisha</u> no denwa-bangō wa nan-ban desu ka.**

        A: <u>3742–8920</u> desu.

      1. **ginkō, 3325–8871**

      2. **gakkō, (03) 3781–6493**

      3. **Tanaka-san no uchi, 3956–4158**

Vocabulary

hon	book	**nan**	what
shimbun	newspaper	**dare no**	whose
kagi	key	**nan-ban**	what number
kuruma	car	**-ban**	number
jūsho	address	**gakkō**	school

SHORT DIALOGUES

1. **Hayashi:** Kore wa Sumisu-san no tokei desu ka.
   Tanaka: Hai, Sumisu-san no tokei desu.

   Hayashi: Is this Mr. Smith's watch?
   Tanaka: Yes, it's Mr. Smith's watch.

2. **Hayashi:** Kore wa Sumisu-san no tokei desu ka.
   Sumisu: Hai, watashi no tokei desu.

   Hayashi: Is this your watch?
   Smith: Yes, it's my watch.

3. **Hayashi:** Kore wa Tanaka-san no hon desu ka.
   Sumisu: Iie, Tanaka-san no dewa arimasen. Watashi no desu.

   Hayashi: Is this Mr. Tanaka's book?
   Smith: No, it's not Mr. Tanaka's. It's mine.

4. **Sumisu:** Taishikan no denwa-bangō wa nan-ban desu ka.
   Hisho: 3325–7634 desu.
   Sumisu: Ginkō no denwa-bangō wa?
   Hisho: 3423–6502 desu.

   Smith: What is the telephone number of the embassy?
   Secretary: It's 3325–7634.
   Smith: What about the telephone number of the bank?
   Secretary: It's 3423–6502.

QUIZ ▓▓▓▓▒▒░░

I Look at the illustrated business card and answer the questions.

1. **Kore wa nan desu ka.**
2. **Kore wa kaisha no namae desu ka.**
3. **Kore wa Tanaka-san no uchi no jūsho desu ka, kaisha no desu ka.**

4. Kore wa Tanaka-san no uchi no denwa-bangō desu ka.

5. Tanaka-san no kaisha no denwa-bangō wa nan-ban desu ka.

II Complete the questions so that they fit the answers.

1. Kore wa (   ) no denwa-bangō desu ka.
   Iie; kaisha no dewa arimasen. Uchi no desu.

2. Kore wa (   ) no jūsho desu ka.
   Tanaka-san no desu.

3. Kore wa (   ) desu ka.
   Tokei desu.

4. Tanaka-san no uchi no denwa-bangō wa (   ) desu ka.
   3325–7634 desu.

III Put the appropriate particles in the parentheses.

1. Kochira (   ) donata desu ka.

2. Kore (   ) nan desu (   ).
   Kaisha (   ) denwa-bangō desu.
   Kore (   )?
   Kaisha (   ) jūsho desu.

3. Kore (   ) watashi (   ) kuruma dewa arimasen. Kaisha (   )
   desu.

IV Translate into Japanese.

1. This is Mr. Tanaka.

2. This is Mr. Tanaka's business card.

3. This is not Mr. Tanaka's home telephone number. It is that of his company.

4. What is your company's telephone number?

LESSON 3 DAY AND TIME

Mr. Smith goes to a department store. It is not open yet.

スミス：　　　　　すみません。いま　なんじですか。
おんなの　ひと：9じ50ぷんです。
スミス：　　　　　デパートは　なんじからですか。
おんなの　ひと：10じからです。
スミス：　　　　　なんじまでですか。
おんなの　ひと：ごご　6じまでです。
スミス：　　　　　どうも　ありがとう。
おんなの　ひと：どういたしまして。

■デパートは　10じから　6じまでです。

Sumisu: Sumimasen. Ima nan-ji desu ka.
Onna no hito: Ku-ji gojuppun desu.
Sumisu: Depāto wa nan-ji kara desu ka.
Onna no hito: Jū-ji kara desu.
Sumisu: Nan-ji made desu ka.
Onna no hito: Gogo roku-ji made desu.
Sumisu: Dōmo arigatō.
Onna no hito: Dō itashimashite.

■ Depāto wa jū-ji kara roku-ji made desu.

Smith: Excuse me. What time is it now?
Woman: It's 9:50.
Smith: What time does the store open?
Woman: It opens at 10:00.
Smith: How late does it stay open?
Woman: It stays open until 6 P.M.
Smith: Thank you very much.
Woman: Don't mention it.

■ The department store's hours are from 10:00 to 6:00.

Vocabulary

すみません	sumimasen	Excuse me./I'm sorry.
いま	ima	now
なんじ	nan-ji	what time
〜じ	-ji	o'clock
おんなの ひと	onna no hito	woman
おんな	onna	woman, female
ひと	hito	person
9じ	ku-ji	9 o'clock
50ぷん	gojuppun/gojippun	50 minutes
〜ふん、〜ぷん	-fun, -pun	minute
デパート	depāto	department store
から	kara	from (particle)
10じ	jū-ji	10 o'clock
まで	made	until (particle)
ごご	gogo	P.M.
6じ	roku-ji	6 o'clock
どう いたしまして	dō itashimashite	Don't mention it./You're welcome. (*lit.* "What have (I) done?")

NOTES

1. **Sumimasen.**
   Sumimasen, "Excuse me," prefaces a request, such as asking a stranger for information. It can also mean "Thank you," "I'm sorry," or "Pardon me."

2. **Jū-ji kara desu. Gogo roku-ji made desu.**
   "From 10 o'clock." "Until 6 P.M."
   Particles follow words, rather than proceed them. (See Grammar II, p. 53.)
   Note that instead of **Jū-ji kara hirakimasu,** "It is open from 10 o'clock," the word "open" is omitted. When the verb is understood, only the key words, (here **jū-ji kara, roku-ji made**) followed by **desu** are often used.

3. When
   Hour. **Nan-ji,** "what time?"
   Day of the week. **Nan-yōbi,** "which day of the week?"
   Day of the month. **Nan-nichi,** "which day of the month?"
   Month. **Nan-gatsu,** "which month?"
   Time in general. **Itsu,** "when?"

PRACTICE

KEY SENTENCES

1. Ima gozen 10-ji desu.
2. Hiru-yasumi wa 12-ji kara 1-ji han made desu.
3. Kyō wa 6-gatsu 18-nichi desu.
4. Ashita wa Hayashi-san no tanjōbi desu.
5. Kinō wa kin-yōbi deshita.
6. Kinō wa moku-yōbi dewa arimasendeshita.

1. It's 10 A.M. now.
2. Lunch time is from 12:00 to 1:30.
3. Today is June 18.
4. Tomorrow is Mr. Hayashi's birthday.
5. Yesterday was Friday.
6. Yesterday was not Thursday.

Vocabulary

gozen	A.M.	**-nichi**	day (See Exercise VI, p. 35.)
hiru-yasumi	lunch time		
hiru	noon	**ashita**	tomorrow
yasumi	rest (period)	**tanjōbi**	birthday
1-ji han	half past 1 (*lit.* "1 o'clock half")	**kinō**	yesterday
		kin-yōbi	Friday
han	half	**-yōbi**	day of the week (See Exercise V, p. 35.)
kyō	today		
6-gatsu 18 nichi	June 18		
6-gatsu	June (*lit.* sixth month)	**deshita**	was
-gatsu	month (See Exercise VII, p. 35.)	**moku-yōbi**	Thursday
		arimasendeshita	was not
18-nichi	18 day		

EXERCISES

I Numbers: Memorize the numbers from 20 to 100.

20, **nijū**	50, **gojū**	80, **hachijū**
30, **sanjū**	60, **rokujū**	90, **kyūjū**
40, **yonjū**	70, **shichijū, nanajū**	100, **hyaku**

Intermediate numbers are made by adding to the above numbers, the numbers from 1 to 9.

ex. 21, **nijū-ichi**

II Look at the pictures and practice the following pattern as in the example given.

    ex. **Ima gozen 1-ji desu.**

      1. **3-ji**
      2. **gogo 4-ji 10-pun**
      3. **gozen 6-ji 15-fun**
      4. **9-ji han**

ex.

1.   2.   3.   4.

III Time: Practice telling time.

    A. **Ima nan-ji desu ka?**

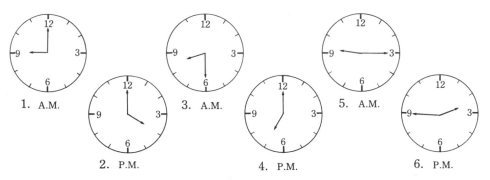

1. A.M.   3. A.M.   5. A.M.

    2. P.M.   4. P.M.   6. P.M.

    B. **Nan-ji kara nan-ji made desu ka?**

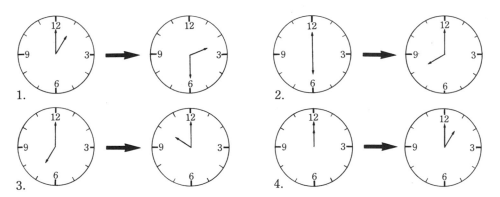

1.   2.

3.   4.

IV Make dialogues by changing the underlined parts as in the examples given.

    A. *ex.* **Q: Ima nan-ji desu ka.**

          A: <u>8-ji</u> desu.

      1. **6:00**
      2. **3:00 P.M.**
      3. **9:30 A.M.**

B. *ex.* **Q: Pātī wa nan-ji kara desu ka.**

    A: 7-ji kara desu.

    1. **ginkō, 9:00**

    2. **eiga, 4:45**

    3. **kaigi, 9:30**

C. *ex.* **Q: Depāto wa nan-ji made desu ka.**

    A: Gogo 6-ji made desu.

    1. **hiru-yasumi, 1:30**

    2. **yūbinkyoku, gogo 5:00**

    3. **shigoto, 5:15**

D. *ex.* **Q: Hiru-yasumi wa nan-ji kara nan-ji made desu ka.**

    A: 12-ji kara 1-ji made desu.

    1. **eiga, 3:30, 4:45**

    2. **ginkō, 9:00, 3:00**

V Days of the week: Memorize the names of the days of the week.

nichi-yōbi, Sunday	**sui-yōbi,** Wednesday	**do-yōbi,** Saturday
getsu-yōbi, Monday	**moku-yōbi,** Thursday	
ka-yōbi, Tuesday	**kin-yōbi,** Friday	

VI Days of the month: Memorize the days of the month.

1st, **tsuitachi**	11th, **jūichi-nichi**	21st, **nijūichi-nichi**
2nd, **futsuka**	12th, **jūni-nichi**	22nd, **nijūni-nichi**
3rd, **mikka**	13th, **jūsan-nichi**	23rd, **nijūsan-nichi**
4th, **yokka**	14th, **jūyokka**	24th, **nijūyokka**
5th, **itsuka**	15th, **jūgo-nichi**	25th, **nijūgo-nichi**
6th, **muika**	16th, **jūroku-nichi**	26th, **nijūroku-nichi**
7th, **nanoka**	17th, **jūshichi-nichi**	27th, **nijūshichi-nichi**
8th, **yōka**	18th, **jūhachi-nichi**	28th, **nijūhachi-nichi**
9th, **kokonoka**	19th, **jūku-nichi**	29th, **nijūku-nichi**
10th, **tōka**	20th, **hatsuka**	30th, **sanjū-nichi**
		31st, **sanjūichi-nichi**

VII Months. Memorize the names of the months.

ichi-gatsu, January	**go-gatsu,** May	**ku-gatsu,** September
ni-gatsu, February	**roku-gatsu,** June	**jū-gatsu,** October
san-gatsu, March	**shichi-gatsu,** July	**jūichi-gatsu,** November
shi-gatsu, April	**hachi-gatsu,** August	**jūni-gatsu,** December

VIII Make dialogues by changing the underlined parts as in the examples given.

    A. *ex.* **Q: Kyō wa nan-nichi desu ka.**

        A: 15-nichi desu.

1. 19-nichi
2. 23-nichi
3. 27-nichi

B. *ex.* Q: Ashita wa nan-yōbi desu ka.

A: <u>Ka-yōbi</u> desu.

1. sui-yōbi
2. moku-yōbi

C. *ex.* Q: Kinō wa nan-nichi deshita ka.

A: <u>11-nichi</u> deshita.

1. 12-nichi
2. 13-nichi

D. *ex.* Q: [Anata no] Tanjōbi wa itsu desu ka.

A: <u>3-gatsu</u> desu.

Q: <u>3-gatsu</u> nan-nichi desu ka.

A: <u>3-gatsu 26-nichi</u> desu.

1. 4-gatsu, 15-nichi
2. 9-gatsu, 21-nichi
3. 12-gatsu, 18-nichi

E. *ex.* Q: Kinō wa <u>moku-yōbi</u> deshita ka.

A: Iie, <u>moku-yōbi</u> dewa arimasendeshita. <u>Kin-yōbi</u> deshita.

1. getsu-yōbi, ka-yōbi
2. sui-yōbi, moku-yōbi
3. do-yōbi, nichi-yōbi

Vocabulary			
pātī	party	**shigoto**	work
eiga	movie	**nan-nichi**	which day (of the month)
kaigi	conference, meeting	**nan-yōbi**	which day (of the week)
yūbinkyoku	post office	**itsu**	when

SHORT DIALOGUES

1. Sumisu: Ima nan-ji desu ka.
   Hisho: 9-ji han desu.
   Sumisu: Kaigi wa nan-ji kara desu ka.
   Hisho: 10-ji kara desu.

   Smith: What time is it now?
   Secretary: It's 9:30.
   Smith: What time does the meeting begin?
   Secretary: It's from 10:00.

2. **Tanaka:** **Natsu-yasumi wa itsu kara desu ka.**

   Sumisu: **7-gatsu 15-nichi kara desu.**

   Tanaka: **7-gatsu 15-nichi wa nan-yōbi desu ka.**

   Sumisu: **Do-yōbi desu.**

   Tanaka: When does summer vacation begin?
   Smith: It's from July 15.
   Tanaka: What day is July 15?
   Smith: It's a Saturday.

| Vocabulary |

natsu-yasumi   summer vacation
   natsu   summer

QUIZ ▰▰▰▰▰▰

I Read this lesson's opening dialogue and answer the following questions.

   1. **Ima 10-ji desu ka.**
   2. **Depāto wa nan-ji kara desu ka.**
   3. **Depāto wa 7-ji made desu ka.**

II Complete the questions so that they fit the answers.

   1. **Hiru-yasumi wa (   ) kara desu ka.**
      12-ji han kara desu.
   2. **Kyō wa (   ) desu ka.**
      Ka-yōbi desu.
   3. **Kinō wa (   ) deshita ka.**
      11-nichi deshita.

III Put the appropriate particles in the parentheses.

   1. **Kinō (   ) kin-yōbi deshita.**
   2. **Watashi (   ) kaisha no hiru-yasumi (   ) 12-ji kara desu.**
   3. **Depāto (   ) nan-ji (   ) nan-ji (   ) desu ka.**

IV Translate into Japanese.

   1. Thank you very much.
   2. You're welcome.
   3. Excuse me. Until what time does the post office stay open?
   4. Today is the 15. Tomorrow is the 16.
   5. Today is Thursday. Yesterday was Wednesday.

LESSON 4 HOW MUCH?

Mr. Smith goes shopping in the department store.

デパートの　てんいん：いらっしゃいませ。

スミス：　　　　　　それを　みせてください。

デパートの　てんいん：はい、どうぞ。

スミス：　　　　　　これは　いくらですか。

デパートの　てんいん：3,000えんです。

スミス：　　　　　　それは　いくらですか。

デパートの　てんいん：これも　3,000えんです。

スミス：　　　　　　じゃ、それを　ください。

デパートの　てんいん：はい、ありがとうございます。

Depāto no ten'in:	**Irasshaimase.**
Sumisu:	**Sore o misete kudasai.**
Depāto no ten'in:	**Hai, dōzo.**
Sumisu:	**Kore wa ikura desu ka.**
Depāto no ten'in:	**Sanzen-en desu.**
Sumisu:	**Sore wa ikura desu ka.**
Depāto no ten'in:	**Kore mo sanzen-en desu.**
Sumisu:	**Ja, sore o kudasai.**
Depāto no ten'in:	**Hai, arigatō gozaimasu.**

Store Clerk:	May I help you, sir? (*lit.* "Welcome!")
Smith:	Would you show me that, please?
Store Clerk:	Certainly, sir. Here you are.
Smith:	How much is this?
Store Clerk:	3,000 yen.
Smith:	How much is that one?
Store Clerk:	This one's 3,000 yen, too.
Smith:	Well then, please give me that one.
Store Clerk:	Very well, sir. Thank you.

Vocabulary		
てんいん	**ten'in**	store clerk
いらっしゃいませ	**irasshaimase**	Come in!/Welcome! (greeting to customers in stores/restaurants)
それ	**sore**	that, that one
を	**o**	(object marker, particle)
みせて　ください	**misete kudasai**	Please show me
みせます（みせる）	**misemasu (miseru)**	show
いくら	**ikura**	how much
3,000えん	**sanzen-en**	3,000 yen
〜えん	**-en**	yen (¥)
も	**mo**	too (particle)
じゃ	**ja**	Well then . . .
ください	**kudasai**	Please give me . . .

NOTES

1. Kore, sore

Whereas English has only "this" and "that," Japanese has three separate indicators: **Kore**, **sore**, and **are**. (See Note 5, p. 46.)

Kore indicates something near the speaker.

Sore indicates something near the person spoken to.

Are indicates something not near either person.

ex. **Kore wa watashi no meishi desu.** "This is my business card."

2. Mo

The particle **mo** means "too, also, either." It is used in both affirmative and negative sentences.

ex. **Sore wa 3,000-en desu. Kore mo 3,000-en desu.** "That one is ¥3,000. This one is ¥3,000, too."

Kore wa watashi no kasa ja arimasen. Sore mo watashi no ja arimasen. "This is not my umbrella. That's not mine either."

3. Ja, sore o kudasai.

Dewa and **ja** correspond to "well" or "well then," an interjection expressing conclusion or resignation.

4. Sore o kudasai.

Kudasai, "please give me," follows the object (a noun referring to concrete things only) + object marker **o**. In this case, **onegaishimasu** can be used instead of **kudasai**.

ex. **Banana o kudasai.** "Please give me some bananas."

5. Ikura, "how much"

ex. **Kono fuirumu wa ikura desu ka.** "How much is this film?"

PRACTICE

KEY SENTENCES ──────────────

1. **Kore wa tokei desu.**
2. **Sore mo tokei desu.**
3. **Are wa 3,000-en desu.**
4. **Kore o kudasai.**
5. **Are mo kudasai.**

1. This is a watch.
2. That is a watch, too.
3. That one (over there) is ¥3,000.
4. Give me this one, please.
5. Give me that one (over there), too, please.

Vocabulary

are   that (over there)

EXERCISES ──────────────

I Look at the pictures and practice the following patterns.

   A. Imagine you are Mr. A and say the following.

   1. **Kore wa tokei desu.**
   2. **Sore wa kasa desu.**
   3. **Are wa terebi desu.**

   B. Now imagine you are Mr. B and say the following.

   1. **Kore wa kasa desu.**
   2. **Sore wa tokei desu.**
   3. **Are wa terebi desu.**

C. Imagine you are the clerk and state the prices of the objects illustrated.

   1. Kore wa 3,000-en desu.

   2. Sore wa 3,500-en desu.

   3. Are mo 3,500-en desu.

II Numbers: Memorize the numbers from 100 to 1,000,000,000,000 and note how decimals and fractions are read.

100. **hyaku**	1,000. **sen**	10,000. **ichiman**
200. **nihyaku**	2,000. **nisen**	100,000. **jūman**
300. **sambyaku**	3,000. **sanzen**	1,000,000. **hyakuman**
400. **yonhyaku**	4,000. **yonsen**	10,000,000. **senman**
500. **gohyaku**	5,000. **gosen**	100,000,000. **ichioku**
600. **roppyaku**	6,000. **rokusen**	1,000,000,000. **jūoku**
700. **nanahyaku**	7,000. **nanasen**	10,000,000,000. **hyakuoku**
800. **happyaku**	8,000. **hassen**	100,000,000,000. **sen'oku**
900. **kyūhyaku**,	9,000. **kyūsen**	1,000,000,000,000. **itchō**

Intermediate numbers are made by combining the numbers composing them.

ex. 135, **hyaku-sanjū-go**   1,829, **sen-happyaku-nijū-kyū**

Decimals. (The word for "decimal point" is **ten**.)

    0, **rei, zero**

    0.7, **rei ten nana**

    0.29, **rei ten ni kyū**

    0.538, **rei ten go san hachi**

Fractions. (**Bun** means "part.")

    1/2, **nibun no ichi**   1/4, **yombun no ichi**   2/3, **sambun no ni**

III Make dialogues by changing the underlined parts as in the examples given.

  A. *ex.* **Q: Kore wa ikura desu ka.**

      A: [Sore wa] 2,000-en desu.

     1. **1,800-en**

     2. **1,200-en**

     3. **7,500-en**

  B. *ex.* **Q: Sore wa hon desu ka.**

      A: Hai, kore wa hon desu.

      Q: Are mo hon desu ka.

      A: Hai, are mo hon desu.

     1. **tokei**

     2. **rajio**

  C. *ex.* **Q: Kore wa ikura desu ka.**

      A: Sore wa 3,500-en desu.

      Q: Are mo 3,500-en desu ka.

      A: Hai, are mo 3,500-en desu.

1. ikura, 5,000-en
2. nan, rajio

D. *ex.* Q: Sore wa <u>3,000-en</u> desu ka.

A: Hai, kore wa <u>3,000-en</u> desu.

Q: Are mo <u>3,000-en</u> desu ka.

A: Iie, are wa <u>3,000-en</u> dewa arimasen. <u>3,500-en</u> desu.

1. tēpurekōdā, rajio
2. Tanaka-san no hon, Sumisu-san no hon

IV Practice the following pattern by changing the underlined part as in the example given.

ex. <u>Kore</u> o kudasai.

1. sore
2. haizara
3. mizu
4. ringo
5. reshīto

Vocabulary

kasa	umbrella	**haizara**	ashtray
terebi	TV (set)	**mizu**	water
rajio	radio	**ringo**	apple
tēpurekōdā	tape recorder	**reshīto**	receipt

SHORT DIALOGUE

Sumisu: Sumimasen. Are wa rajio desu ka.
Ten'in: Iie, rajio dewa arimasen. Tēpurekōdā desu.
Sumisu: Kore wa rajio desu ka.
Ten'in: Hai, rajio desu.
Sumisu: Ikura desu ka.
Ten'in: 28,000-en desu.
Sumisu: Dewa, kore o kudasai.

Smith: Excuse me. Is that a radio?
Clerk: No, it's not a radio. It's a tape recorder.
Smith: Is this a radio?
Clerk: Yes, it's a radio.
Smith: How much is it?
Clerk: It's ¥28,000.
Smith: Then, I'll take this.

Vocabulary

dewa well then

QUIZ

I Imagine you are B in the illustration and answer A's questions.

1. **Kore wa tokei desu.**
   Sore mo tokei desu ka.
2. **Are wa nan desu ka.**
3. **Are wa ikura desu ka.**
4. **Kore mo 50,000-en desu ka.**
5. **Kore wa ikura desu ka.**
6. **Sore mo 5,000-en desu ka.**

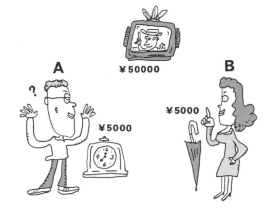

II Complete the questions so that they fit the answers.

1. **Sore wa (   ) desu ka.**
   Kore wa tēpurekōdā desu.
2. **Kore wa (   ) desu ka.**
   Sore wa 13,000-en desu.
3. **Kochira wa (   ) desu ka.**
   Tanaka-san desu.
4. **(   ) wa ikura desu ka.**
   Are wa 3,500-en desu.

III Put the appropriate particles in the parentheses.

1. **Kore (   ) kudasai.**
2. **Kore (   ) ikura desu ka.**
   5,000-en desu.
   Sore (   ) 5,000-en desu ka.
   Hai, kore (   ) 5,000-en desu.
   Are (   ) 5,000-en desu ka.
   Iie, are (   ) 5,000-en dewa arimasen. Are (   ) 3,500-en desu.

IV Answer with the appropriate expressions in Japanese.

1. When you want a store clerk to show you an article that is near him, what do you say?
2. When you have decided to buy an article that is near you, what do you say to the clerk?
3. When you want to know the price of an article near you, what do you say?
4. What does a store clerk say when a customer enters the store?

LESSON 5 COUNTING OBJECTS

Mr. Smith buys a camera at a camera shop.

スミス： すみません。その　カメラは　いくらですか。

カメラや：どれですか。

スミス： その　ちいさい　カメラです。

カメラや：これですか。25,000えんです。どうぞ。

スミス： これを　ください。それから　フイルムを　みっつ
　　　　　ください。

■ちいさい　カメラは　25,000えんです。

Sumisu: Sumimasen. Sono kamera wa ikura desu ka.
Kamera-ya: Dore desu ka.
Sumisu: Sono chiisai kamera desu.
Kamera-ya: Kore desu ka. 25,000-en desu. Dōzo.
Sumisu: Kore o kudasai. Sorekara fuirumu o mittsu kudasai.

■ **Chiisai kamera wa 25,000-en desu.**

Smith: Excuse me. How much is that camera?
Salesman: Which one, sir?
Smith: That small camera.
Salesman: This one? It's ¥25,000. Here you are.
Smith: I'll take this. And please let me have three (rolls of) film.

■ The small camera is ¥25,000.

Vocabulary		
その	**sono**	that
カメラ	**kamera**	camera
カメラや	**kamera-ya**	camera store, camera seller
〜や	**-ya**	store, seller
どれ	**dore**	which
ちいさい	**chiisai**	small (**-i** adj.)

それから	**sorekara**	and
フイルム	**fuirumu**	film
みっつ	**mittsu**	3

NOTES

1. Kamera-ya

Kamera-ya means not only "camera store" but also the store owner or store clerk. **Ya** is added to many things to mean the store or the person selling something.

ex. **Hana-ya**, "flower shop, florist"; **sakana-ya**, "fish shop, fish seller"; **hon-ya**, "book store, book seller."

2. Sorekara

Sorekara, "and, and also, and then, after that, in addition," is a connective placed at the beginning of a new sentence to connect it to the previous one.

3. Mittsu

In Japanese there are two numerical systems, the **hitotsu, futatsu, mittsu** system and the abstract **ichi, ni, san** system. Counting things can be done in two ways:

1. Using the **hitotsu, futatsu, mittsu** system independently. (See Exercise III, p. 48.)

ex. **Fuirumu o mittsu kudasai.** "Please give me three (rolls of) film."

2. Using the **ichi, ni, san** system combined with a counter. Two counters are **-mai**, for thin, flat objects such as paper, records, etc., and **-hon (-bon, -pon)**, for long, slender objects such as pencils, bottles, etc. Other counters appear in the appropriate place in the text, and they are given comprehensively in Appendix I.

-mai (how many . . . nan-mai)		-hon (how many . . . nan-bon)	
ichi-mai	shichi-mai, nana-mai	ippon	nana-hon
ni-mai	hachi-mai	ni-hon	happon
san-mai	kyū-mai	sam-bon	kyū-hon
yon-mai	jū-mai	yon-hon	juppon
go-mai	jūichi-mai	go-hon	jūippon
roku-mai	jūni-mai	roppon	jūni-hon

ex. **Hagaki o san-mai kudasai.** "Please give me three postcards." (*lit.* "three 'sheets of' ")

Note: The **hitotsu, futatsu, mittsu** system only goes as far as **tō** (10), after which the **ichi, ni, san** system is used: **jū-ichi, jū-ni, jū-san**, etc.

4. **Fuirumu o mittsu kudasai.**

   Note the word order: thing + **o** + numeral (or numeral and counter) + **kudasai.**

5. **Kono chiisai kamera**

   Chiisai is an adjective. Adjectives will be given in detail in Lesson 13 and Lesson 14.

   In Lesson 4 it was pointed out that there are three words for this and that: **kore, sore** and **are.** The demonstratives **kono, sono** and **ano** are used with nouns and have similar meanings from the viewpoint of the speaker. Study the following diagram and the chart (see Appendix F) to understand the meaning of these words.

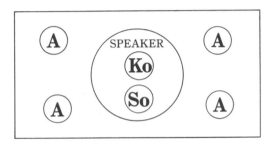

6. **Ikutsu,** "How many?"
   ex. **Fuirumu o kudasai.** "Please give me some film."
   Hai, ikutsu desu ka. "Certainly sir, how many do you wish?"

PRACTICE

KEY SENTENCES

1. **Kono kamera wa 25,000-en desu.**
2. **Kono ringo wa hitotsu 200-en desu.**
3. **Kore wa Nihon no kamera desu.**
4. **Sono chiisai denchi o mittsu kudasai.**

1. This camera is ¥25,000.
2. One of these apples is ¥200.
3. This is a Japanese camera.
4. Please give me three of those small batteries.

| Vocabulary |

kono   this
hitotsu 1
denchi   battery

EXERCISES

I Look at the picture and practice how to use **kore/kono**, **sore/sono** and **are/ano**.

    1. **Kore wa 30,000-en desu.**

      Kono kamera wa 30,000-en desu.

    2. **Sore wa 20,000-en desu.**

      Sono tokei wa 20,000-en desu.

    3. **Are wa 10,000-en desu.**

      Ano tēpurekōdā wa 10,000-en desu.

II Make dialogues by changing the underlined parts as in the examples given.

    A. *ex.* **Q:** <u>Sono kamera</u> **wa ikura desu ka.**

          A: <u>Kore</u> **wa 30,000-en desu.**

        1. **kono rajio, sore**

        2. **ano tēpurekōdā, are**

    B. *ex.* **Kore wa** <u>Nihon</u> **no kuruma desu ka.**

          A: Iie, <u>Nihon</u> **no dewa arimasen.** <u>Doitsu</u> **no desu.**

        1. **Amerika, Igirisu**

        2. **Itaria, Furansu**

    C. *ex.* **Q: Kore wa doko no kamera desu ka.**

          A: <u>Nihon</u> **no kamera desu.**

        1. **Doitsu**

        2. **Amerika**

D. *ex.* Q: Ano <u>akai kasa</u> wa ikura desu ka.

    A: Are wa <u>5,000-en</u> desu.

    1. chiisai kamera, 20,000-en

    2. Doitsu no tokei, 10,000-en

E. *ex.* Q: Hayashi-san no kasa wa <u>kore</u> desu ka.

    A: Hai, <u>sore</u> desu.

    1. sore, kore

    2. are, are

F. *ex.* <u>Hayashi-san no kasa wa dore desu ka.</u>

    A: Kore desu.

    1. Nihon-go no tēpu

    2. Sumisu-san no kuruma

III Practice how to count things.

1, **hitotsu**	4, **yottsu**	7, **nanatsu**	10, **tō**
2, **futatsu**	5, **itsutsu**	8, **yattsu**	11, **jūichi**
3, **mittsu**	6, **muttsu**	9, **kokonotsu**	12, **jūni**

IV Look at the pictures and practice the following pattern by changing the underlined parts as in the example given.

    ex. **Kono <u>fuirumu</u> o <u>futatsu</u> kudasai.**

        1. kono denchi, hitotsu

        2. sono ōkii ringo, itsutsu

        3. kono mikan, 2-kiro

        4. 100-en no kitte, 10-mai

        5. bīru, 12-hon

1   2   3   4   5

Vocabulary

ano	that, that one (over there)	**akai**	red (**-i** adj.)
Igirisu	United Kingdom	**Nihon-go**	Japanese language
Itaria	Italy	**-go**	language
Furansu	France	**tēpu**	tape
doko	where, belonging to or coming from what place?	**futatsu**	2
		ōkii	big (**-i** adj.)

itsutsu	5	**10-mai**	*lit.* 10 (sheets)
mikan	tangerine	**-mai**	(counter)
2-kiro	2 kilograms	**bīru**	beer
-kiro	kilogram	**12-hon**	12 bottles
kitte	postage stamp	**-hon, -bon, -pon**	(counter)

SHORT DIALOGUES

1. **Sumisu:** **Sumimasen. Rajio o misete kudasai.**
   Ten'in: **Dono rajio desu ka.**
   Sumisu: **Ano chiisai rajio desu.**
   Ten'in: **Hai, dōzo.**

   Smith: Excuse me. Would you show me that radio?
   Clerk: Which radio?
   Smith: That small radio (over there).
   Clerk: Certainly, sir. Here you are.

2. **Sumisu:** **Ano kasa wa ikura desu ka.**
   Ten'in: **Dore desu ka.**
   Sumisu: **Ano aoi kasa desu.**
   Ten'in: **Are wa 5,000-en desu.**
   Sumisu: **Ano kuroi kasa mo 5,000-en desu ka.**
   Ten'in: **Iie, are wa 7,000-en desu.**
   Sumisu: **Ja, ano aoi kasa o kudasai.**

   Smith: How much is that umbrella (over there)?
   Clerk: Which one?
   Smith: That blue one.
   Clerk: That's ¥5,000.
   Smith: Is that black umbrella ¥5,000, too?
   Clerk: No, it's ¥7,000.
   Smith: Well then, I'll take that blue one.

> **Vocabulary**

dono which
aoi blue (**-i** adj.)
kuroi black (**-i** adj.)

QUIZ

I Supposing you are the store clerk in the illustration. Answer the customer's questions.

1. **Kono Doitsu no kamera wa ikura desu ka.**
2. **Sono kamera mo Doitsu no desu ka.**
3. **Sono kamera wa ikura desu ka.**
4. **Ano chiisai rajio wa doko no desu ka.**

II Complete the questions so that they fit the answers.

1. **Kono denchi wa (   ) desu ka.**
   100-en desu.
2. **(   ) wa ikura desu ka.**
   Are wa 30,000-en desu.
3. **Are wa (   ) no kitte desu ka.**
   Iie, Igirisu no dewa arimasen.
   (   ) no desu ka.
   Amerika no desu.

III Put the appropriate particles in the parentheses. (If a particle is not required, put an X in the parentheses.)

1. **Kore (   ) Nihon (   ) tēpurekōdā desu. Sono tēpurekōdā (   )**
   Nihon (   ) desu.
2. **Kamera (   ) misete kudasai.**
3. **Bīru (   ) 15-hon (   ) kudasai.**
4. **Kore (   ) 150-en desu.**
5. **Kono (   ) ringo (   ) hitotsu (   ) 200-en desu.**

IV Translate into Japanese.

1. How much is this?
2. How much is this radio?
3. My watch is not Japanese. It is American.
4. Please show me that small tape recorder.
5. Please give me 3 (rolls of) film.
   Which film?
   That film.

LESSON 6 GOING AND COMING

Mr. Tanaka meets Mr. Hayashi at Tokyo Station. Mr. Hayashi looks as if he is going on a trip.

たなか：あ、はやしさん。しゅっちょうですか。

はやし：ええ。

たなか：どこに　いきますか。

はやし：きょうとの　ししゃに　いきます。

たなか：ひとりで　いきますか。

はやし：いいえ、かいしゃの　ひとと　いきます。

たなか：おおさかにも　いきますか。

はやし：いいえ、おおさかには　いきません。

たなか：いつ　とうきょうに　かえりますか。

はやし：あさって　かえります。

■はやしさんは　かいしゃの　ひとと　きょうとの　ししゃに
　いきます。そして　あさって　とうきょうに　かえります。

Tanaka:	A, Hayashi-san. Shutchō desu ka.
Hayashi:	Ee.
Tanaka:	Doko ni ikimasu ka.
Hayashi:	Kyōto no shisha ni ikimasu.
Tanaka:	Hitori de ikimasu ka.
Hayashi:	Iie, kaisha no hito to ikimasu.
Tanaka:	Ōsaka ni mo ikimasu ka.
Hayashi:	Iie, Ōsaka ni wa ikimasen.
Tanaka:	Itsu Tōkyō ni kaerimasu ka.
Hayashi:	Asatte kaerimasu.

■ Hayashi-san wa kaisha no hito to Kyōto no shisha ni ikimasu. Soshite asatte Tōkyō ni kaerimasu.

Tanaka: Ah, Mr. Hayashi, is it a business trip (you're going on)?
Hayashi: Yes.
Tanaka: Where are you going?
Hayashi: I'm going to our branch office in Kyoto.
Tanaka: Are you going alone?
Hayashi: No, I'm going with a person from the company.
Tanaka: Are you going to Osaka, too?
Hayashi: No, we're not going to Osaka.
Tanaka: When are you coming back to Tokyo?
Hayashi: We're returning the day after tomorrow.

■ Mr. Hayashi is going to the company's branch office in Kyoto with a colleague. They will return to Tokyo the day after tomorrow.

Vocabulary		
あ	**a**	ah
しゅっちょうですか	**shutchō desu ka**	is it a business trip (you're going on)?
しゅっちょう	**shutchō**	business trip
に	**ni**	to (particle)
いきます（いく）	**ikimasu (iku)**	go, is going
きょうと	**Kyōto**	Kyoto (city and prefecture)
ししゃ	**shisha**	branch office
ひとりで	**hitori de**	alone
と	**to**	with (particle)
おおさか	**Ōsaka**	Osaka (city and prefecture)
とうきょう	**Tōkyō**	Tokyo (city and prefecture)
かえります（かえる）	**kaerimasu (kaeru)**	return, come back
あさって	**asatte**	the day after tomorrow
そして	**soshite**	and then

GRAMMAR II

Lessons 6–7   NI/E verb

1. noun **wa** place **NI/E IKIMASU**
2. noun **wa** place **NI/E IKIMASU KA**

   Hai, (noun **wa** place **ni**) **ikimasu.**

   Iie, (noun **wa** place **ni**) **ikimasen.**

- Particles **ni/e**

  Particles are an important part of Japanese sentence structure. They resemble English prepositions in the way they connect words, but unlike English *pre*positions, which come before nouns, Japanese particles are *post*positions, always coming after nouns. Particles show the grammatical role of nouns in Japanese.

The role of the preposition "to" in English is played by the particles **ni** and **e** in Japanese, placed after the noun—something like the English suffix "-ward," as in "northward."

ex. **Tōkyō ni/e ikimasu.** "I am going to Tokyo." (*lit.* " 'Tokyo-ward' I am going.")

Theoretically the use of **ni** and **e** are divided as given below, but in actual practice they are interchangeable. In this book, in situations where either might occur, we use **ni**.

> **e**: expresses direction
>> *ex.* **Higashi e ikimasu.** "(I) am going toward the east."
>
> **ni**: expresses arrival at a destination
>> *ex.* **Kyonen no 12-gatsu ni Nihon ni kimashita.** "(I) came to Japan last December."

Note that some particles, like **ka**, may come at the end of phrases, clauses or sentences. See Lesson 1, **ka**; Lesson 9, **kara**, **yo**, **ne**; Lesson 10, **ne**; Lesson 12, **ga**; and Lesson 16, **ni**.

- Verbs

Japanese sentences end with the verb. (**Desu** in Grammar I is not strictly speaking a verb, but its use in sentences is similar to that of a verb and so it comes at the end.) The endings of verbs show the tense and whether they are positive or negative.

Tenses of Japanese verbs can be divided roughly into two large categories:

1. Present Form

> Habitual action: *ex.* **Tanaka-san wa mainichi kaisha ni ikimasu.** "Mr. Tanaka goes to the office (*lit.* company) every day."
>
> Future: *ex.* **[Watashi wa] Ashita kaerimasu.** "I return/am returning/will return tomorrow."

2. Past Form

> Past: *ex.* **[Watashi wa] Senshū Kyōto ni ikimashita.** "Last week (I) went to Kyoto."
>
> Present perfect: *ex.* **Ima kimashita.** "(He) has just come."

In simple sentences like the above, tenses of Japanese verbs closely resemble those in English. However, verbs that occur within a sentence in addition to the main verb at the end (i.e., Before I *left* home, I turned off the TV), do not necessarily take the same form they would in English. But that kind of sentence is outside the scope of this book and must be studied in Book II.

Note: The **-u** form of the verb given in the vocabulary lists (**-u**, **-ku**, **-su**, **-ru**, etc.) is the form found in dictionaries, so it is often called the dictionary form. Used at the end of a sentence, it is less formal in conversations than the **-masu** form. This book uses only the more polite **-masu** form.

NOTES

1. A. **Hitori de ikimasu.**

Number of people takes the particle **de**.

ex. **Hitori de**, "alone, by oneself"

San-nin de, "three of us/them"

B. Kaisha no hito to ikimasu.
Individual or individuals take the particle **to**, "with."
ex. **Tanaka-san to**, "with Mr. Tanaka"

2. **Ōsaka ni mo ikimasu ka.**
   Iie, Ōsaka ni wa ikimasen.
   Mr. Hayashi says he is going to Kyoto, which is close to the important industrial, city of Osaka, so Mr. Tanaka asks him if he is going to Osaka too. **Ōsaka ni mo . . .?** Note the position after the noun of the particles **ni**, "to, towards," and **mo**, "too, also."
   In his reply, Mr. Hayashi uses the topic marker particle **wa** to show that **Ōsaka ni** is the topic, "As for Osaka, I am not going there." (See Grammar III, p. 66.) Note that while two particles may normally follow one another, as do **ni mo** and **ni wa** above, **wa** and **mo** never follow the particles **ga** and **o**, but simply take their place. Similarly, **wa** and **mo** are never used together. One or the other is used.
   ex. **Sumisu-san wa bengoshi desu.** "Mr. Smith is a lawyer." **Buraun-san mo bengoshi desu.** "Mr. Brown, too, is a lawyer."
   Mo can follow any of the other particles such as **ni, kara, de**, etc.

3. **Asatte kaerimasu.**
   Relative time expressions like "yesterday," "next week," "this month" and "last year" do not take particles.

4. **Soshite, asatte Tōkyō ni kaerimasu.**
   In Japanese many sentences begin with connectives, like **soshite**, meaning "and then," which link them to the previous sentence.

5. **A. Doko**, "where"
   ex. **Doko ni ikimasu ka.** "Where are you going?"
   B. Itsu, "when." Time in general.
   ex. **Itsu kimasu ka.** "When are you coming?"
   C. Dare/donata (ga), "who"
   ex. **Dare ga Ōsaka ni ikimasu ka.** "Who is going to Osaka?" When the subject is unknown, the particle **ga** should be used after **dare/donata** instead of the topic marker **wa**. (See Grammar III, p. 66.)

PRACTICE

KEY SENTENCES

1. **Watashi wa ashita ginkō ni ikimasu.**
2. **Kono densha wa Tōkyō Eki ni ikimasen.**
3. **Watashi wa kinō yūbinkyoku ni ikimashita.**
4. **Watashi wa senshū gakkō ni ikimasendeshita.**
5. **Sumisu-san wa kyonen Amerika kara Nihon ni kimashita.**
6. **Sumisu-san wa rainen Amerika ni kaerimasu.**

1. I'm going to the bank tomorrow.
2. This train doesn't go to Tokyo Station.
3. I went to the post office yesterday.
4. I didn't go to school last week.
5. Mr. Smith came to Japan from America last year.
6. Mr. Smith will go back to America next year.

Vocabulary

densha	(electric) train	kara	from (particle)
Tōkyō Eki	Tokyo Station	kimashita	came
eki	station	kimasu (kuru)	come
senshū	last week	rainen	next year
kyonen	last year		

EXERCISES

I Verbs: Memorize the following verbs in their present and past forms.

	Present Form		Past Form	
	aff.	*neg.*	*aff.*	*neg.*
go	ikimasu	ikimasen	ikimashita	ikimasendeshita
come	kimasu	kimasen	kimashita	kimasendeshita
return	kaerimasu	kaerimasen	kaerimashita	kaerimasendeshita

II Practice the following by changing the underlined part as in the example given.

   ex. **A. [Watashi wa] Ginkō ni ikimasu.**

   1. **kaisha**
   2. **Amerika**

III Make dialogues by changing the underlined part as in the examples given.

   A. *ex.* **Q: [Anata wa] Ashita kaisha ni ikimasu ka.**

   A*a*: Hai, ikimasu.

   A*n*: Iie, ikimasen.

   1. **tomodachi no uchi**
   2. **depāto**
   3. **taishikan**

   B. *ex.* **Q: Kono densha wa Tōkyō Eki ni ikimasu ka.**

   A*a*: Hai, ikimasu.

   A*n*: Iie, ikimasen.

    1. **basu**

    2. **chikatetsu**

C. *ex.* **Q: Sumisu-san wa <u>kinō</u> Amerika ni kaerimashita ka.**

    A*a*: Hai, kaerimashita.

    A*n*: Iie, kaerimasendeshita.

    1. **senshū**

    2. **sengetsu**

    3. **kyonen**

D. *ex.* **Q: Dare ga kyō taishikan ni ikimasu ka.**

    A: <u>Tanaka-san</u> ga ikimasu.

    1. **tomodachi**

    2. **Tanaka-san no hisho**

E. *ex.* **Q: [Anata wa] Itsu Nihon ni kimashita ka.**

    A: <u>Sengetsu</u> kimashita.

    1. **senshū**

    2. **kyonen**

F. *ex.* **Q: Tanaka-san wa kinō doko ni ikimashita ka.**

    A: <u>Depāto</u> ni ikimashita.

    1. **yūbinkyoku**

    2. **tomodachi no uchi**

    3. **ginkō**

G. *ex.* **Q: Sumisu-san wa dare to Narita Kūkō ni ikimashita ka.**

    A: <u>Tanaka-san to</u> ikimashita.

    1. **tomodachi to**

    2. **kaisha no hito to**

    3. **hitori de**

Vocabulary

tomodachi	friend	**sengetsu**	last month
basu	bus	**ga**	(subject marker, particle)
chikatetsu	subway, *lit.* underground railway	**Narita Kūkō**	Narita Airport
		kūkō	airport

SHORT DIALOGUES

1. **Tanaka:**   **Kyō ginkō ni ikimasu ka.**

    Hisho: **Hai, ikimasu.**

    Tanaka: **Yūbinkyoku ni mo ikimasu ka.**

    Hisho: **Iie, yūbinkyoku ni wa ikimasen.**

    Tanaka: Are you going to the bank today?

    Secretary: Yes, I am.

Tanaka: Will you go to the post office, too?

Secretary: No, I'm not going to the post office.

2. **Sumisu:**   **Kono densha wa Tōkyō Eki ni ikimasu ka.**

   Otoko no hito: Iie, ikimasen.

   Sumisu: **Dono densha ga ikimasu ka.**

   Otoko no hito: Ano aoi densha ga ikimasu.

   Smith: Does this train go to Tokyo Station?

   Man: No, it doesn't.

   Smith: Which train goes there?

   Man: That blue train over there does.

Vocabulary

otoko no hito   man

  otoko   man, male

QUIZ

I Read this lesson's opening dialogue and answer the following questions.

   1. **Hayashi-san wa Ōsaka no shisha ni ikimasu ka, Kyōto no shisha ni ikimasu ka.**

   2. **Hayashi-san wa dare to Kyōto no shisha ni ikimasu ka.**

   3. **Hayashi-san wa itsu Tōkyō ni kaerimasu ka.**

II Complete the questions so that they fit the answers.

   1. **(   ) ni ikimasu ka.**

     Hai, ginkō ni ikimasu.

     (   ) ni mo ikimasu ka.

     Iie, yūbinkyoku ni wa ikimasen.

   2. **(   ) Nihon ni kimashita ka.**

     Kyonen kimashita.

   3. **(   ) ni ikimashita ka.**

     Kūkō ni ikimashita.

     (   ) to ikimashita ka.

     Hitori de ikimashita.

III Put the appropriate particles in the parentheses. (If a particle is not required, put an X in the parentheses.)

   1. **Tanaka-san wa ashita (   ) Ōsaka (   ) ikimasu.**

   2. **Yamada-san wa kaisha no hito (   ) kūkō (   ) ikimashita.**

3. Tanaka-san (　　) itsu (　　) Ōsaka kara kaerimasu ka.
4. Tomodachi wa senshū hitori (　　) Amerika ni kaerimashita.
5. Ashita Kyōto (　　) ikimasu.
   Ōsaka ni (　　) ikimasu ka.
   Iie, Ōsaka ni (　　) ikimasen.
6. Dare (　　) kimashita ka.
   Yamada-san ga kimashita.

IV Translate into Japanese.

1. Excuse me, does this bus go to Tokyo Station?
2. Mr. Tanaka went to Osaka yesterday with a person from his company. And he will return to Tokyo the day after tomorrow.
3. Mr. Smith came to Japan alone last year.
4. Who went to the airport?
   Mr. Tanaka's secretary went.

LESSON 7 GOING BY TAXI

Mr. Smith visits Mr. Tanaka on Sunday.

たなか：スミスさん、よく　いらっしゃいました。

スミス：こんにちは。

たなか：どうぞ　おはいりください。

スミス：しつれいします。

たなか：どうぞ　こちらへ。バスで　きましたか。

スミス：いいえ、タクシーで　きました。

たなか：どうぞ　おかけください。

スミス：ありがとうございます。

■スミスさんは　にちようびに　タクシーで　たなかさんの　うちに
　いきました。

Tanaka:	**Sumisu-san, yoku irasshaimashita.**
Sumisu:	**Konnichiwa.**
Tanaka:	**Dōzo ohairi kudasai.**
Sumisu:	**Shitsurei shimasu.**
Tanaka:	**Dōzo kochira e. Basu de kimashita ka.**
Sumisu:	**Iie, takushī de kimashita.**
Tanaka:	**Dōzo okake kudasai.**
Sumisu:	**Arigatō gozaimasu.**

■ **Sumisu-san wa nichiyōbi ni takushi de Tanaka-san no uchi ni ikimashita.**

Tanaka:	Mr. Smith, how nice of you to come.
Smith:	Hello.
Tanaka:	Do come in.
Smith:	May I?
Tanaka:	This way, please. Did you come by bus?
Smith:	No. I came by taxi.
Tanaka	Do sit down.
Smith:	Thank you.

■ Mr. Smith went to Mr. Tanaka's house by taxi on Sunday.

よく いらっしゃいました	**yoku irasshaimashita**	How nice of you to come. (*lit.* "Welcome!")
よく	**yoku**	well
いらっしゃいました	**irasshaimashita**	came
いらっしゃいます (いらっしゃる)	**irasshaimasu (irassharu)**	come (polite word for **kuru**)
おはいり ください	**ohairi kudasai**	Do come in.
はいります (はいる)	**hairimasu (hairu)**	enter
しつれいします	**shitsurei shimasu**	May I? (I'm afraid I'll be disturbing you.)
こちらへ	**kochira e**	this way
こちら	**kochira**	this direction
で	**de**	by (particle)
タクシー	**takushi**	taxi
おかけ ください	**okake kudasai**	Please have a seat. (*lit.* "Please sit down.")
かけます (かける)	**kakemasu (kakeru)**	sit
に	**ni**	on (particle)

NOTES

1. **Shitsurei shimasu.**

   "May I." (*lit.* "I'll be so bold as to do so.")
   Shitsurei essentially means "rudeness" and is used when entering a house or room, passing in front of someone, leaving in the middle of a gathering and so on, in other words, when creating some sort of disturbance and interrupting the status quo. Some people use it as a form of "good-bye," instead of **sayōnara**, when leaving a house or room.

2. **Basu de kimashita ka.**

   The particle **de** follows nouns to express means.
   ex. **basu de**, (travel) "by bus"
   pen de, (write) "with pen"
   Nihon-go de, (speak) "in Japanese"
   iyahōn de, (listen) "with earphones"
   funabin de, (send) "by sea mail"

3. **Nichi-yōbi ni ikimashita.**

   Specific expressions of time take the particle **ni** as in the following:
   5-ji ni, "at 5 o'clock"
   do-yōbi ni, "on Saturday"
   12-nichi ni, "on the 12th"
   1960-nen ni, "in 1960"

4. **Nani/nan de**, "how"

    ex. **Nan de ikimasu ka.** "How will you go?"

      Basu de ikimasu. "I'll go by bus."

    An exception to this pattern is **aruite ikimasu**, "I'll walk."

PRACTICE

KEY SENTENCES

1. **Kurāku-san wa 5-gatsu 18-nichi ni Kanada kara Nihon ni kimashita.**
2. **Kurāku-san wa rainen no 3-gatsu ni Kanada ni kaerimasu.**
3. **Watashi wa chikatetsu de kaisha ni ikimasu.**

1. Mr. Clark came to Japan on May 18 from Canada.
2. Mr. Clark will go back to Canada in March of next year.
3. I go to the office by subway.

Vocabulary

Kurāku   Clark
Kanada   Canada

EXERCISES

I Practice the following pattern by changing the underlined part as in the example given.

    ex. **Howaito-san wa 5-gatsu 18-nichi ni Nihon ni kimashita.**

      1. **15-nichi ni**
      2. **1980 nen ni**
      3. **senshū no moku-yōbi ni**
      4. **sengetsu**
      5. **ototoi**
      6. **senshū**

II Make dialogues by changing the underlined part as in the examples given.

    A. *ex.* **Q: Howaito-san wa itsu Nihon ni kimasu ka.**

        A: 5-gatsu 18-nichi ni kimasu.

      1. **getsu-yōbi**
      2. **raishū no do-yōbi**
      3. **raigetsu no 15-nichi**
      4. **rainen no 10-gatsu**

    B. *ex.* **Q: Tanaka-san wa nan de uchi ni kaerimashita ka.**

        A: Kuruma de kaerimashita.

      1. **takushi**

2. **basu**

3. **densha**

C. *ex.* **Q: Hayashi-san wa nan-nen ni Igirisu ni ikimashita ka.**

　　A: <u>**1981-nen**</u> **ni ikimashita.**

1. **1975-nen**

2. **1982-nen**

D. *ex.* **Q: Dare ga kyō Kyōto no shisha ni ikimasu ka.**

　　A: <u>**Hayashi-san**</u> **ga ikimasu.**

　　Q: Hayashi-san wa itsu Tōkyō ni kaerimasu ka.

　　A: Asatte kaerimasu.

1. **Tanaka-san**

2. **Sumisu-san**

Vocabulary

Howaito	White	**raishū**	next week
1980-nen	(the year) 1980	**raigetsu**	next month
-nen	year (See Appendix K.)	**nan de**	how, by what means
ototoi	the day before yesterday	**nan-nen**	what year?

SHORT DIALOGUE

Tanaka:　**Kurāku-san wa itsu Nihon ni kimashita ka.**

Kurāku:　**Kyonen no 5-gatsu 18-nichi ni kimashita.**

Tanaka:　**Kyōto ni ikimashita ka.**

Kurāku:　**Ee, senshū Shinkansen de ikimashita. Kin-yōbi ni Tōkyō ni kaerimashita.**

Tanaka:　When did you come to Japan?

Clark:　I came on May 18 last year.

Tanaka:　Did you go to Kyoto?

Clark:　Yes, I went (there) by Shinkansen last week. I returned to Tokyo on Friday.

Vocabulary

Shinkansen　　Shinkansen, New Trunk Line

QUIZ ▰▰▰▰▨

I Read this lesson's opening dialogue and answer the following questions.

1. **Dare ga Tanaka-san no uchi ni ikimashita ka.**

2. **Sumisu-san wa itsu Tanaka-san no uchi ni ikimashita ka.**

3. **Sumisu-san wa Tanaka-san no uchi ni densha de ikimashita ka.**

4. **Sumisu-san wa Tanaka-san no uchi ni nan de ikimashita ka.**

II Complete the questions so that they fit the answers.

   1. **Nichi-yōbi ni (   ) ni ikimashita ka.**
     Tomodachi no uchi ni ikimashita.

   2. **Tanaka-san wa (   ) Kyōto kara kaerimashita ka.**
     Senshū no do-yōbi ni kaerimashita.

   3. **Kurāku-san wa (   ) ni Osaka ni ikimasu ka.**
     18-nichi ni ikimasu.
     (   ) de ikimasu ka.
     Shinkansen de ikimasu.
     (   ) to ikimasu ka.
     Hitori de ikimasu.

III Put the appropriate particles in the parentheses. (If a particle is not required, put an X in the parentheses.)

   1. **Watashi wa basu (   ) kaisha (   ) kimasu. Anata (   ) basu de kimasu ka.**

   2. **Itsu (   ) Nihon ni kimashita ka.**
     5-gatsu 18-nichi (   ) kimashita.

IV Answer with the appropriate expressions in Japanese.

   1. How does one greet a person one meets in the daytime?

   2. What does one say to a guest who has just arrived?

   3. How does one offer a chair to a guest?

V Translate into Japanese.

   1. Please come this way.

   2. Do come in.

   3. Mr. Tanaka went home yesterday by taxi.

   4. Miss White is going to the Osaka branch office on Friday.

Volume I

Provides survival skills for beginners, and builds a solid basic understanding of all aspects of the language. Students will master both phonetic syllabaries and a vocabulary of around 750 words. Completion of the text requires about 60 hours.

NEW FEATURES:

- New English-Japanese glossary
- Short *kanji* lessons from the end of Volume I.
- Grammar explanations have been re-edited for greater clarity.
- Dialogues are shorter and easier to memorize.
- Additional appendices for grammar usage.

Text	paperback, 232 pages	ISBN 4-7700-1882-7
Tapes	three 40-min. audio cassettes	ISBN 4-7700-1883-5
Compact Discs	two 60-min. CD's	ISBN 4-7700-1909-2
Workbook	paperback, 184 pages	ISBN 4-7700-1907-6
Workbook Tapes	two 50-min. audio cassettes	ISBN 4-7700-1908-4
Japanese Teacher's Manual	paperback, 160 pages	ISBN 4-7700-1906-8

Volume II & *NEW* Volume III

Teaches the basic language skills necessary to function in an adult environment. Volume II stresses daily conversational skills and introduces a vocabulary of about 900 new words and 130 *kanji*. Completion of Volume II requires about 120 hours. Volume III brings the student to the intermediate level and emphasizes accurate, natural Japanese. Completion of Volume III requires about 120 hours.

NEW FEATURES:

- Volume II of original edition has been separated into two volumes.
- Transition in difficulty level from Volume I to Volume II is more gradual.
- Short *kanji* study sections included in each lesson.
- Dialogues in earlier lessons are easier.
- New English-Japanese glossary in each volume.
- New supplementary reading sections.
- New, larger type size is easier to read

Volume II	Text	paperback, 232 pages	ISBN 4-7700-1884-3
	Tapes	three 80-min. audio cassettes	ISBN 4-7700-1885-1
Volume III	Text	paperback, 240 pages	ISBN 4-7700-1886 X
	Tapes	three 80-min. audio cassettes	ISBN 4-7700-1887-8

Published by:
KODANSHA INTERNATIONAL LTD.
17-14, Otowa 1-Chome, Bunkyo-ku, Tokyo 112, Japan   Tel: (03)3944-6492 Fax: (03)3944-6323

Distributed in America by:
KODANSHA AMERICA INC.
114 Fifth Avenue, New York, New York 10011   Tel: (212)727-6460 Fax: (212)727-9177

Distributed in Europe, the Near and Middle East by:
KODANSHA EUROPE LTD.
95 Aldwych, London WC2B 4JF   Tel: (071)304-4095 Fax: (071)304-4096

Distributed in Australia and New Zealand by:
BOOKWISE INTERNATIONAL
54 Crittenden Road, Findon 5023, South Australia   Tel: (08)268-8222 Fax: (08)268-8704

Printed in Japan

JAPANESE FOR BUSY PEOPLE

Revised Edition

Now in 3 Volumes!!

改訂版 コミュニケーションのための日本語 全3巻
Association for Japanese-Language Teaching (AJALT)

The completely revised JAPANESE FOR BUSY PEOPLE series is a concise yet comprehensive language course, offering the most practical means available of acquiring a working knowledge of real Japanese. In the three progressive levels from "survival" level through intermediate study, lessons emphasize words and patterns which can be put to immediate use in conversational situations. And now, as a result of intensive review by the editors of the Association for Japanese-Language Teaching, the series has been revised, improved and expanded to make it easier than ever to acquire Japanese language skills.

LESSON 8

EXISTENCE OF PEOPLE AND THINGS

Let's have a look at Mr. Tanaka's house.

いまに　いすや　テーブルや　テレビが　あります。テーブルの
うえに　しんぶんと　はなが　あります。いまに　たなかさんの
おくさんが　います。にわに　たなかさんと　おとこの　こが　います。
だいどころに　だれも　いません。

Ima ni isu ya tēburu ya terebi ga arimasu. Tēburu no ue ni shimbun to hana ga arimasu. Ima ni Tanaka-san no okusan ga imasu. Niwa ni Tanaka-san to otoko no ko ga imasu. Daidokoro ni dare mo imasen.

There is a chair, a table, a TV set (etc.) in the living room. There are some flowers and a newspaper on (top of) the table. Mrs. Tanaka is in the living room. Mr. Tanaka and a boy are in the garden. There isn't anybody in the kitchen.

いま	**ima**	living room
に	**ni**	in (particle)
いす	**isu**	chair
や	**ya**	and (etc.) (particle)
テーブル	**tēburu**	table
あります（ある）	**arimasu (aru)**	are (for inanimate things)
うえ	**ue**	top
と	**to**	and (particle)
はな	**hana**	flower
おくさん	**okusan**	(his) wife (See Note 2, p. 168.)
います（いる）	**imasu (iru)**	is (for living things)
にわ	**niwa**	garden
おとこのこ	**otoko no ko**	boy (*lit.* "male child")
こ	**ko**	child
だいどころ	**daidokoro**	kitchen
だれも〜ません	**dare mo . . . -masen**	nobody . . . is

GRAMMAR III

Lessons 8–9   Existence of People and Things

1. place NI noun GA ARIMASU/IMASU
2. noun WA place NI ARIMASU/IMASU
3. place NI WA noun GA ARIMASU/MASU

- **Arimasu/Imasu**
  Both verbs express "being." **Arimasu** is used for inanimate things (books, buildings, tree, etc.) and **imasu** for animate things (people, animals, insects, etc.)

- Particle **ni**
  Existence in a place is indicated by the particle **ni**, not **e**.
  ex. **Niwa ni Tanaka-san ga imasu.** "Mr. Tanaka is in the garden."

- Particle **ga**. Subject marker.
  When a subject is introduced for the first time, or when the speaker believes the information to be new to the listener, the subject marker **ga** is used after the noun.
  ex. **Basu ga kimasu.** "The bus is coming."
  Kinō Yamada-san ga kimashita. "Mr. Yamada came yesterday."
  Ga is also used when the subject is unknown, i.e., with question words like "who" and "what." (See Note 4, below.)
  ex. **Dare ga kimashita ka.** "Who came?"

Ga is used similarly in the reply.

ex. **Hayashi-san ga kimashita.** "Mr. Hayashi came."

● **Ga→wa/ni→ni wa**

For a neutral description, the following pattern is used.

ex. **Ikkai ni resutoran ga arimasu.** "There is a restaurant on the first floor."

When you want to talk about the restaurant, "the restaurant" becomes the topic.

ex. **Resutoran wa ikkai ni arimasu.** "The restaurant is on the first floor."

When you want to talk about what is on the first floor, "on the first floor" becomes the topic.

ex. **Ikkai ni wa resutoran ga arimasu.** "On the first floor, there is a restaurant."

● **Verb⸺→desu**

When the verb is understood, **desu** sometimes takes its place at the end of the sentence. In Lesson 6 we see the sentence, **"Shutchō desu ka?"** and **desu** here is used in place of **shimasu**.

ex. **Terebi wa doko ni arimasu ka.** "Where is the TV set?"

Tēburu no ue desu. (for **Tēburu no ue ni arimasu.**) "It's on the table."

If it is not certain whether there is a TV or not, **desu** cannot be substituted and **arimasu** must be repeated to make the meaning clear.

ex. **Tēburu no ue ni terebi ga arimasu ka.** "Is there a TV set on the table?"

Hai, arimasu./Hai, terebi ga arimasu. "Yes, there is./Yes, there is a TV set."

In this case, one may not say: **Hai, terebi desu./Hai, tēburu no ue desu.**

NOTES

1. **Ima ni isu ya tēburu ya terebi ga arimasu.**

   The particle **ya** is used for "and" when listing two or more things or people and implying the existence of others as well.

2. **Tēburu no ue ni shimbun to hana ga arimasu.**

   The particle **to** is used for "and" when the existence of nothing or nobody else is implied. From the Japanese sentence it is clear that there is nothing on the table besides the newspaper and the flowers. Note that unlike "and," both **to** and **ya** are used only to connect nouns.They cannot be used to connect verbs or clauses.

3. **Dare mo imasen.**

   Dare, "who," combines with the particle **mo** to mean "nobody" when followed by a verb with the negative ending **-masen**. Similarly, **nani mo**, "nothing," and **doko ni mo**, "nowhere," take the negative verb ending **-masen**.

   ex. **Dare mo kimasen deshita.** "Nobody came."

   Tanaka-san wa ashita doko ni mo ikimasen. "Mr. Tanaka is not going anywhere tomorrow."

4. Nani ga

Like **dare**, ''who'' (see Note 5, p. 55), **nani**, ''what,'' is never followed by the topic maker **wa**. It always takes the subject marker **ga**.

ex. **Isu no ue ni nani ga arimasu ka.** ''What is there on the chair?''
Hon ga arimasu. ''There is a book.''

PRACTICE

KEY SENTENCES

1. **Ikkai ni ima ga arimasu.**
2. **Hako no naka ni kitte to hagaki ga arimasu.**
3. **Tana no ue ni shashin ya hon ga arimasu.**
4. **Mado no chikaku ni onna no ko ga imasu.**
5. **Genkan ni dare mo imasen.**
6. **Todana no mae ni nani mo arimasen.**

1. There is a living room on the first floor.
2. There are stamps and postcards in the box.
3. There are pictures, books (etc.) on the shelf.
4. There is a girl near the window.
5. There isn't anybody in the entrance hall.
6. There isn't anything in front of the cabinet.

Vocabulary			
ikkai	first floor, ground floor	**mado**	window
-kai	floor (See Appendix I.)	**chikaku**	near, close to
hako	box	**onna no ko**	girl (*lit.* ''female child'')
naka	inside	**genkan**	entrance hall
hagaki	postcard	**todana**	cabinet
tana	shelf	**mae**	in front of, before
shashin	photograph		

EXERCISES

I Verbs: Memorize the following verbs and their present and past forms.

	Present Form		Past Form	
	aff.	*neg.*	*aff.*	*neg.*
be be	**arimasu** **imasu**	**arimasen** **imasen**	**arimashita** **imashita**	**arimasendeshita** **imasendeshita**

II Practice the following pattern by changing the underlined parts as in the examples given.

   A. *ex.* **Ima ni <u>terebi</u> ga arimasu.**

      1. **todana**
      2. **isu**
      3. **denwa**

   B. *ex.* **Ima ni <u>kodomo</u> ga imasu.**

      1. **otoko no ko**
      2. **onna no ko**

III Make dialogues by changing the underlined parts as in the examples given.

   A. *ex.* **Q: Ikkai ni <u>nani</u> ga arimasu ka.**

      A: <u>Ima</u> ga arimasu.

      1. **daidokoro**
      2. **shokudō**
      3. **o-tearai**

   B. *ex.* **Q: <u>Hako no naka</u> ni nani ga arimasu ka.**

      A: <u>Hagaki to kitte</u> ga arimasu.

      1. **tēburu no ue, hana to shimbun**
      2. **tana no ue, shashin ya hon**

   C. *ex.* **Q: Niwa ni dare ga imasu ka.**

      A: <u>Otoko no ko</u> ga imasu.

      1. **otoko no ko to onna no ko**
      2. **Tanaka-san**

   D. *ex.* **Q: <u>Daidokoro</u> ni dare ga imasu ka.**

      A: Dare mo imasen.

      1. **genkan**
      2. **shokudō**

   E. *ex.* **Q: <u>Todana no mae</u> ni nani ga arimasu ka.**

      A: Nani mo arimasen.

      1. **isu no ue**
      2. **isu no shita**

Vocabulary

kodomo	child	**nani mo . . . -masen**	nothing is
shokudō	dining room	**shita**	under
o-tearai	lavatory		
o-	(Traditionally added to certain words to give them elegance.) (prefix)		

SHORT DIALOGUE

Otoko no hito: Kono biru ni wa denwa ga arimasu ka.

Onna no hito: Hai, arimasu. Asoko ni uketsuke ga arimasu ne. Ano uketsuke no mae ni arimasu.

Otoko no hito: Dōmo arigatō.

Man: Is there a telephone in this building?

Woman: Yes, there is. There's a reception desk over there, you see? It's in front of the reception desk.

Man: Thank you.

Vocabulary

biru building

asoko over there, that place (over there)

uketsuke reception (desk)

ne You see . . . (*lit.* . . . "isn't there?")

QUIZ ▰▰▰▰▱▱

I Read this lesson's opening text and answer the following questions.

1. **Ima ni nani ga arimasu ka.**
2. **Tēburu no ue ni nani ga arimasu ka.**
3. **Ima ni dare ga imasu ka.**
4. **Daidokoro ni dare ga imasu ka.**

II Complete the questions so that they fit the answers.

1. **Niwa ni (   ) ga imasu ka.**
   Tanaka-san ga imasu.
2. **Ima ni (   ) ga arimasu ka.**
   Isu ya tēburu ga arimasu.
3. **Daidokoro ni (   ) ga imasu ka.**
   Dare mo imasen.
4. **Isu no ue ni (   ) ga arimasu ka.**
   Nani mo arimasen.

III Circle the correct verb of the two in parentheses.

1. **Tana no ue ni shashin ya hon ga (arimasu, imasu).**
2. **Niwa ni Tanaka-san ga (arimasu, imasu).**
3. **Daidokoro ni dare mo (imasu, imasen).**

4. **Terebi no ue ni nani mo (arimasu, arimasen).**

IV Put the appropriate particles in the parentheses. (If a particle is not required, put an X in the parentheses.)

1. **Hako (   ) naka (   ) kitte (   ) arimasu.**
2. **Tēburu (   ) ue ni hana (   ) shimbun (   ) arimasu.** (There is nothing else there besides the flowers and the newspapers.)
3. **Hako no naka ni hagaki (   ) kitte (   ) arimasu.** (There are other things besides postcards and stamps.)
4. **Genkan ni dare (   ) imasu ka.**
   Dare (   ) imasen.

V Translate into Japanese.

1. There are chairs, tables (etc.) in the living room.
2. In the garden (there) are Mr. Tanaka and a boy.
3. Who is in the kitchen?
   There isn't anybody (there).
4. There isn't anything on the chair.

LESSON 9 PLACE, LOCATION

Mr. Smith wants to send a parcel home. He is in front of the apartment building asking the superintendent how to go about it.

スミス： この　ちかくに　ゆうびんきょくが　ありますか。

かんりにん：ええ、ありますよ。

スミス： どこですか。

かんりにん：あそこに　スーパーが　ありますね。ゆうびんきょくは
あの　スーパーの　となりです。あかい　ポストが　あり
ますから、わかりますよ。

スミス： どうも　ありがとう。

■ゆうびんきょくは　スーパーの　となりです。

Sumisu: Kono chikaku ni yūbinkyoku ga arimasu ka.
Kanrinin: Ee, arimasu yo.
Sumisu: Doko desu ka.
Kanrinin: Asoko ni sūpā ga arimasu ne. Yūbinkyoku wa ano sūpā no tonari desu. Akai posuto ga arimasu kara, wakarimasu yo.
Sumisu: Dōmo arigatō.

■ Yūbinkyoku wa supā no tonari desu.

Smith:	Is there a post office near here?
Superintendent:	Yes, there is.
Smith:	Where is it?
Superintendent:	See that supermarket over there? The post office is next to that super-market. There's a red mail box, so you can't miss it.
Smith:	Thank you.

■ The post office is next to the supermarket.

かんりにん	**kanrinin**	superintendent
よ	**yo**	I tell you (particle)
スーパー	**sūpā**	supermarket
となり	**tonari**	next to
ポスト	**posuto**	mail box, post box
から	**kara**	so, because (particle)
わかります（わかる）	**wakarimasu (wakaru)**	understand, see

NOTES

1. **Ee, arimasu yo.**

   The particle **yo** is added to the end of a sentence to call attention to information the speaker thinks the other person does not know.

2. **Doko desu ka.**

   The same as **doko ni arimasu ka**. **Desu** is used in place of **ni arimasu**. (See Grammar III, p. 66.)

3. **Asoko ni sūpā ga arimasu ne.**

   "See that supermarket over there?" (*lit.* "There's a supermarket over there, isn't there?")

   The particle **ne** comes at the end of a sentence or phrase and, like "you see?" or "isn't there/it?" in English, seeks the confirmation and agreement of the other person. The particle **yo** *tells*, while the particle **ne** *asks*.

4. **Akai posuto ga arimasu kara**

   The particle **kara** means "because, so, therefore" and comes after the phrase or clause. The Japanese meaning can be expressed in English in two ways: "Because there's a red mail box," or "There's a red mail box, so . . ."

5. **Dōshite, "why"**

   ex. **Dōshite byōin wa 12-ji made desu ka.** Why is the hospital (only open) until 12 o'clock?

   Kyō wa do-yōbi desu kara. "Because today is Saturday."

PRACTICE

KEY SENTENCES

1. **Eki no chikaku ni tatemono ga takusan arimasu.**
2. **Hon-ya no mae ni kodomo ga 5-nin imasu.**

3. Takushī-noriba wa eki no mae desu.

4. Kyō wa do-yōbi desu kara, byōin wa 12-ji made desu.

1. There are many buildings near the station.

2. There are 5 children in front of the book store.

3. The taxi stand is in front of the station.

4. Today is Saturday, so the hospital is (only open) until 12:00.

Vocabulary

tatemono	building	**takushī-noriba**	taxi stand
takusan	many, lots of	**noriba**	*lit.* "boarding place"
hon-ya	book store	**byōin**	hospital
5-nin	5 people		
-nin	(counter for people)		
	(See Appendix I.)		

EXERCISES

I Practice the following patterns by changing the underlined parts as in the examples given.

    A. *ex.* **Tēburu no ue ni <u>ringo</u> ga <u>itsutsu</u> arimasu.**

        1. **hagaki, 3-mai**

        2. **bîru, 2-hon**

        3. **hana, takusan**

    B. *ex.* **Niwa ni <u>otoko no ko</u> ga <u>futari</u> imasu.**

        1. **onna no ko, 3-nin**

        2. **otoko no hito, hitori**

II Make dialogues by changing the underlined parts as in the examples given.

    A. *ex.* **Q: Tēburu no ue ni <u>ringo</u> ga <u>ikutsu</u> arimasu ka.**

        A: <u>Mittsu</u> arimasu.

        1. **hagaki, nan-mai, 3-mai**

        2. **bîru, nan-bon, 2-hon**

        3. **hana, nan-bon, takusan**

    B. *ex.* **Q: Niwa ni <u>otoko no hito</u> ga nan-nin imasu ka.**

        A: <u>Hitori</u> imasu.

        1. **onna no ko, 3-nin**

        2. **otoko no ko, futari**

    C. *ex.* **Q: Kono chikaku ni <u>takushī-noriba</u> ga arimasu ka.**

        A: Hai, arimasu. <u>Takushī-noriba</u> wa <u>eki no mae</u> ni arimasu.

        1. **kippu-uriba, eki no naka**

        2. **chikatetsu no iriguchi, depāto no mae**

        3. **byōin, asoko**

        4. **kusuri-ya, soko**

D. *ex.* **Q: Kuruma no kagi wa doko ni arimasu ka.**

   A: Koko ni arimasu.

   1. watashi no megane

   2. kono heya no kagi

E. *ex.* **Q: Tanaka-san wa doko ni imasu ka.**

   A: 2-kai ni imasu.

   1. niwa

   2. tonari no heya

F. *ex.* **Q: Basu-noriba wa doko desu ka.**

   A: Eki no mae desu.

   1. hon-ya, depāto no tonari

   2. kaisatsuguchi, eki no naka

   3. kusuri-ya, kōban no tonari

   4. byōin, eki no chikaku

III A. Connect the following sentences using **kara**, "because," as in the example given.

   ex. **Kyō wa yasumi desu. Watashi wa gakkō ni ikimasen.**

   Kyō wa yasumi desu kara, watashi wa gakkō ni ikimasen.

   1. **Kyō wa nichi-yōbi desu. Watashi wa kaisha ni ikimasen.**

B. Read the short dialogues and make the appropriate statements (S) using **kara**.

  ex. **Q: Dōshite kyō byōin wa 12-ji made desu ka.**
  A: Kyō wa do-yōbi desu kara.
  S: Kyō wa do-yōbi desu kara, byōin wa 12-ji made desu.

  1. **Q: Dōshite anata wa kyō gakkō ni ikimasen ka.**
    A: Kyō wa nichi-yōbi desu kara.
    S:

  2. **Q: Dōshite Sumisu-san wa kūkō ni ikimasu ka.**
    A: Okusan ga hikōki de kimasu kara.
    S:

Vocabulary

futari	2 people (See Appendix I.)	**yaoya**	vegetable store
		sakana-ya	fish store
hitori	1 person	**sakana**	fish
ikutsu	how many	**pan-ya**	bread store, bakery
nan-mai	how many sheets	**pan**	bread
nan-bon	how many bottles	**saka-ya**	liquor store
nan-nin	how many people	**soko**	there, that place
kippu-uriba	ticket office	**koko**	here, this place
kippu	ticket	**megane**	(eye) glasses
-uriba	*lit.* "selling place"	**heya**	room
iriguchi	entrance	**basu-noriba**	bus terminal
byōin	hospital	**kaisatsuguchi**	ticket gate
kusuri-ya	pharmacy, drug store	**kōban**	police box
kusuri	medicine	**yasumi**	holiday
niku-ya	meat store	**dōshite**	why
niku	meat	**hikōki**	airplane

SHORT DIALOGUE

Sumisu: **Kyō no shimbun wa doko ni arimasu ka.**
Yamada: **Koko ni arimasu. Hai, dōzo.**

Smith: Where is today's paper?
Yamada: It's here. Here you are.

QUIZ

I Read this lesson's opening dialogue and answer the following questions.

    1. **Sumisu-san wa doko ni ikimasu ka.**

    2. **Yūbinkyoku wa sūpā no mae desu ka.**

II Complete the questions so that they fit the answers.

    1. **Takushi-noriba wa (   ) desu ka.**
       Asoko desu.

    2. **Eki no chikaku ni (   ) ga arimasu ka.**
       Basu-noriba ya yūbinkyoku ya depāto ga arimasu.

    3. **Hon-ya wa (   ) ni arimasu ka.**
       Sūpā no tonari ni arimasu.

    4. **(   ) Narita Kūkō ni ikimasu ka.**
       Tomodachi ga kimasu kara.

    5. **Tēburu no ue ni ringo ga (   ) arimasu ka.**
       Mittsu arimasu.

    6. **Eki no mae ni otoko no hito ga (   ) imasu ka.**
       Futari imasu.

III Put the appropriate particles in the parentheses. (If a particle is not required, put an X in the parentheses.)

    1. **Basu-noriba (   ) doko (   ) desu ka.**
       Depāto (   ) mae (   ) arimasu.

    2. **Tēburu no ue (   ) bīru ga nan-bon (   ) arimasu ka.**
       2-hon (   ) arimasu.

    3. **Dōshite kyō kaisha (   ) ikimasen ka.**
       Do-yōbi desu (   ).

    4. **O-tearai (   ) doko (   ) arimasu ka.**
       Asoko desu.

IV Translate into Japanese.

    1. The liquor store is next to the vegetable store.

    2. Excuse me, where is the lavatory?
       It's over there.

    3. Miss White went to Osaka, so she isn't in the office today.

    4. Why is the hospital (only open) until 12:00 today?
       Because it's Saturday.

    5. There are five children in front of the book store.

LESSON 10 TICKETS BOUGHT

Mr. Smith and Mr. Tanaka are talking about their plans for the weekend.

たなか：しゅうまつに　なにを　しますか。

スミス：にちようびに　ともだちと　かぶきを　みます。

たなか：いいですね。もう　きっぷを　かいましたか。

スミス：ええ、せんしゅう　ぎんざの　プレイガイドで　かいました。

■スミスさんは　せんしゅう　ぎんざの　プレイガイドで　かぶきの
　きっぷを　かいました。にちようびに　ともだちと　かぶきを
　みます。

Tanaka: Shūmatsu ni nani o shimasu ka.
Sumisu: Nichi-yōbi ni tomodachi to kabuki o mimasu.
Tanaka: Ii desu ne. Mō kippu o kaimashita ka.
Sumisu: Ee, senshū Ginza no pureigaido de kaimashita.

■ Sumisu-san wa senshū Ginza no pureigaido de kabuki no kippu o kaimashita. Nichi-yōbi ni tomodachi to kabuki o mimasu.

Tanaka: What are you doing this weekend?
Smith: I'm going to see the Kabuki with friends on Sunday.
Tanaka: How nice. Have you bought your tickets yet?
Smith: Yes, I bought them last week at a theater booking agency in the Ginza.

■ Mr. Smith bought tickets for the Kabuki at a theater booking agency in the Ginza last
week. He is going to see the Kabuki with friends on Sunday.

Vocabulary		
しゅうまつ	**shūmatsu**	weekend
します（する）	**shimasu (suru)**	do
かぶき	**kabuki**	Kabuki (Japanese theater)
みます（みる）	**mimasu (miru)**	see

いいですね	ii desu ne	*lit.* It's nice (good, all right).
いい	ii	good (**-i** adj.)
もう	mō	already
かいました	kaimashita	bought
かいます（かう）	kaimasu (kau)	buy
ぎんざ	Ginza	Ginza (place name)
プレイガイド	pureigaido	theater booking agency
で	de	at (particle)

GRAMMAR IV

Lessons 10–12   . . . O verb/ . . . NI . . . O verb

1. person **WA** noun **O** verb
2. person **WA** person **NI** noun **O** verb

• Verbs

	Present Form		Past Form	
	aff.	*neg.*	*aff.*	*neg.*
see	**mi-masu**	**mi-masen**	**mi-mashita**	**mi-masendeshita**
buy	**kai-masu**	**kai-masen**	**kai-mashita**	**kai-masendeshita**
read	**yomi-masu**	**yomi-masen**	**yomi-mashita**	**yomi-masendeshita**
show	**mise-masu**	**mise-masen**	**mise-mashita**	**mise-masendeshita**
tele-phone	**denwa o shi-masu**	**denwa o shi-masen**	**denwa o shi-mashita**	**denwa o shi-masen deshita**

• Particle **o**. Object marker.
   Placed after a noun, **o** indicates that the noun is the object. **O** is used with verbs such as "see," "read," "drink," "buy" and many others.
   ex. **Terebi o mimasu**, "(I) watch TV."

• Particle **ni**. Indirect object marker.
   In Japanese, the indirect object, or recipient, in the case of verbs such as "give," "teach," "telephone" and so on is indicated by the particle **ni**.
   ex. **Hayashi-san wa Sumisu-san ni denwa o shimashita.** "Mr. Hayashi telephoned Mr. Smith."

NOTES

1. **Ii desu ne.**
   Here the particle **ne** does not seek confirmation or agreement. It is a sharing of the other persons's pleasure. Nuances can be conveyed by the amount of stress given any syllable. Compare this **ne** with the **ne** in Lesson 9.

2. **Ginza no pureigaido de kaimashita.**
   Nouns and place names concerned with actions such as where things are bought, seen, eaten and so on take the particle **de**.

3. **Doko,** "where"
   ex. **Doko de terebi o mimasu ka.** "Where do you watch television?"
   Ima de mimasu. "I watch it in the living room."

4. **Nani,** "what"
   ex. **Nani o kaimashita ka.** "What did you buy?"
   Kippu o kaimashita. "I bought a/some ticket/tickets."

PRACTICE

KEY SENTENCES

1. **[Watashi wa] Ashita eiga o mimasu.**
2. **Tanaka-san wa mainichi uchi de benkyō o shimasu.**
3. **[Watashi wa] Kinō resutoran de hiru-gohan o tabemashita.**
4. **[Watashi wa] Kinō depāto de nani mo kaimasendeshita.**

1. I am going to see a movie tomorrow.
2. Mr. Tanaka studies at home every day.
3. I had lunch at a restaurant yesterday.
4. I didn't buy anything yesterday at the department store.

Vocabulary

mainichi	every day	**resutoran**	restaurant
mai-	every (See Appendix K.)	**hiru-gohan**	lunch
		gohan	meal
benkyō o shimasu	study	**tabemashita**	ate
(benkyō o suru)		**tabemasu (taberu)**	eat

EXERCISES

I Verbs: Memorize the following verbs and their present and past forms.

	Present Form		Past Form	
	aff.	*neg.*	*aff.*	*neg.*
see	mimasu	mimasen	mimashita	mimasendeshita
listen	kikimasu	kikimasen	kikimashita	kikimasendeshita
eat	tabemasu	tabemasen	tabemashita	tabemasendeshita
drink	nomimasu	nomimasen	nomimashita	nomimasendeshita
buy	kaimasu	kaimasen	kaimashita	kaimasendeshita
read	yomimasu	yomimasen	yomimashita	yomimasendeshita
study	benkyō o shimasu	shimasen	shimashita	shimasendeshita
shop	kaimono o shimasu	shimasen	shimashita	shimasendeshita
give a party	pātī o shimasu	shimasen	shimashita	shimasendeshita
work	shigoto o shimasu	shimasen	shimashita	shimasendeshita
play tennis	tenisu o shimasu	shimasen	shimashita	shimasendeshita

II Practice the following patterns by changing the underlined part as in the examples given.

A. *ex.* [Watashi wa] Eiga o mimasu.

   1. terebi

   2. kabuki

   3. e

B. *ex.* [Watashi wa] Rajio o kikimasu.

   1. nyūsu

   2. ongaku no tēpu

   3. rekōdo ya shīdī

C. *ex.* [Watashi wa] Hiru-gohan o tabemasu.

   1. asa-gohan

   2. ban-gohan

   3. sandoitchi to sarada

D. *ex.* [Watashi wa] O-cha o nomimasu.

   1. o-sake

   2. sūpu

   3. kusuri

E. *ex.* [Watashi wa] <u>Hana</u> o kaimasu.

    1. zasshi

    2. kitte

    3. Nihon no chizu

F. *ex.* [Watashi wa] <u>Hon</u> o yomimasu.

    1. tegami

    2. Nihon-go no shimbun

G. *ex.* [Watashi wa] <u>Benkyō</u> o shimasu.

    1. kaimono

    2. **pātī**

    3. shigoto

    4. tenisu

III Make dialogues by changing the underlined parts as in the examples given. Convert verbs to their appropriate form as necessary.

A. *ex.* Q: [Anata wa] Komban <u>eiga</u> o <u>mimasu</u> ka.

    A*a*: Hai, <u>mimasu</u>.

    A*n*: Iie, <u>mimasen</u>.

    1. hon, yomimasu

    2. Nihon-go no benkyō, shimasu

B. *ex.* Q: [Anata wa] Kinō <u>hon-ya</u> de <u>hon</u> o <u>kaimashita</u> ka.

    A*a*: Hai, <u>kaimashita</u>.

    A*n*: Iie, <u>kaimasendeshita</u>.

    1. kaisha, shigoto, shimasu

    2. kissaten, kōhi, nomimasu

C. *ex.* Q: [Anata wa] Maiasa nani o nomimasu ka.

    A: <u>Kōhī</u> o nomimasu.

    1. kōcha

    2. miruku

    3. jūsu to kōhī

D. *ex.* Q: [Anata wa] Kinō nani o shimashita ka.

    A: <u>Uchi de hon o yomimashita</u>.

    1. depāto de kutsu o kaimasu

    2. uchi de Nihon-go no benkyō o shimasu

    3. byōin ni ikimasu

E. *ex.* Q: [Anata wa] Kyō doko de hiru-gohan o tabemasu ka.

    A: <u>Uchi</u> de tabemasu.

    1. eki no chikaku no resutoran

    2. tomodachi no uchi

F. *ex.* Q: [Anata wa] Itsu Nihon-go no benkyō o shimasu ka.

    A: <u>Mainichi</u> shimasu.

1. maiban
2. getsu-yōbi to ka-yōbi ni
3. maishū ka-yōbi ni

G. *ex.* Q: [Anata wa] Shūmatsu ni dare to tenisu o shimasu ka.

A: <u>Tanaka-san</u> to shimasu.

1. tomodachi
2. kazoku

H. *ex.* Q: [Anata wa] Depāto de nani o <u>kaimashita</u> ka.

A: Nani mo <u>kaimasendeshita</u>.

1. tabemasu
2. nomimasu

Vocabulary

e	picture	zasshi	magazine
kikimasu (kiku)	listen	chizu	map
nyūsu	news	yomimasu (yomu)	read
ongaku	music	tegami	letter
rekōdo	record	kaimono	shopping
shīdī	CD, compact disc	tenisu	tennis
asa-gohan	breakfast (*lit.* "morning meal")	komban	this evening
		kissaten	coffee shop
asa	morning	kōhī	coffee
ban-gohan	dinner (*lit.* "evening meal")	nomimasu (nomu)	drink
		maiasa	every morning
ban	evening	kōcha	black tea
sandoitchi	sandwich	miruku	milk
sarada	salad	jūsu	juice
o-cha	tea	kutsu	shoes
cha	tea	maiban	every evening
o-sake	Japanese rice wine	maishū	every week
sake	Japanese rice wine	kazoku	(my) family
sūpu	soup		

SHORT DIALOGUE

Hayashi: Kinō Nihon-go no benkyō o shimashita ka.

Howaito: Iie, shimasendeshita.

Hayashi: Dōshite benkyō o shimasendeshita ka.

Howaito: Tomodachi ga uchi ni kimashita kara.

Hayashi: Did you study Japanese yesterday?

White: No, I didn't.

Hayashi: Why didn't you study?

White: Because some friends came to my house.

QUIZ ▰▰▰▰

I Read this lesson's opening dialogue and answer the following questions.

  1. Sumisu-san wa nichi-yōbi ni eiga o mimasu ka, kabuki o mimasu ka.

  2. Sumisu-san wa hitori de kabuki o mimasu ka.

  3. Sumisu-san wa itsu kabuki no kippu o kaimashita ka.

  4. Sumisu-san wa doko de kabuki no kippu o kaimashita ka.

II Complete the questions so that they fit the answers.

  1. (   ) ni eiga o mimashita ka.
     Nichi-yōbi ni mimashita.

  2. Kyō (   ) de hiru-gohan o tabemasu ka.
     Eki no chikaku no resutoran de tabemasu.

  3. Do-yōbi ni (   ) o shimasu ka.
     Tomodachi no uchi ni ikimasu. Soshite tomodachi no uchi de ban-gohan o tabemasu.

  4. Depāto de (   ) o kaimashita ka.
     Nani mo kaimasen deshita.

III Put the appropriate particles in the parentheses. (If a particle is not required, put an X in the parentheses.)

  1. Sumisu-san wa shokudō (   ) imasu.

  2. Howaito-san wa chikatetsu (   ) kaisha (   ) ikimasu.

  3. Tanaka-san wa kaisha no chikaku no resutoran (   ) hiru-gohan (   ) tabemashita.

  4. Watashi wa kinō depāto (   ) nani (   ) kaimasen deshita.

  5. Shūmatsu ni nani (   ) shimasu ka.

  6. Watashi wa maiasa (   ) uchi (   ) shimbun (   ) yomimasu.

IV Translate into Japanese.

  1. I bought a camera at the department store on Sunday. It was ¥45,000.

  2. What did you do yesterday?
    I listened to a tape of Japanese at home in the morning. I went to the Ginza in the afternoon and bought a camera (there).

  3. Miss White doesn't eat anything in the morning.

ブラウンさんは　ABCの　べんごしです。そして　スミスさんの
ともだちです。ブラウンさんは　ことしの　6がつに　ひとりで　にほん
に　きました。おくさんは　らいしゅう　にほんに　きます。

　ブラウンさんの　かいしゃは　とうきょうえきの　ちかくに　あります。
しごとは　げつようびから　きんようびまでです。

　ブラウンさんは　まいあさ　コーヒーを　のみますが、なにも　たべ
ません。そして　しんぶんを　よみます。ちかてつで　かいしゃに
いきます。ときどき　ちかてつで　ほんや　ざっしを　よみます。

　かいしゃは　9じから　5じはんまでです。レストランや　かいしゃの
しょくどうで　ひるごはんを　たべます。ひるやすみは　12じはんから
2じまでですから、ときどき　かいしゃの　ひとと　デパートや
きっさてんに　いきます。

　うちに　7じごろ　かえります。きのうは　かいしゃから　スミスさ
んの　うちに　いきましたから、11じごろ　うちに　かえりました。

　ブラウンさんは　あした　しんかんせんで　きょうとに　いきます。
きょうとの　ししゃで　かいぎを　します。そして　きんようびに
とうきょうに　かえります。

Buraun-san wa ABC no bengoshi desu. Soshite Sumisu-san no tomodachi
desu. Buraun-san wa kotoshi no 6-gatsu ni hitori de Nihon ni kimashita.
Okusan wa raishū Nihon ni kimasu.

Buraun-san no kaisha wa Tōkyō Eki no chikaku ni arimasu. Shigoto wa
getsu-yōbi kara kin-yōbi made desu.

Buraun-san wa maiasa kōhî o nomimasu ga, nani mo tabemasen. Soshite
shimbun o yomimasu. Chikatetsu de kaisha ni ikimasu. Tokidoki chikatetsu
de hon ya zasshi o yomimasu.

Kaisha wa 9-ji kara 5-ji han made desu. Resutoran ya kaisha no shokudō de
hiru-gohan o tabemasu. Hiru-yasumi wa 12-ji han kara 2-ji made desu kara,
tokidoki kaisha no hito to depāto ya kissaten ni ikimasu.

Uchi ni 7-ji goro kaerimasu. Kinō wa kaisha kara Sumisu-san no uchi ni ikimashita kara, 11-ji goro uchi ni kaerimashita.

Buraun-san wa ashita Shinkansen de Kyōto ni ikimasu. Kyōto no shisha de kaigi o shimasu. Soshite kin-yōbi ni Tōkyō ni kaerimasu.

Mr. Brown is a lawyer with ABC. And he is a friend of Mr. Smith's. Mr. Brown came to Japan alone this June. His wife will come to Japan next week.

Mr. Brown's company is near Tokyo Station. He works from Monday to Friday.

Mr. Brown drinks coffee every morning, but he doesn't eat anything. And he reads the paper. He goes to his office by subway. Sometimes he reads a book or a magazine on the subway.

His office hours are from 9:00 to 5:30. He has lunch at a restaurant or in the company cafeteria. Lunch time is from 12:30 to 2:00, so sometimes he goes to a department store or a cafe with people from the office.

He gets home about 7:00. Last night he got home about 11:00 because he went from the office to the Smiths' house.

Mr. Brown is going to Kyoto tomorrow on the Shinkansen. He is holding a meeting at the branch office in Kyoto. He will return to Tokyo on Friday.

| Vocabulary |

ブラウン	**Buraun**	Brown
ことし	**kotoshi**	this year
が	**ga**	but (particle)
ときどき	**tokidoki**	sometimes (See Appendix J.)
しょくどう	**shokudō**	cafeteria
7じごろ	**7-ji goro**	about 7:00
～ごろ	**goro**	about
かいぎを　します	**kaigi o shimasu**	hold a meeting/conference
（かいぎを　する）	**(kaigi o suru)**	

LESSON 12 TELEPHONING

Mr. Katō telephones Mr. Smith.

かとう：もしもし、スミスさんの　おたくですか。

スミス：はい、そうです。

かとう：かとうですが、ごしゅじんは　いらっしゃいますか。

スミス：いま　いません。9じごろ　かえります。

かとう：そうですか。では　また　あとで　でんわを　します。

スミス：はい、おねがいします。

かとう：しつれいします。

スミス：さようなら。

■かとうさんは　スミスさんの　うちに　でんわを　しましたが、スミ
　スさんの　ごしゅじんは　いませんでした。

Katō:	Moshi moshi, Sumisu-san no o-taku desu ka.
Sumisu:	Hai, sō desu.
Katō:	Katō desu ga, go-shujin wa irasshaimasu ka.
Sumisu:	Ima imasen. 9-ji goro kaerimasu.
Kato:	Sō desu ka. Dewa mata ato de denwa o shimasu.
Sumisu:	Hai, onegaishimasu.
Katō:	Shitsurei shimasu.
Sumisu:	Sayōnara.

■Katō-san wa Sumisu-san no uchi ni denwa o shimashita ga, Sumisu-san no
go-shujin wa imasendeshita.

Katō:	Hello. Is that Mr. Smith's residence?
Smith:	Yes, it is.
Katō:	This is Katō. Is your husband there?
Smith:	He's not here now. He'll be back about 9:00.
Katō:	I see. Then I'll call again later.
Smith:	Yes. Please do.
Katō:	Good-bye.
Smith:	Good-bye.

■Mr. Katō telephoned the Smiths' house but Mr. Smith was not there.

Vocabulary

かとう	**Katō**	a surname
もしもし	**moshi moshi**	hello
おたく	**o-taku**	(his) residence
が	**ga**	(particle) (See Note 3 below.)
ごしゅじん	**go-shujin**	(your) husband
ご〜	**go-**	(honorific, referring to some-one else's . . .)
いらっしゃいます （いらっしゃる）	**irasshaimasu (irassharu)**	is (polite word for **imasu**)
そうですか	**sō desu ka**	I see.
また	**mata**	again
あとで	**ato de**	afterwards
おねがいします	**onegaishimasu**	Please (do).
しつれいします	**shitsurei shimasu**	good-bye (*lit.* "I'll be rude.")
に	**ni**	to (particle)

NOTES

1. Moshi moshi.

This is the conventional beginning of a telephone conversation and may be repeated during the call to confirm whether the other party is still on the line. It is sometimes also like "I say!" used to attract the attention of someone one does not know. (See Lesson 24.) It is best to confine its use to the telephone.

2. Sumisu-san no o-taku

The honorific **o** (or **go** as in **go-shujin**) is often prefixed to nouns to mean "your," i.e., **o-namae**, "your name." Similarly, **o-taku** means "your house," or, as here, "Mr. Smith's residence." It is very polite.

The word **taku** alone is seldom used. **Uchi**, "house," is more common. I.e., **Are wa dare no uchi desu ka.** "Whose house is that?" **Uchi** is also used to mean "my/our house" or simply "our," as in **uchi no kuruma**, "our car."

3. A. Katō desu ga, go-shujin wa irasshaimasu ka.
B. Katō-san wa Sumisu-san ni denwa o shimashita ga, Sumisu-san wa imasendeshita.

This **ga** is a connective, joining two clauses. It can usually be translated as "but," as in B, but sometimes it cannot, as in A. In A, it has no particular meaning. It is just a kind of courteous hesitation and indicates that the phrase before it is merely a preliminary to the principal matter.

4. 9-ji goro

The suffix **goro**, "about," is used to indicate approximate time.

ex. **3-ji goro**, "about 3 o'clock"

   9-gatsu goro, "about September"

5. Sō desu ka.

When **Sō desu ka** means "I see," as here, it is said with a falling intonation. It can also mean "Oh, really?" or "Is that so?" and be a question expecting an answer. In that case, it is said with a rising intonation.

6. Onegaishimasu

A very convenient phrase, used when making a request. Literally, it means "I beg you," and the verb may be simply implied, as here, where it means "I beg you (to do that)."

ex. **Taipu o onegaishimasu.** "Could you type this, please?"

   Ginza made onegaishimasu. "Please take me to the Ginza." (Said to a taxi driver.)

The reply to **onegaishimasu** is often **Hai, wakarimashita.** "Certainly./I see."

PRACTICE

KEY SENTENCES

1. **[Watashi wa] Ashita bengoshi ni aimasu.**
2. **[Watashi wa] Hayashi-san ni denwa o shimasu.**
3. **[Watashi wa] Yoku tomodachi ni tegami o kakimasu.**
4. **[Watashi wa] Amari eiga o mimasen.**
5. **[Watashi wa] Sumisu-san no kaisha ni denwa o shimashita ga, Sumisu-san wa imasendeshita.**

1. I am going to see the lawyer tomorrow.
2. I will telephone Mr. Hayashi.
3. I often write to (my) friends.
4. I don't see movies very often.
5. I telephoned Mr. Smith's office, but he wasn't there.

Vocabulary

aimasu (au)	meet
denwa o shimasu	make a phone call
(denwa o suru)	
yoku	often (See Appendix J.)
kakimasu (kaku)	write
amari . . . -masen	does not . . . often (See Appendix J.)

I Verbs: Memorize the following verbs and their present and past forms.

	Present Form		Past Form	
	aff.	*neg.*	*aff.*	*neg.*
telephone	**denwa o shimasu**	**shimasen**	**shimashita**	**shimasendeshita**
write	**kakimasu**	**kakimasen**	**kakimashita**	**kakimasendeshita**
ask	**kikimasu**	**kikimasen**	**kikimashita**	**kikimasendeshita**
tell	**oshiemasu**	**oshiemasen**	**oshiemashita**	**oshiemasendeshita**
meet	**aimasu**	**aimasen**	**aimashita**	**aimasendeshita**

II Practice the following pattern by changing the underlined part as in the example given.

  ex. **[Watashi wa] Hayashi-san ni denwa o shimasu.**

  1. **Sumisu-san**
  2. **gakkō**
  3. **kaisha**

III Make dialogues by changing the underlined parts as in the examples given.

  A. *ex.* **Q: [Anata wa] Mainen tomodachi ni kurisumasu kādo o kakimasu ka.**
  A*a*: Hai, kakimasu.
  A*n*: Iie, kakimasen.

  1. **nengajō**

  B. *ex.* **Q: [Anata wa] Dare ni denwa o shimasu ka.**
  A: Tanaka-san ni shimasu.

  1. **tomodachi**
  2. **haha**

  C. *ex.* **Q: [Anata wa] Doko ni denwa o shimasu ka.**
  A: Kaisha ni shimasu.

  1. **gakkō**
  2. **hoteru**

  D. *ex.* **Q: Tanaka-san wa Sumisu-san ni nani o oshiemashita ka.**
  A: Tanaka-san no uchi no denwa-bangō o oshiemashita.

  1. **mise no namae**
  2. **naisen-bangō**

  E. *ex.* **Q: Tanaka-san wa dare ni Hayashi-san no jūsho o kikimashita ka.**
  A: Hisho ni kikimashita.

1. Sumisu-san

　　　2. kaisha no hito

F. *ex.* Q: [Anata wa] Ashita dare ni aimasu ka.

　　A: <u>Tomodachi</u> ni aimasu.

　　1. gakkō no sensei

　　2. Hayashi-san no otōsan to okāsan

G. *ex.* Q: [Anata wa] Yoku tomodachi ni tegami o kakimasu ka.

　　A*a*: <u>Hai, yoku</u> kakimasu.

　　A*n*: <u>Iie, amari</u> kakimasen.

　　1. hai, tokidoki. iie, zenzen

IV　Connect the following sentences using **ga**, "but," as in the example given.

　　ex. Ashita wa nichi-yōbi desu. [Watashi wa] Kaisha de shigoto o shimasu.

　　Ashita wa nichi-yōbi desu ga, [watashi wa] kaisha de shigoto o shimasu.

　　1. Watashi wa kinō Tanaka-san no uchi ni ikimashita. Tanaka-san wa ima-sendeshita.

　　2. Watashi wa kinō depāto ni ikimashita. Depāto wa yasumi deshita.

Vocabulary

mainen	every year	**naisen-bangō**	extension num-
kurisumasu kādo	Christmas card		ber
nengajō	New Year's card	**kikimasu (kiku)**	ask
haha	(my) mother	**sensei**	teacher
hoteru	hotel	**otōsan**	(your) father
oshiemasu (oshieru)	tell	**okāsan**	(your) mother
mise	store, shop	**zenzen . . . -masen**	never (do) (See Appendix J.)

SHORT DIALOGUES

1. On the telephone.

　Otoko no hito:　Moshi moshi, Tanaka-san no o-taku desu ka.

　Onna no hito:　Iie, chigaimasu.

　Otoko no hito:　Dōmo sumimasen.

　Onna no hito:　Iie. Dō itashimashite.

　Man:　　　Hello. Is this Mr. Tanaka's residence?

　Woman:　No, you have the wrong number.

　Man:　　　Sorry to have troubled you.

　Woman:　That's quite all right.

2. On the telephone.

　Kōkanshu:　Tōkyō Denki de gozaimasu.

Hayashi: Tanaka-san o onegaishimasu.
Kōkanshu: Hai, shōshō omachi kudasai.

Operator: This is Tokyo Electric.
Hayashi: May I speak to Mr. Tanaka, please?
Operator: Just a moment, please.

3. Sumisu: Watashi wa maiasa jogingu o shimasu ga, Hayashi-san mo jogingu o
shimasu ka.
Hayashi: Hai, watashi mo yoku shimasu.

Smith: I jog every morning. Do you jog, too?
Hayashi: Yes, I often do.

Vocabulary

chigaimasu (chigau)	That's wrong.
kōkanshu	switchboard operator
Tōkyō Denki de gozaimasu	This is Tokyo Electric.
de gozaimasu	(polite word for **desu**)
shōshō	a moment
omachi kudasai	Please wait.
machimasu (matsu)	wait
jogingu o shimasu	jog
(jogingu o suru)	

QUIZ

I Read this lesson's opening dialogue and answer the following questions.

1. **Dare ga Sumisu-san no uchi ni denwa o shimashita ka.**
2. **Sumisu-san no go-shujin wa uchi ni imashita ka, imasendeshita ka.**
3. **Sumisu-san no go-shujin wa nan-ji goro uchi ni kaerimasu ka.**
4. **Katō-san wa mata ato de Sumisu-san ni denwa o shimasu ka.**

II Complete the questions so that they fit the answers.

1. **Kinō (   ) o shimashita ka.**
   Tegami o kakimashita.
   (   ) ni kakimashita ka.
   Haha ni kakimashita.
2. **Hayashi-san wa (   ) ni Kurāku-san no jūsho o kikimashita ka.**
   Howaito-san ni kikimashita.

3. (   ) ga Kyōto no shisha ni denwa o shimashita ka.
   Sumisu-san ga shimashita.

III Circle the correct word of the two in parentheses.

1. **Yoku kono resutoran ni kimasu ka.**
   (Hai, Iie), amari (kimasu, kimasen).
2. **Yoku terebi o (mimasu, mimasen) ka.**
   (Hai, Iie), zenzen (mimasu, mimasen).
3. **Yamada-san wa (yoku, amari) tomodachi ni denwa o shimasu.**
4. **Sumisu-san wa yoku densha de shimbun o (yomimasu, yomimasen)**
   ga, Kurāku-san wa zenzen (yomimasu, yomimasen).

IV Put the appropriate particles in the parentheses. (If a particle is not required, put an X in the parentheses.)

1. **Sumisu-san wa Hayashi-san (   ) denwa o shimashita.**
2. **Doko (   ) denwa o shimasu ka.**
   Gakkō ni shimasu.
3. **Yoku (   ) dare (   ) tenisu o shimasu ka.**
   Kazoku to shimasu.
4. **Tanaka-san wa Howaito-san (   ) Yamada-san no uchi no denwa-**
   bangō (   ) oshiemashita.
5. **Moshi moshi, Sumisu desu (   ), Hayashi-san (   ) irasshaimasu**
   ka.

V Translate into Japanese.

1. Hello. Is this the Tanaka residence?
2. This is Tanaka of Tokyo Electric. Is Mr. Hayashi there?
3. I'll call again later.
4. I asked Mr. Clark for his office telephone number.
5. Mr. Clark doesn't write letters to his friends very often but Miss White does (write often).

LESSON 13 DELICIOUS CAKES

Mr. Tanaka is offering Mr. Smith a cup of tea.

たなか：おちゃを　どうぞ。

スミス：ありがとうございます。

たなか：おかしは　いかがですか。

スミス：はい、いただきます。きれいな　おかしですね。にほんの
　　　　おかしですか。

たなか：ええ、そうです。どうぞ　めしあがってください。

スミス：とても　おいしいです。

たなか：おちゃを　もう　いっぱい　いかがですか。

スミス：いいえ、もう　けっこうです。

■スミスさんは　たなかさんの　うちで　きれいな　にほんの　おかし
　を　たべました。　おちゃを　いっぱい　のみました。

Tanaka:　O-cha o dōzo.
Sumisu:　Arigatō gozaimasu.
Tanaka:　O-kashi wa ikaga desu ka.
Sumisu:　Hai, itadakimasu. Kireina o-kashi desu ne. Nihon no o-kashi desu
　　　　ka.
Tanaka:　Ee, sō desu. Dōzo meshiagatte kudasai.
Sumisu:　Totemo oishii desu.
Tanaka:　O-cha o mō ippai ikaga desu ka.
Sumisu:　Iie, mō kekkō desu.

■Sumisu-san wa Tanaka-san no uchi de kireina Nihon no o-kashi o tabemashita. O-cha o ippai nomimashita.

Tanaka:　Do have some tea.
Smith:　　Thank you.
Tanaka:　Will you have a cake?
Smith:　　Yes, I'd love one. What pretty cakes! Are they Japanese cakes?
Tanaka:　Yes, they are. Please, help yourself.
Smith:　　They are delicious.

94

Tanaka: Will you have another cup of tea?
Smith: No (thank you). That was enough.

■ Mr. Smith ate (some) pretty Japanese cakes at Mr. Tanaka's house. He drank a cup of tea.

Vocabulary

おかし	**o-kashi**	cake
いかがですか	**ikaga desu ka**	How about . . . ?
いかが	**ikaga**	how
いただきます（いただく）	**itadakimasu (itadaku)**	eat (polite word for **tabemasu**)
きれい（な）	**kireina**	pretty, clean (**-na** adj.)
めしあがって　ください	**meshiagatte kudasai**	Please eat/have (some)
とても	**totemo**	very (See Appendix J.)
おいしい	**oishii**	good, tasty (**-i** adj.)
もう	**mō**	more (another)
1ぱい	**ippai**	1 cupful
〜はい、ばい、ぱい	**-hai, -bai, -pai**	(counter. See Appendix I.)
いいえ、もう けっこうです	**iie, mō kekkō desu**	No (thank you). That was enough.

GRAMMAR V

Lessons 13–14   Adjectives

1. **ADJECTIVE** + noun
2. noun **wa ADJECTIVE desu**

1. Modifying Nouns: Adjective + Noun		
-i adj.	**ōkii kōen**	big park
-na adj.	**yūmeina kōen**	famous park

2. Adjective as Predicate: Adjective + **Desu**				
	Present Form		Past Form	
	aff.	*neg.*	*aff.*	*neg.*
-i adj.	ōkii desu	ōkikunai desu	ōkikatta desu	ōkikunakatta desu
-na adj.	yūmei desu	yūmei dewa arimasen	yūmei deshita	yūmei dewa arimasendeshita

• Japanese adjectives can either modify nouns by immediately preceding them or act as predicates. In this they resemble English.

There are two kinds of adjectives: **-i** adjectives and **-na** adjectives. Unlike English adjectives, Japanese adjectives are inflected as shown above. Either **-i** or **-na** adjectives can take the place of noun 2 in the noun 2 + **desu** construction given in Grammar I.

NOTES

1. **Dōzo.**

   Dōzo, "please (accept/do)," is used when making an offer to someone or when begging their kindness and consideration.

2. **Ikaga desu ka.**

   A politer way of saying **Dō desu ka,** *lit.* "How is it?" This phrase is often used when offering things like food and drink, meaning "Would you like one?" or "How about some?" It can be used in a variety of situations, such as when enquiring about a person's preferences or circumstances, when asking whether the person is free to do something (Lesson 18), or his state of health (Lesson 22).

3. **Itadakimasu.**

   A polite equivalent of **tabemasu,** "I eat," and **moraimasu,** "I receive." Said when taking something that is offered, implying both acceptance and gratitude. Japanese mealtime conventions:

   Before eating: **Itadakimasu.** "I gratefully partake."
   After eating: **Gochisōsama.** "Thank you for a lovely meal." (*lit.* "It was indeed a feast!")

4. **Iie, mō kekkō desu.**

   The polite way of refusing something offered. **Kekkō** means "good, fine, splendid." **Mō** in this case means "already." The expression **kekkō desu** implies, "I am all right as I am," or "What I've had was fine. It was enough."

5. **Donna,** "what kind of"

   When one wants to know more about things, people or places, one uses **donna** + noun. Answers can be given in various ways.

   ex. Q: **Donna okashi o tabemashita ka.** "What kind of cakes did (you) eat?"
   A1: **Oishii okashi o tabemashita.** "(I) had (some) delicious cakes."
   A2: **Kireina okashi o tabemashita.** "(I) ate (some) pretty cakes."
   A3: **Nihon no okashi o tabemashita.** "(I) ate Japanese cakes."
   A4: **Kukkī o tabemashita.** "(I) ate cookies."

PRACTICE

KEY SENTENCES

1. **Kono ringo wa totemo oishii desu.**
2. **Ano ringo wa amari oishikunai desu.**
3. **[Watashi wa] Oishii ringo o tabemashita.**
4. **Kono heya wa shizuka desu.**
5. **Ano heya wa shizuka dewa arimasen.**
6. **[Watashi wa] Shizukana heya de benkyō o shimasu.**

1. This apple is very good.
2. That apple doesn't taste very good.
3. I ate some delicious apples.
4. This room is quiet.
5. That room is not quiet.
6. I study in a quiet room.

Vocabulary

amari . . . -nai/-masen   not very . . . (See Appendix J.)
shizukana   quiet (**-na** adj.)

EXERCISES

I **-i** adjective: Memorize the following **-i** adjectives.

	As Predicate: Present Form		Modifying Noun
	aff.	*neg.*	
big	**ōkii desu**	**ōkikunai desu**	**ōkii**
expensive	**takai desu**	**takakunai desu**	**takai**
good	**ii desu**	**yokunai desu***	**ii**
new, fresh	**atarashii desu**	**atarashikunai desu**	**atarashii**
small	**chiisai desu**	**chiisakunai desu**	**chiisai**
cheap	**yasui desu**	**yasukunai desu**	**yasui**
bad	**warui desu**	**warukunai desu**	**warui**
old	**furui desu****	**furukunai desu**	**furui**
interesting	**omoshiroi desu**	**omoshirokunai desu**	**omoshiroi**
difficult	**muzukashii desu**	**muzukashikunai desu**	**muzukashii**
far	**tōi desu**	**tōkunai desu**	**tōi**
good, tasty	**oishii desu**	**oishikunai desu**	**oishii**
busy	**isogashii desu**	**isogashikunai desu**	**isogashii**

boring	tsumaranai desu	tsumaranakunai desu	tsumaranai
easy	yasashii desu	yasashikunai desu	yasashii
near	chikai desu	chikakunai desu	chikai

*All inflected forms of **ii** come from the **i**-adjective **yoi**, which also means "good."
**Not used for people.

II Practice the following patterns by changing the underlined parts in the examples given.

A. *ex.* **Kono kamera** wa ōkii desu.

Ano kamera wa chiisai desu.

1. kono kuruma, ano kuruma

2. kono tamago, ano tamago

B. *ex.* **Kono rajio** wa takai desu.

Ano rajio wa yasui desu.

1. kono tokei, ano tokei

2. gyūniku, toriniku

C. *ex.* Kore wa atarashii uchi desu.

Are wa furui uchi desu.

1. terebi

2. sakana

3. yasai

III Make dialogues by changing the underlined part as in the examples given.

A. *ex.* **Q:** Nihon-go wa yasashii desu ka.

A*a*: Hai, yasashii desu.

A*n*: Iie, yasashikunai desu.

1. muzukashii

2. omoshiroi

B. *ex.* **Q:** Kono hon wa omoshiroi desu ka.

A*a*: Hai, omoshiroi desu.

A*n*: Iie, amari omoshirokunai desu.

1. takai

2. ii

C. *ex.* **Q:** Kore wa ii hon desu ka.

A*a*: Hai, totemo ii hon desu.

A*n*: Iie, amari ii hon dewa arimasen.

1. omoshiroi

2. muzukashii

D. *ex.* **Q:** Kōen wa koko kara tōi desu ka.

A: Iie, tōkunai desu. Chikai desu.

1. basu-noriba

2. gakkō

3. chikatetsu no eki

IV **-na** adjective: Memorize the following **-na** adjectives.

	As Predicate: Present Form		Modifying Noun
	aff.	*neg.*	
pretty, clean	**kirei desu**	**kirei dewa arimasen**	**kireina**
quiet	**shizuka desu**	**shizuka dewa arimasen**	**shizukana**
famous	**yūmei desu**	**yūmei dewa arimasen**	**yūmeina**
kind, helpful	**shinsetsu desu**	**shinsetsu dewa arimasen**	**shinsetsuna**
free	**hima desu**	**hima dewa arimasen**	**himana**
lively	**nigiyaka desu**	**nigiyaka dewa arimasen**	**nigiyakana**
convenient	**benri desu**	**benri dewa arimasen**	**benrina**
well, healthy	**genki desu**	**genki dewa arimasen**	**genkina**

V Practice the following patterns by changing the underlined parts as in the examples given.

    A. *ex.* <u>Kono hana</u> wa kirei desu.

        1. **Howaito-san**

        2. **ano kissaten**

    B. *ex.* <u>Kono daidokoro</u> wa benri desu.

        1. **kono kamera**

        2. **Tokyo no chikatetsu**

    C. *ex.* **Watashi-tachi wa <u>kireina</u> resutoran de shokuji o shimashita.**

        1. **shizukana**

        2. **yūmeina**

VI Make dialogues by changing the underlined part as in the examples given.

    A. *ex.* **Q: Tanaka-san wa <u>genki</u> desu ka.**

        A*a*: Hai, <u>genki</u> desu.

        A*n*: Iie, <u>genki</u> dewa arimasen.

        1. **shinsetsu**

    B. *ex.* **Q: Are wa <u>yūmeina</u> resutoran desu ka.**

        A*a*: Hai, totemo <u>yūmeina</u> resutoran desu.

        A*n*: Iie, amari <u>yūmeina</u> resutoran dewa arimasen.

        1. **kireina**

        2. **shizukana**

    C. *ex.* **Q: [Anata wa] <u>Ashita</u> hima desu ka.**

        A: Iie, hima dewa arimasen. Isogashii desu.

1. ashita no gogo
2. raishū no kin-yōbi

D. *ex.* Q: Tōkyō Hoteru wa donna hoteru desu ka.

A: <u>Atarashii</u> hoteru desu.

1. ōkii
2. shizukana
3. totemo ii

E. *ex.* Q: Hayashi-san wa donna hito desu ka.

A: <u>Shinsetsuna</u> hito desu.

1. omoshiroi
2. genkina

Vocabulary

tamago	egg	watashi-tachi	we
takai	expensive (**-i** adj.)	-tachi	(plural suffix for peo-
yasui	cheap (**-i** adj.)		ple)
gyū-niku	beef	shokuji o shimasu	have a meal
tori-niku	chicken meat	(shokuji o suru)	
atarashii	new, fresh (**-i** adj.)	shokuji	meal
furui	old, not fresh (**-i** adj.)	yūmeina	famous (**-na** adj.)
yasai	vegetable	genkina	well, healthy (**-na** adj.)
yasashii	easy (**-i** adj.)	shinsetsuna	kind, helpful (**-na** adj.)
muzukashii	difficult (**-i** adj.)	himana	free (**-na** adj.)
omoshiroi	interesting (**-i** adj.)	isogashii	busy (**-i** adj.)
kōen	park	Tōkyō Hoteru	Tokyo Hotel
benrina	convenient (**-na** adj.)	donna	what kind of

SHORT DIALOGUES

1. **Tanaka:** Sumisu-san, o-genki desu ka.
   Sumisu: Ee, arigatō gozaimasu. Genki desu.

   Tanaka: How are you, Mr. Smith?
   Smith: Fine, thank you.

2. **Tanaka:** Kyō wa ii tenki desu ne.
   Sumisu: Ee, hontō ni ii tenki desu ne.
   Tanaka: Kyō wa isogashii desu ka.
   Sumisu: Iie, amari isogashikunai desu.

   Tanaka: It's a fine day today, isn't it?
   Smith: Yes, it really is lovely weather.
   Tanaka: (Are you) busy today?
   Smith: No, (I'm) not so busy.

3. **Tanaka:** Sumisu-san no uchi wa kaisha kara tōi desu ka.
   Sumisu: Iie, tōkunai desu. Chikai desu. Chikatetsu de 20-pun gurai desu.
   Tanaka: Sō desu ka. Benri desu ne.

   Tanaka: Is your house far from your office?
   Smith: No, it isn't. It's near by. It's about 20 minutes by subway.
   Tanaka: I see. How convenient.

4. **Howaito:** Koko wa shizukana kōen desu ne.
   Yamada: Ee, ōkii ki ya kireina hana ga takusan arimasu ne. Howaito-san wa yoku kōen ni ikimasu ka.
   Howaito: Ee, nichi-yōbi no asa tokidoki uchi no chikaku no kōen ni ikimasu.

   White: This is a quiet park, isn't it?
   Yamada: Yes. There are lots of big trees and beautiful flowers (etc.), aren't there? Do you go to parks often?
   White: Yes. I sometimes go to the park near my house on Sunday morning.

Vocabulary

tenki	weather
hontō ni	really, truly
20-pun gurai	about 20 minutes (for about 20 minutes)
gurai	about, approximately
ki	tree

QUIZ

I Read this lesson's opening dialogue and answer the following questions.

1. **Sumisu-san wa o-kashi o tabemashita ka.**
2. **Sumisu-san wa doko no o-kashi o tabemashita ka.**
3. **Sumisu-san wa nani o nomimashita ka.**

II Complete the questions so that they fit the answers.

1. **Tanaka-san wa (   ) desu ka.**
   Hai, genki desu.
2. **Sono hon wa (   ) desu ka.**
   Iie, amari omoshirokunai desu.
3. **Ano hito wa (   ) desu ka.**
   Tanaka-san desu.
4. **Ano hito wa (   ) hito desu ka.**
   Shinsetsuna hito desu.

III Circle the correct adjective in the parentheses.

1. **Ano kissaten no kōhī wa amari (oishii desu, oishikunai desu).**
2. **Uchi no chikaku ni (kirei, kireina) kōen ga arimasu.**
3. **Kono hon wa (omoshirokunai desu, omoshiroi dewa arimasen).**
4. **Watashi no rajio wa (ikunai desu, yokunai desu, ii dewa arimasen).**
5. **Are wa (yūmei, yūmeina) resutoran desu.**
6. **Yamada-san no uchi wa koko kara totemo (chikai desu, chikakunai desu).**

IV Translate into Japanese.

1. Would you like some coffee?
   Thank you, I'll have some.
2. Would you like another cup of coffee?
   No, thank you. That was enough.
3. We had dinner at a famous restaurant.
4. That cafe is clean, but it isn't quiet.
5. I am busy today.

LESSON 14 YESTERDAY'S ENJOYABLE KABUKI

Mr. Tanaka is asking Mr. Smith about the Kabuki he saw.

たなか：かぶきは　どうでしたか。

スミス：とても　きれいでした。

たなか：にほんごが　わかりましたか。

スミス：いいえ、ぜんぜん　わかりませんでしたから、イヤホーンで
　　　　えいごの　せつめいを　ききました。とても　おもしろかった
　　　　です。

■スミスさんは　かぶきを　みました。イヤホーンで　えいごの　せつ
　めいを　ききました。かぶきは　とても　おもしろかったです。

Tanaka:　Kabuki wa dō deshita ka.
Sumisu:　Totemo kirei deshita.
Tanaka:　Nihon-go ga wakarimashita ka.
Sumisu:　Iie, zenzen wakarimasendeshita kara, iyahōn de Ei-go no setsumei
　　　　o kikimashita. Totemo omoshirokatta desu.

■Sumisu-san wa kabuki o mimashita. Iyahōn de Ei-go no setsumei o kikimashita. Kabuki wa totemo omoshirokatta desu.

Tanaka:　How was the Kabuki?
Smith:　It was very beautiful.
Tanaka:　Did you understand the Japanese?
Smith:　No, I didn't understand it at all, so I listened to the English explanation with ear-
　　　　phones. It was fascinating.

■Mr. Smith saw a Kabuki play. He listened to the English explanation with earphones. He
enjoyed the Kabuki very much.

Vocabulary		
どうでしたか	**dō deshita ka**	How was it?
どう	**dō**	how

わかりました	**wakarimashita**	understood
わかります (わかる)	**wakarimasu (wakaru)**	understand
ぜんぜん 〜ません	**zenzen . . . -masen**	(not) at all (See Appendix E.)
イヤホーン	**iyahōn**	earphones
えいご	**Ei-go**	English language
せつめい	**setsumei**	explanation

NOTES

1. **Dō deshita ka.**

Used when asking a person his impression of something.

ex. **Eiga wa dō deshita ka.** "How was the movie?"

Omoshirokatta desu. "It was delightful."

2. **Nihon-go ga wakarimashita ka.**

Note that with the verb **wakarimasu**, the noun usually takes the particle **ga** rather than **o**. (See Grammar X, p. 174.)

PRACTICE

KEY SENTENCES

1. **Kinō wa samukatta desu.**
2. **Kinō wa atsukunakatta desu.**
3. **Kinō no pātī wa nigiyaka deshita.**
4. **[Watashi wa] Senshū hima dewa arimasendeshita.**

1. It was cold yesterday.
2. It wasn't hot yesterday.
3. Yesterday's party was lively.
4. I had no free time last week.

Vocabulary	
samukatta	was cold
samui	cold (**-i** adj.)
atsukunakatta	was not hot
atsui	hot (**-i** adj.)
nigiyakana	lively (**-na** adj.)

EXERCISES

I A. **-i** adjectives: Memorize the following **-i** adjectives and their present and past forms.

	Present Form		Past Form	
	aff.	*neg.*	*aff.*	*neg.*
cold	samui desu	samukunai desu	samukatta desu	samukunakatta desu
hot	atsui desu	atsukunai desu	atsukatta desu	atsukunakatta desu
enjoyable	tanoshii desu	tanoshiku-nai desu	tanoshikatta desu	tanoshikunakatta desu
good	ii desu	yokunai desu	yokatta desu	yokunakatta desu
interesting	omoshiroi desu	omoshiroku-nai desu	omoshirokatta desu	omoshiroku-nakatta desu
tasty	oishii desu	oishikunai desu	oishikatta desu	oishikunakatta desu
expensive	takai desu	takakunai desu	takakatta desu	takakunakatta desu

B. **-na** adjectives: Study the following **-na** adjectives.

	Present		Past	
	aff.	*neg.*	*aff.*	*neg.*
quiet	shizuka desu	shizuka dewa arimasen	shizuka deshita	shizuka dewa arimasendeshita
well, healthy	genki desu	genki dewa arimasen	genki deshita	genki dewa arimasendeshita

II Practice the following patterns by changing the underlined part as in the examples given.

    A. *ex.* **Kinō no eiga wa <u>omoshirokatta</u> desu.**

        1. **ii**

        2. **tanoshii**

    B. *ex.* **Kinō machi wa <u>shizuka</u> deshita.**

        1. **nigiyaka**

III Make dialogues by changing the underlined parts as in the examples given.

    A. *ex.* **Q: <u>Kinō no pātī</u> wa tanoshikatta desu ka.**

        A*a*: Hai, tanoshikatta desu.

        A*n*: Iie, tanoshikunakatta desu.

1. ryokō
2. gorufu

B. *ex.* Q: <u>Tanaka-san</u> wa genki deshita ka.

A*a*: Hai, totemo genki deshita.

A*n*: Iie, amari genki dewa arimasendeshita.

1. sensei
2. Tanaka-san no hisho

C. *ex.* Q: Kono hon wa <u>yokatta</u> desu ka.

A*a*: Hai, <u>yokatta</u> desu.

A*n*: Iie, <u>yokunakatta</u> desu.

1. omoshiroi
2. muzukashii

D. *ex.* Q: Kinō no pāti wa dō deshita ka.

A*a*: Totemo <u>tanoshikatta</u> desu.

A*n*: Amari <u>tanoshikunakatta</u> desu.

1. omoshiroi
2. nigiyaka

E. *ex.* Q: <u>Ryokō</u> wa dō deshita ka.

A: Totemo <u>tanoshikatta</u> desu.

1. eiga, omoshiroi
2. ryōri, oishii

Vocabulary

tanoshii	enjoyable (**-i** adj)
machi	town, street
ryokō	trip
gorufu	golf
ryōri	food, cooking

SHORT DIALOGUE

Tanaka:　Kinō eki no chikaku no resutoran ni ikimashita.

Sumisu:　Donna resutoran deshita ka.

Tanaka:　Shizukana resutoran deshita.

Sumisu:　Ryōri wa dō deshita ka.

Tanaka:　Totemo oishikatta desu.

Sumisu:　Yokatta desu ne.

Tanaka:　Yesterday I went to the restaurant near the station.

Smith:　What was the restaurant like?

Tanaka:　It was a quiet restaurant.

Smith: How was the food?

Tanaka: It was very good.

Smith: It turned out well (then), didn't it?

QUIZ ▪▪▪▪▪

I Read this lesson's opening dialogue and answer the following questions.

   1. **Sumisu-san wa nani o mimashita ka.**

   2. **Kabuki wa omoshirokatta desu ka, omoshirokunakatta desu ka.**

   3. **Sumisu-san wa nan de Ei-go no setsumei o kikimashita ka.**

II Give the antonyms of the following.

   1. **muzukashii**   4. **chiisai**   7. **samui**   10. **ii**

   2. **tōi**   5. **yasui**   8. **nigiyakana**

   3. **omoshiroi**   6. **himana**   9. **atarashii**

III Complete the questions so that they fit the answers.

   1. **Shūmatsu ni (   ) o shimashita ka.**

       Kyōto ni ikimashita.

       Kyōto wa (   ) deshita ka.

       Totemo kirei deshita.

       Tenki wa (   ) desu ka.

       Ee, totemo yokatta desu.

   2. **(   ) hiru-gohan o tabemasen ka.**

       Isogashii desu kara.

   3. **Ano hito wa (   ) hito desu ka.**

       Omoshiroi hito desu.

IV Circle the correct words in the parentheses.

   1. **Kinō no tenki wa totemo (yokatta desu, ii deshita, ikatta desu).**

   2. **Ryokō wa (nan, dō) deshita ka.**

       Tanoshikatta desu.

   3. **Do-yōbi no pātī wa (nigiyakatta desu, nigiyaka deshita).**

   4. **Ano resutoran wa amari (kirekunai desu, kirei desu, kirei dewa arimasen).**

   5. **Kinō eiga o mimashita ga, zenzen (omoshirokatta desu, omoshirokunai deshita, omoshirokunakatta desu).**

   6. **Tanaka-san wa senshū (genkikatta desu, genki deshita).**

V Translate into Japanese.

   1. How was yesterday's meeting?

   2. Yesterday's weather was good.

   3. That restaurant's food was not very good.

LESSON **15** GIVING AND RECEIVING

Mr. Tanaka and Mr. Smith are talking about a vase Mr. Tanaka received from Mr. Clark.

スミス：きれいな　かびんですね。

たなか：ええ、たんじょうびに　ともだちの　クラークさんに
　　　　もらいました。

スミス：いい　いろですね。

たなか：ええ、わたしの　すきな　いろです。

■たなかさんは　クラークさんに　かびんを　もらいました。クラークさんは　たなかさんに　かびんを　あげました。

Sumisu:　Kireina kabin desu ne.
Tanaka:　Ee, tanjōbi ni tomodachi no Kurāku-san ni moraimashita.
Sumisu:　Ii iro desu ne.
Tanaka:　Ee, watashi no sukina iro desu.

■ Tanaka-san wa Kurāku-san ni kabin o moraimashita. Kurāku-san wa Tanaka-san ni kabin o agemashita.

Smith:　　What a lovely vase!
Tanaka:　Yes. My friend Mr. Clark gave it to me on my birthday.
Smith:　　It's a nice color, isn't it?
Tanaka:　Yes, it's a favorite color of mine.

■ Mr. Tanaka received a vase from Mr. Clark. Mr. Clark gave Mr. Tanaka a vase.

Vocabulary		
かびん	**kabin**	vase
に	**ni**	from (particle)
もらいました	**moraimashita**	received
もらいます（もらう）	**moraimasu (morau)**	receive
いろ	**iro**	color

108

すき（な）	**sukina**	likable, favorite (**-na** adj.)
に	**ni**	to (particle)
あげました	**agemashita**	gave
あげます（あげる）	**agemasu (ageru)**	give

GRAMMAR VI

Lesson 15   Giving and Receiving

. . . NI . . . O verb

1. person **WA** person **NI** noun **O AGEMASU**
2. person **WA** person **NI** noun **O MORAIMASU**

- **Agemasu/Kuremasu**, "give"

  Moraimasu, "receive"

  There are two words in Japanese meaning "give," and great care must be taken in their correct use. **Agemasu,** *lit.* "to raise up," implies "to humbly present," and can never be used when speaking of something that someone gives *you*. **Kuremasu,** on the other hand, literally means "to hand down" and must *only* be used in connection with things given to you.

  ex. **Watashi wa Tanaka-san ni kabin o agemashita.** "I gave Mr. Tanaka a vase."

  Kurāku-san wa watashi ni kabin o kuremashita. "Mr. Clark gave me a vase."

  Watashi wa Kurāku-san ni kabin o moraimashita. "I received a vase from Mr. Clark."

  Note: **Kuremasu** is not used in this book since **moraimasu**, "receive," is more frequently used. Also, **kara** is often used with **moraimasu** instead of **ni**.

  Agemasu may also be freely used when the speaker is not involved in the giving.

  ex. **Kurāku-san wa Tanaka-san ni kabin o agemashita.** "Mr. Clark gave Mr. Tanaka a vase."

NOTE

1. **Tomodachi no Kurāku-san**

   This is not the possessive **no**. It is the appositive, "my friend, Mr. Clark."

PRACTICE

KEY SENTENCES

1. **Hayashi-san wa Sumisu-san ni hon o agemashita.**
2. **Sumisu-san wa Hayashi-san ni hon o moraimashita.**

1. Mr. Hayashi gave Mr. Smith a book.
2. Mr. Smith received a book from Mr. Hayashi.

EXERCISES

I Verbs: Memorize the following verbs and their present and past forms.

	Present Form		Past Form	
	aff.	*neg.*	*aff.*	*neg.*
give receive	**agemasu** **moraimasu**	**agemasen** **moraimasen**	**agemashita** **moraimashita**	**agemasendeshita** **moraimasendeshita**

II Practice the following pattern by changing the underlined parts as in the example given.

> *ex.* <u>Hayashi-san</u> wa <u>Sumisu-san</u> ni hon o agemasu. <u>Sumisu-san</u> wa <u>Hayashi-san</u> ni hon o moraimasu.

> 1. Sumisu-san, Sumisu-san no hisho
> 2. Nihon-go no sensei, Kurāku-san

III Make dialogues by changing the underlined part as in the examples given.

> A. *ex.* **Q:** [Anata wa] Kurāku-san ni <u>hon</u> o agemashita ka.
>
> **A*a*:** Hai, agemashita.
>
> **A*n*:** Iie, agemasendeshita.
>
> 1. kireina kitte
> 2. atarashii jisho
> 3. ryokō no shashin

> B. *ex.* **Q:** Dare ga Kurāku-san ni atarashii jisho o agemasu ka.
>
> **A:** <u>Tanaka-san</u> ga agemasu.
>
> 1. Haruko-san
> 2. kaisha no hito

> C. *ex.* **Q:** [Anata wa] Dare ni eiga no kippu o moraimashita ka.
>
> **A:** <u>Tomodachi</u> ni moraimashita.
>
> 1. chichi
> 2. ane

> D. *ex.* **Q:** [Anata wa] Otōsan no tanjōbi ni otōsan ni nani o agemasu ka.
>
> **A:** <u>Nekutai</u> o agemasu.
>
> 1. tokei
> 2. rekishi no hon

Vocabulary

jisho	dictionary	**ane**	(my) elder sister
Haruko	a given name (female)	**nekutai**	necktie
chichi	(my) father	**rekishi**	history

SHORT DIALOGUES

1. **Hayashi:** Ii nekutai desu ne.

   Kurāku: Dōmo arigatō. Kinō kanai ni moraimashita. Kinō wa watashi no tanjōbi deshita.

   Hayashi: What a nice necktie.
   Clark: Thank you. I received it from my wife yesterday. Yesterday was my birthday.

2. **Sumisu:** Watashi wa Amerika de Nihon-go no benkyō o shimashita.

   Tanaka: Hiragana ya kanji no benkyō mo shimashita ka.

   Sumisu: Haí, shimashita. Kanji wa totemo omoshiroi desu. Watashi wa yoku Nihon-go no hon o yomimasu. Nihon-go no sensei ni kono hon o moraimashita. Totemo omoshiroi hon desu.

   Smith: I studied Japanese in America.
   Tanaka: Did you study *hiragana, kanji* (and so on), too?
   Smith: Yes, I did. Kanji is fascinating. I often read books in Japanese. I was given this book by my Japanese teacher. It's a very entertaining book.

Vocabulary

kanai	(my) wife
hiragana	*hiragana* (Japanese script)
kanji	*kanji* (Chinese characters)

QUIZ

I Read this lesson's opening dialogue and answer the following questions.

1. Tanaka-san wa itsu kireina kabin o moraimashita ka.
2. Tanaka-san wa dare ni kireina kabin o moraimashita ka.
3. Dare ga Tanaka-san ni kireina kabin o agemashita ka.
4. Kurāku-san wa dare ni kireina kabin o agemashita ka.

II Complete the questions so that they fit the answers.

1. Tanaka-san wa (   ) ni ryokō no shashin o agemashita ka.
   Kurāku-san ni agemashita.
2. Hayashi-san wa (   ) ni eiga no kippu o moraimashita ka.
   Sumisu-san ni moraimashita.
3. Tomodachi ni (   ) o agemashita ka.
   Nihon-go no jisho o agemashita.

III Put the appropriate particles in the parentheses. (If a particle is not required, put an X in the parentheses.)

1. **Watashi wa kono kabin o kaimasen deshita. Tomodachi (   ) morai-mashita.**

2. **Dare (   ) Hayashi-san ni eiga no kippu (   ) agemashita ka.**

3. **Sumisu-san wa tomodachi (   ) Amerika no kireina kitte (   ) agemashita.**

4. **Tanjōbi (   ) nani (   ) moraimashita ka.**

   Nani (   ) moraimasen deshita.

IV Translate into Japanese.

1. Mr. Tanaka received a pretty vase from Mr. Clark.

2. Mr. Hayashi gave Mr. Smith a map of Kyoto.

3. Did you give that person a business card?

   Yes, I did (give him one).

LESSON 16　ASKING PREFERENCES

Mr. Hayashi invites Mr. Smith to go skiing.

はやし：どようびに　にっこうに　スキーに　いきます。スミスさん、
　　　　いっしょに　いきませんか。

スミス：いいですね。いきましょう。なんで　いきますか。

はやし：でんしゃで　いきます。とうきょうえきで　あいませんか。

スミス：はい。なんじに　あいましょうか。

はやし：あさの　7じに　とうきょうえきの　かいさつぐちで
　　　　あいましょう。

スミス：はい、わかりました。じゃ、どようびに。

■はやしさんは　スミスさんと　にっこうに　スキーに　いきます。
　どようびの　あさ　7じに　とうきょうえきの　かいさつぐちで
　スミスさんに　あいます。

Hayashi:　Do-yōbi ni Nikkō ni sukī ni ikimasu. Sumisu-san, issho ni iki-
　　　　masen ka.
Sumisu:　Ii desu ne. Ikimashō. Nan de ikimasu ka.
Hayashi:　Densha de ikimasu. Tōkyō Eki de aimasen ka.
Sumisu:　Hai. Nan-ji ni aimashō ka.
Hayashi:　Asa no 7-ji ni Tōkyō Eki no kaisatsuguchi de aimashō.
Sumisu:　Hai, wakarimashita. Ja, do-yōbi ni.

■ Hayashi-san wa Sumisu-san to Nikkō ni sukī ni ikimasu. Do-yōbi no asa 7-ji
ni Tōkyō Eki no kaisatsuguchi de Sumisu-san ni aimasu.

Hayashi:　I'm going to Nikko on Saturday to ski. Mr. Smith, wouldn't you like to go with
　　　　me?
Smith:　How nice! I'd love to go. (*lit.* "Let's go.") How do we get there?
Hayashi:　We'll go by train. Shall we meet at Tokyo Station?
Smith:　All right. What time shall we meet?
Hayashi:　Let's meet by the ticket gate in Tokyo Station at 7:00 in the morning.
Smith:　Sure. That's fine. Well, see you Saturday!

■ Mr. Hayashi is going skiing in Nikko with Mr. Smith. He is meeting Mr. Smith at 7:00 on Saturday morning by the ticket gate at Tokyo Station.

Vocabulary

にっこう	**Nikkō**	Nikko (city name)
スキー	**sukī**	skiing
に	**ni**	to (particle)
いっしょに	**issho ni**	together with
あいましょうか	**aimashō ka**	Shall we meet . . .
わかりました	**wakarimashita**	sure, certainly

GRAMMAR VII

Lessons 16–17   Inviting and Offering to Do Something

1. verb **-MASHŌ**
2. verb **-MASHŌ KA**
3. verb **-MASEN KA**

- Inviting and Suggesting

  verb **-mashō**

  ex. **12-ji ni eki no mae de aimashō.** "Let's meet at 12:00 in front of the station."
  Verb **-mashō** is generally translatable as "let's," "we'll," "I'll."

  verb **-mashō ka**

  ex. **Nan-ji ni aimashō ka.** "What time shall we meet?"
  Verb **-mashō ka** is used when you are inviting someone to decide a time, place, etc., for something.

  verb **-masen ka**

  ex. **Issho ni Nikkō ni ikimasen ka.** "Won't you go to Nikko with me?"
      Nichi-yōbi ni uchi ni kimasen ka. "Won't you come to my house on Sunday?"
  Verb **-masen ka** is used to invite someone to do something. Appropriate replies are as follows.

     Acceptance: 1. **Ee/Hai, verb -mashō.** "Yes, let's."
                    2. **Ee/Hai, arigatō gozaimasu.** "Yes, thank you."
                    3. **Ee/Hai, zehi.** "Yes, I'd love to."
     Refusal: 1. **Zannen desu ga, tsugō ga warui desu.** "I'm sorry, I'm afraid it's not convenient." (*lit.* "Unfortunately the circumstances are unfavorable.")
                2. **Arigatō gozaimasu. Demo (mō yomimashita).** "Thank you. But (I've already read it)." (State your reason after **demo**.)
                3. **Iie, kekkō desu.** "No, thank you." (See Note 4, p. 96)

- Offering to do something
  verb **-mashō ka**

ex. **Chizu o kakimashō ka.** "Shall I draw you a map?"
Verb **-mashō ka** is used when offering to do something for someone.
Appropriate replies are as follows.
   Acceptance: **Hai, onegaishimasu.** "Yes, please."
   Refusal: **Iie, kekkō desu.** "No, thank you."

NOTES

1. **Sukī ni ikimasu.**
   Sukī, "skiing," is a purpose, not a place. Therefore it takes the particle **ni,** not **e.**

2. **Sumisu-san, issho ni ikimasen ka.**
   Sumisu-san is simply being addressed by name and hence is not the topic of the sentence. In this case, the name, or title, usually comes at the beginning of the Japanese sentence.
   ex. **Tanaka-san, dōzo kochira ni.** "This way, please, Mr. Tanaka."

3. **Ja, do-yōbi ni.**
   Do-yōbi ni is short for **Do-yōbi ni aimashō,** "Let's meet on Saturday." Japanese often refer to the next meeting rather than saying "Goodbye."
   ex. **Ja, mata ashita.** "Well then, (see you) again tomorrow."

PRACTICE

KEY SENTENCES

1. **Do-yōbi ni issho ni tenisu o shimasen ka.**
2. **Issho ni shokuji ni ikimasen ka.**
3. **12-ji ni eki no mae de aimashō.**

1. Won't you play tennis with me on Saturday?
2. Won't you go out for a meal with me?
3. Let's meet at 12:00 in front of the station.

EXERCISES

I Verbs: Memorize the following **-mashō, -mashō ka,** and **-masen ka** forms.

	go	see	do	meet
V-masu	ikimasu	mimasu	shimasu	aimasu
V-mashō	ikimashō	mimashō	shimashō	aimashō
V-mashō ka	ikimashō ka	mimashō ka	shimashō ka	aimashō ka
V-masen ka	ikimasen ka	mimasen ka	shimasen ka	aimasen ka

II Practice the following patterns:

ex. **eiga ni ikimasu** ⟶ **Eiga ni ikimashō.**
Eiga ni ikimashō ka.
Eiga ni ikimasen ka.

1. **shokuji o shimasu**
2. **kōhī o nomimasu**

III Make dialogues by changing the underlined parts as in the examples given.

A. *ex* A: **B-san, ashita issho ni <u>shokuji</u> ni ikimasen ka.**
B*a*: **Ee, ikimashō.**
B*n*: **Zannen desu ga, tsugō ga warui desu.**

1. **kaimono**
2. **haikingu**
3. **doraibu**

B. *ex.* A: **B-san, issho ni <u>eiga o mimasen</u> ka.**
B: **Ee, <u>mimashō</u>.**

1. **sampo o shimasu**
2. **takushī de kaerimasu**
3. **ano resutoran de hiru-gohan o tabemasu**

C. *ex.* A: **Nan de kaerimashō ka.**
B: **<u>Takushī</u> de kaerimasen ka.**
A: **Ee, sō shimashō.**

1. **chikatetsu**
2. **basu**

D. *ex.* A: **Nan-ji ni aimashō ka.**
B: **<u>12-ji</u> goro wa dō desu ka.**
A: **Ee, ii desu.**

1. **3-ji**
2. **5-ji han**

E. *ex.* A: **Doko ni <u>doraibu</u> ni ikimashō ka.**
B: **<u>Umi no chikaku</u> ni ikimasen ka.**
A: **Ee, ikimashō.**

1. **kaimono, Ginza**
2. **sukī, Nikkō**

F. *ex.* A: **Nani o shimashō ka**
B: **<u>Tenisu o shimashō</u>.**

1. **sampo ni ikimasu**
2. **eiga o mimasu**

| Vocabulary |

zannen desu ga	I'm sorry, but . . .	**doraibu**	driving/a drive
zannenna	regrettable (**-na** adj.)	**sampo o shimasu**	take a walk
tsugō ga warui	(I) am unable (*lit.* "Con-	**(sampo o suru)**	
desu	ditions are bad.")	**sampo**	a walk
tsugō	condition	**umi**	sea
haikingu	hiking		

SHORT DIALOGUES

1. **Sumisu:** Hayashi-san, sampo ni ikimasen ka.
   Hayashi: Ee, ikimashō.
   Sumisu: Kono chikaku ni ōkii kōen ga arimasu. Kōen ni ikimashō.

   Smith: Mr. Hayashi, wouldn't you like to go for a walk?
   Hayashi: Yes, let's go.
   Smith: There is a big park near here. Let's go to the park.

2. Discussing what to give the Tanakas for their new baby.
   Yamada: Tanaka-san no akachan ni nani o agemashō ka.
   Howaito: Supūn to koppu wa dō desu ka.
   Yamada: Ii desu ne. Ashita depāto de kaimasen ka.
   Howaito: Ee, sō shimashō.

   Yamada: What shall we give the Tanakas for their (new) baby?
   White: How about a spoon and a mug?
   Yamada: All right. Shall we buy them tomorrow at the department store?
   White: Yes, let's do that.

| Vocabulary |

akachan	baby (other than speaker's own)
supūn	spoon
koppu	mug

QUIZ ▰▰▰▰▰▰

I Read this lesson's opening dialogue and answer the following questions.

1. **Hayashi-san wa doko ni sukī ni ikimasu ka.**
2. **Hayashi-san wa hitori de sukī ni ikimasu ka.**
3. **Hayashi-san wa Sumisu-san ni doko de aimasu ka.**
4. **Hayashi-san wa Sumisu-san ni 7-ji ni aimasu ka, 8-ji ni aimasu ka.**
5. **Hayashi-san to Sumisu-san wa nan de ikimasu ka.**

II Complete the questions so that they fit the answers.

1. **Do-yōbi ni eiga ni ikimasen ka.**
   Ee, ikimashō. (   ) de aimashō ka.
   Tōkyō Eki no kaisatsuguchi de aimashō.
   (   ) ni aimashō ka.
   4-ji ni aimasen ka.
   Ee, ii desu. 4-ji ni aimashō.
2. **Kinō tenisu ni ikimashita.**
   Sō desu ka. (   ) to shimashita ka.
   Sumisu-san to shimashita.

III Put the appropriate particle in the parentheses. (If a particle is not required, put an X in the parentheses.)

1. **Issho (   ) tenisu (   ) shimasen ka.**
2. **Issho (   ) tenisu (   ) ikimasen ka.**
3. **Raishū no do-yōbi (   ) doraibu (   ) ikimasen ka.**
4. **Shokuji (   ) ikimasen ka.**
   Ee. Doko (   ) tabemashō ka.

IV Translate into Japanese.

1. I went shopping at a department store on Saturday.
2. Won't you have a meal with me?
   Yes, let's (do that). Where shall we go?
   Wouldn't you like to go to the new restaurant near the station?
   Yes, let's do that.

LESSON **17** INVITATION TO A PARTY

Mr. Tanaka invites Mr. Smith to a farewell party for Mr. Clark.

たなか：どようびの　ばん　うちで　クラークさんの　そうべつかいを
　　　　します。スミスさん、きませんか。

スミス：ええ、ぜひ。ありがとうございます。おたくは　どちらですか。

たなか：あざぶです。ちずを　かきましょうか。

スミス：ええ、おねがいします。

■スミスさんは　どようびの　ばん　クラークさんの　そうべつかいに
　いきます。

Tanaka: Do-yōbi no ban uchi de Kurāku-san no sōbetsukai o shimasu.
　　　　Sumisu-san, kimasen ka.
Sumisu: Ee, zehi. Arigatō gozaimasu. O-taku wa dochira desu ka.
Tanaka: Azabu desu. Chizu o kakimashō ka.
Sumisu: Ee, onegaishimasu.

■ Sumisu-san wa do-yōbi no ban Kurāku-san no sōbetsukai ni ikimasu.

Tanaka: I'm giving a farewell party for Mr. Clark at my house on Saturday evening.
　　　　Won't you come, Mr. Smith?
Smith: Yes, I'd like to. Thank you very much. Where is your house?
Tanaka: It's in Azabu. Shall I draw you a map?
Smith: Yes, please.

■ Mr. Smith is going to a farewell party for Mr. Clark on Saturday evening.

Vocabulary		
そうべつかい	**sōbetsukai**	farewell party
ぜひ	**zehi**	I'd like to. (*lit.* "by all means")
どちら	**dochira**	where (polite word for **doko**)
あざぶ	**Azabu**	Azabu (place name)
かきましょうか	**kakimashō ka**	Shall (I) draw . . .

NOTES

1. Sōbetsukai o shimasu.

Since Mr. Tanaka is the host, he says **Sōbetsukai o shimasu,** "I'm giving a farewell party," rather than **sōbetsukai ga arimasu,** "There will be a farewell party." (See Grammar VIII, p. 124.)

PRACTICE

KEY SENTENCES

1. Nichi-yōbi ni uchi ni kimasen ka.
2. Mado o akemashō ka.

1. Won't you come to my house on Sunday?
2. Shall I open the window?

Vocabulary

akemashō ka	Shall I open . . . ?
akemasu (akeru)	open

EXERCISES

I Verbs: Memorize the following verbs and their **-mashō** forms.

	open	close	turn on	turn off	make a copy
V-masu	akemasu	shimemasu	tsukemasu	keshimasu	kopī o shimasu
V-mashō	akemashō	shimemashō	tsukemashō	keshimashō	kopī o shi-mashō
V-mashō ka	akema-shō ka	shimema-shō ka	tsukema-shō ka	keshima-shō ka	kopī o shi-mashō ka

II Practice the following patterns.

   ex. **mado o akemasu ⟶ Mado o akemashō.**
                           Mado o akemashō ka.

     1. **rajio o keshimasu**
     2. **doa o shimemasu**

III Make dialogues by changing the underlined parts as in the examples given.

    A. *ex.* **A: Do-yōbi ni uchi de <u>Kurāku-san no sōbetsukai</u> o shimasu. Uchi ni kimasen ka.**

B*a*: Ee, zehi.

B*n*: Zannen desu ga, tsugō ga warui desu.

1. pātī

2. Kurāku-san no kangeikai

B. *ex.* A: Kono <u>hon</u> wa omoshiroi desu yo. <u>Yomimasen</u> ka.

B*a*: Ee, arigatō gozaimasu.

B*n*: Arigato gozaimasu. Demo mō yomimashita.

1. zasshi, yomimasu

2. bideo, mimasu

C. *ex.* A: <u>Atsui</u> desu ne. <u>Mado o akemashō ka.</u>

B*a*: Ee, onegaishimasu.

B*n*: Iie, kekkō desu.

1. kurai, denki o tsukemasu

2. urusai, doa o shimemasu

3. atsui, hītā o keshimasu

Vocabulary

keshimasu (kesu)	turn off	**kurai**	dark (**-i** adj.)
doa	door	**denki**	(electric) light
shimemasu (shimeru)	close	**tsukemasu (tsukeru)**	turn on
kangeikai	welcome party	**urusai**	noisy (**-i** adj.)
demo	but	**hītā**	heater
bideo	video		

SHORT DIALOGUE

Yamada: Kopī o shimashō ka.

Sumisu: Hai, onegaishimasu.

Yamada: Nan-mai shimashō ka.

Sumisu: 3-mai onegaishimasu.

Yamada: Shall I make a copy?

Smith: Yes, please.

Yamada: How many copies shall I make?

Smith: Three copies, please.

Vocabulary

kopī   photocopy

QUIZ ▌▒▒▒▒▒

I Read this lesson's opening dialogue and answer the following questions.

1. Kurāku-san no sōbetsukai wa itsu desu ka.

2. Sumisu-san wa Kurāku-san no sōbetsukai ni ikimasu ka, ikimasen ka.

3. Tanàka-san wa doko de Kurāku-san no sōbetsukai o shimasu ka.

4. Tanaka-san no uchi wa doko ni arimasu ka.

5. Tanaka-san wa Sumisu-san ni chizu o kakimasu ka.

II Put the appropriate particles in the parentheses. (If a particle is not required, put an X in the parentheses.)

1. **Raishū no do-yōbi (　　) okusan to issho (　　) uchi (　　) kimasen ka.**

   Ee, zehi.

   Issho (　　) ban-gohan (　　) tabemashō.

2. **Tenisu (　　) ikimasen ka. Ii tenki desu kara.**

   Zannen desu (　　), tsugō (　　) warui desu.

3. **Atsui desu ne. Mado (　　) akemashō ka.**

   Hai, onegaishimasu.

III Translate into Japanese.

1. Won't you come to my house on Sunday?

2. We're having a farewell party for Mr. Clark at our house on Friday. Won't you come?

   Yes, I'd like to.

3. Won't you have a meal with me?

4. It's cold, isn't it? Shall I close the window?

   Yes, please.

5. Shall I draw you a map?

LESSON 18 OWNERSHIP AND EVENTS

Mr. Hayashi and Mr. Smith are making a date to go to the movies.

はやし：えいがの　きっぷが　2まい　あります。こんばん　いっしょ
　　　　に　いきませんか。

スミス：ざんねんですが、こんばん　7じに　たいしかんに　いきます。
　　　　たいしかんで　パーティーが　ありますから。

はやし：そうですか。あしたは　どうですか。

スミス：あしたは　じかんが　あります。

はやし：じゃ、あした　いきませんか。

スミス：ええ、あした　おねがいします。

■スミスさんは　こんばん　たいしかんで　パーティーが　ありますか
　ら、あした　はやしさんと　えいがに　いきます。

Hayashi:	Eiga no kippu ga 2-mai arimasu. Komban issho ni ikimasen ka.
Sumisu:	Zannen desu ga, komban 7-ji ni taishikan ni ikimasu. Taishikan de pātī ga arimasu kara.
Hayashi:	Sō desu ka. Ashita wa dō desu ka.
Sumisu:	Ashita wa jikan ga arimasu.
Hayashi:	Ja, ashita ikimasen ka.
Sumisu:	Ee, ashita onegaishimasu.

■ Sumisu-san wa komban taishikan de pātī ga arimasu kara, ashita Hayashi-san to eiga ni ikimasu.

Hayashi:	I have two tickets for the movie. Wouldn't you like to go with me tonight?
Smith:	I'm sorry, but I'm going to the embassy tonight at 7:00. There's a party at the embassy.
Hayashi:	I see. What about tomorrow?
Smith:	I'm free tomorrow.
Hayashi:	Well then, would you like to go tomorrow?
Smith:	Yes, let's make it tomorrow.

■There is a party at the embassy tonight, so Mr. Smith is going to the movie with Mr. Hayashi tomorrow.

| Vocabulary |

あります（ある）	**arimasu (aru)**	have
じかん	**jikan**	time

GRAMMAR VIII

Lesson 18   Ownership and Events

1. person WA noun GA ARIMASU
2. place DE event GA ARIMASU

- Grammar III covers the main uses of the verb **arimasu**. The following are additional uses.
    1. To have, to own
        - *ex.* **Kuruma ga arimasu kara issho ni ikimashō.** "I have a car, so let's go together."
        - *ex.* **Tanaka-san wa kodomo ga futari arimasu.** "Mr. Tanaka has two children."
    2. To take place, to happen
        - *ex.* **Koko de 2-ji kara kaigi ga arimasu.** "There will be a meeting here from 2 o'clock."

    Note: Remember that in the case of "giving a party" or "holding a meeting," etc., the verb **shimasu** is used. (See Note 1, p. 120.)

    Note also, **koko de**. When **arimasu** means "take place" or "occur," the particle used with the place is **de**, rather than **ni**.

NOTE

1. **Ashita wa dō desu ka.**
    The questioner is asking about his friend's arrangements for tomorrow. **Ashita** ("tomorrow"), though not the grammatical subject, is the topic in question, so it takes the topic marker **wa**.

PRACTICE

KEY SENTENCES

1. [Watashi wa] Kyō jikan ga arimasu.
2. [Watashi wa] Eiga no kippu ga 2-mai arimasu.
3. Sumisu-san wa kodomo ga futari arimasu.
4. Do-yōbi ni taishikan de pātī ga arimasu.

1. I have time today.
2. I have two tickets for the movie.
3. Mr. Smith has two children.
4. On Saturday there will be a party at the embassy.

EXERCISES

I Practice the following pattern by changing the underlined part as in the example given.

> ex. [Watashi wa] Jikan ga arimasu.
>
>   1. kaigi
>   2. eiga no kippu
>   3. kodomo
>   4. kyōdai

II Make dialogues by changing the underlined parts as in the examples given.

> A. ex. Q: [Anata wa] Ima jikan ga arimasu ka.
>
>   Aa: Hai, arimasu.
>   An: Iie, arimasen.
>
>   1. ima, o-kane
>   2. ashita, kaigi
>   3. kongetsu, yasumi
>
> B. ex. Q: [Anata wa] Eiga no kippu ga arimasu ka.
>
>   A: Hai, arimasu.
>
>   1. kuruma
>   2. kyōdai
>
> C. ex. Q: Hayashi-san wa kyō kaigi ga arimasu ka.
>
>   Aa: Hai, arimasu. 3-ji kara kaisha de arimasu.
>   An: Iie, arimasen. Ashita arimasu.
>
>   1. Nihon-go no jugyō
>   2. pātī
>
> D. ex. Q: [Anata wa] Itsu yasumi ga arimasu ka.
>
>   A: Raigetsu arimasu.
>
>   1. Nihon-go no jugyō, getsu-yōbi to ka-yōbi ni

E. *ex.* A: Do-yōbi ni <u>pātī</u> ga arimasu.

B: <u>Pātī</u> wa doko de arimasu ka.

A: <u>Taishikan</u> de arimasu.

1. kaigi, kaisha

2. tomodachi no kekkon-shiki, hoteru

F. *ex.* Q: Sumisu-san wa <u>kyōdai</u> ga nan-nin arimasu ka.

A: <u>3-nin</u> arimasu.

1. kodomo, futari

2. imōto-san, hitori

Vocabulary

kyōdai	brothers and/or sisters	**kekkon-shiki**	wedding
o-kane	money	**kekkon**	marriage
kongetsu	this month	**shiki**	ceremony
yasumi	vacation, day off	**imōto-san**	(your) younger sister
jugyō	class		

SHORT DIALOGUES

1. **Yamada:** Hayashi-san, ima jikan ga arimasu ka.
   Hayashi: Iie, ima chotto isogashii desu. Ima kara kaigi ga arimasu kara.

   Yamada: Mr. Hayashi, do you have time, now?
   Hayashi: No, I'm afraid I'm busy now. There's a conference (starting) now.

2. **Yamada:** Kurāku-san no sōbetsukai wa doko de arimasu ka.
   Howaito: Hayashi-san no uchi de arimasu.
   Yamada: Itsu arimasu ka.
   Howaito: Kin-yōbi no gogo 7-ji kara desu.

   Yamada: Where is the farewell party for Mr. Clark being held?
   White: It's being held at Mr. Hayashi's house.
   Yamada: When is it?
   White: On Friday evening, from 7 o'clock.

3. **Tanaka:** Sumisu-san, okosan ga arimasu ka.
   Sumisu: Ee, futari arimasu. Musuko to musume desu.
   Tanaka: Musuko-san wa nan-sai desu ka.
   Sumisu: Musuko wa 15-sai desu.
   Tanaka: Ojō-san wa?
   Sumisu: 13-sai desu.

   Tanaka: Mr. Smith, do you have any children?
   Smith: Yes, I have two. A son and a daughter.

Tanaka: How old is your son?
Smith: My son is 15.
Tanaka: (And) Your daughter?
Smith: (She's) Thirteen.

Vocabulary

chotto	a little	**nan-sai**	how many years old
okosan	(your) child	**-sai**	years old (used only for
musuko	(my) son		people and pets)
musume	(my) daughter	**ojō-san**	(your) daughter
musuko-san	(your) son		

QUIZ

I Read this lesson's opening dialogue and answer the following questions.

   1. **Hayashi-san wa nan no kippu ga arimasu ka.**

   2. **Hayashi-san wa kippu ga nan-mai arimasu ka.**

   3. **Sumisu-san wa komban eiga ni ikimasu ka, pātī ni ikimasu ka.**

   4. **Komban taishikan de nani ga arimasu ka.**

   5. **Hayashi-san wa komban hitori de eiga ni ikimasu ka.**

   6. **Hayashi-san wa itsu, dare to eiga ni ikimasu ka.**

II Complete the questions so that they fit the answers.

   1. **Hayashi-san wa kyōdai ga (   ) arimasu ka.**
     3-nin arimasu.

   2. **Anata wa (   ) yasumi ga arimasu ka.**
     Raigetsu arimasu.

   3. **Kyō taishikan de (   ) ga arimasu ka.**
     Pātī ga arimasu.

   4. **Tomodachi no kekkon-shiki wa (   ) de arimasu ka.**
     Hoteru de arimasu.

III Put the appropriate particles in the parentheses. (If a particle is not required, put an X in the parentheses.)

   1. **Tanaka-san wa kuruma (   ) arimasu.**

   2. **Tanaka-san no kuruma wa asoko (   ) arimasu.**

   3. **Kyō kaigi wa doko (   ) arimasu ka.**

   4. **Sumisu-san wa kodomo (   ) futari (   ) arimasu.**

   5. **Nichi-yōbi ni tomodachi no uçhi (   ) pātī (   ) arimasu.**

6. **Eiga (   ) kippu (   ) 2-mai (   ) arimasu.**
   Ashita (   ) issho ni ikimasen ka.
   Tsugō ga warui desu. Shigoto (   ) takusan arimasu kara.

IV Translate into Japanese.

1. I have three younger sisters. My sisters are in Tokyo and Osaka.
2. Mr. Tanaka, will you have a vacation in August?
   No, I won't. I'll have (one) in September.
3. There is a meeting at (our) Kyoto branch office next week.

LESSON 19 DOING THIS AND THAT

Mrs. Smith is telling Mr. Hayashi about her friend Linda who has just arrived in Japan.

スミス：きのう　アメリカから　ともだちの　リンダさんが　きました。

はやし：リンダさんは　いつまで　にほんに　いますか。

スミス：こんしゅうの　きんようびまで　とうきょうに　います。とう
きょうに　みっかだけ　います。それから　わたしと　いっ
しょに　りょこうを　します。

はやし：どこに　いきますか。

スミス：きょうとと　ならに　いって、ふるい　おてらや　にわを
みます。そして　リンダさんは　らいしゅうの　もくようびに
アメリカに　かえります。

■スミスさんの　ともだちの　リンダさんは　きのう　アメリカから
きました。らいしゅうの　もくようびまで　にほんに　います。

Sumisu: Kinō Amerika kara tomodachi no Rinda-san ga kimashita.
Hayashi: Rinda-san wa itsu made Nihon ni imasu ka.
Sumisu: Konshu no kin-yobi made Tōkyō ni imasu. Tōkyō ni mikka dake
imasu. Sorekara watashi to issho ni ryokō o shimasu.
Hayashi: Doko ni ikimasu ka.
Sumisu: Kyōto to Nara ni itte, furui o-tera ya niwa o mimasu. Soshite
Rinda-san wa raishū no moku-yōbi ni Amerika ni kaerimasu.

■ Sumisu-san no tomodachi no Rinda-san wa kinō Amerika kara kimashita.
Raishū no moku-yōbi made Nihon ni imasu.

Smith:　　My friend Linda came from America yesterday.
Hayashi:　How long (*lit.* "until when") is Linda staying in Japan?
Smith:　　She'll be in Tokyo until this Friday. She'll only be in Tokyo three days. Then she's taking a trip with me.
Hayashi:　Where are you going?
Smith:　　We'll go to Kyoto and Nara and see (things like) old temples and gardens. Then Linda returns to America on Thursday of next week.

■ Mrs. Smith's friend Linda arrived yesterday from America. She is staying in Japan until Thursday of next week.

Vocabulary

リンダ	**Rinda**	Linda
います（いる）	**imasu (iru)**	stay
こんしゅう	**konshū**	this week
みっか	**mikka**	(for) 3 days
だけ	**dake**	only
それから	**sorekara**	after that
なら	**Nara**	Nara (city and prefecture)
おてら	**o-tera**	temple

GRAMMAR IX

Lessons 19–27   -TE Form, -NAI Form, and Model Verb Conjugation

• All the verbs presented so far have been in, or derived from, the **-masu** form. Here are two other important verb forms, the **-te** form and the **-nai** form.

1. **-te** Form

Regular I					
buy	**kai-masu**	**katte**	go	**iki-masu**	**itte***
return	**kaeri-masu**	**kaette**	read	**yomi-masu**	**yonde**
wait	**machi-masu**	**matte**	call	**yobi-masu**	**yonde**
write	**kaki-masu**	**kaite**	push	**oshi-masu**	**oshite**
Regular II					
eat	**tabe-masu**	**tabete**	see	**mi-masu**	**mite**
show	**mise-masu**	**misete**	get off	**ori-masu**	**orite**
Irregular					
come	**ki-masu**	**kite**	do	**shimasu**	**shite**

*iki-masu, irregular change

• As shown above, the **-te** form can be made from the **-masu** form, although most Regular I verbs undergo a phonetic change.

• Use of **-te** form: The **-te** form of the verb occurs in the middle of sentences or combined with **kudasai** to form the polite imperative. It is used extensively and has various meanings which should be learned. Particular uses are explained in Lessons 19–25.

2. **-nai** Form

Regular I					
buy return wait	**kai-masu** **kaeri-masu** **machi-masu**	**kawanai** **kaeranai** **matanai**	write go	**kaki-masu** **iki-masu**	**kakanai** **ikanai**
Regular II					
eat show	**tabe-masu** **mise-masu**	**tabenai** **misenai**	see get off	**mi-masu** **ori-masu**	**minai** **orinai**
Irregular					
come	**ki-masu**	**konai**	do	**shi-masu**	**shinai**

- Use of the **-nai** form: A negative verb when used in mid-sentence usually takes the **-nai** form, rather than the **-masen** form it has at the end of a sentence. In this book, only the following use of the **-nai** form is given: verb **-nai de kudasai,** "Please do not . . ."
  This verb **-nai** + **de** + **kudasai** is a polite prohibition. (While not included in this book, it should be noted that the **-nai** form does end negative sentences in familiar speech, which uses the dictionary form for present and future and the **-ta** form for the past tense.)

- Model Verb Conjugation
  As can be inferred from the above, the conjugation of Japanese verbs falls into the following three categories:
  Regular I: Five-vowel conjugation
  Regular II: Single-vowel conjugation
  Irregular: There are only two irregular verbs, **shimasu** and **kimasu.**

- Regular I verbs are conjugated according to the Japanese vowel order: **a, i, u, e, o.** Regular II verbs are based on the vowels **i** and **e** only. From the **-nai** form it can be seen whether a verb is Regular I or Regular II. If the vowel preceding **-nai** is **a,** it is a Regular I verb. If it is **i** or **e,** it is a Regular II verb.

	Regular I	Regular II
-nai form	**kaka-nai**	**tabe-nai**
-masu form	**kaki-masu**	**tabe-masu**
dictionary form	**kaku**	**taberu**
conditional form	**kake-ba**	**tabere-ba**
volitional form	**ka-kō**	**tabeyō**
-te form	**kaite**	**tabete**
-ta form	**kaita**	**tabeta**

● Of the seven forms above, this book includes the **-nai**, **-masu** and **-te** forms. These three forms, the dictionary form and the **-ta** form are given comprehensively in Appendix E.

NOTES

1. **Kinō Amerika kara Rinda-san ga kimashita.**
   Rinda-san wa itsu made Nihon ni imasu ka.
   Since we hear about Linda for the first time in the first sentence, she takes the subject marker **ga**. As soon as the existence of Linda is understood by both speaker and listener, she becomes the topic, and then takes the topic marker **wa**.

2. **Kyōto to Nara ni itte, furui o-tera ya niwa o mimasu.**
   When one action is followed by another, the first clause is terminated by the verb **-te** form. The subject of the first clause and the second clause is the same. This cannot be done unless the mood and the tense of both sentences are the same. The following two sentences *cannot* be connected by the verb **-te** form.
   A. Statement: **Watashi wa kippu ga 2-mai arimasu.** "I have two tickets."
   B. Suggestion: **Ashita issho ni eiga ni ikimashō.** "Let's go to the movies tomorrow."

PRACTICE

KEY SENTENCES

1. **[Watashi wa] Kinō shigoto no ato de tomodachi to shokuji o shite, 9-ji ni uchi ni kaerimashita.**
2. **Kurāku-san wa kyonen no 5-gatsu kara Nihon ni imasu. Soshite rainen no 3-gatsu made [Nihon ni] imasu.**
3. **Tanaka-san wa mainichi 2-jikan benkyō o shimasu.**
4. **Hayashi-san wa asa-gohan no mae ni rajio de nyūsu o kikimasu. Shokuji no ato de shimbun o yomimasu.**

1. Yesterday, after work, I had a meal with my friends, and returned home at 9 o'clock.
2. Mr. Clark has been in Japan since last May and will stay until next March.
3. Mr. Tanaka studies two hours every day.
4. Mr. Hayashi listens to the news on the radio before breakfast. After the meal, he reads the newspaper.

| Vocabulary |

shigoto no ato de	after work	**-kan**	for
no ato de	after	**asa-gohan no mae ni**	before breakfast
2-jikan	(for) 2 hours	**no mae ni**	before
-jikan	(counter)		

EXERCISES ───

I Verbs: Memorize the following **-te** forms:

meet	**ai-masu**	**atte**	see	**mi-masu**	**mite**
go	**iki-masu**	itte	do	**shi-masu**	**shite**
read	**yomi-masu**	**yonde**	come	**ki-masu**	**kite**
eat	**tabe-masu**	**tabete**			

II Connect the sentences using the **-te** form as in the example given.

    ex. **Hon-ya ni ikimasu. Jisho o kaimasu.**

    Hon-ya ni itte, jisho o kaimasu.

      1. **Tanaka-san ni aimasu. issho ni eiga ni ikimasu.**

      2. **kabuki o mimasu. shokuji o shimasu. takushī de kaerimasu.**

      3. **eiga o mimashō. shokuji o shimashō.**

      4. **uchi ni kimasen ka. o-cha o nomimasen ka.**

      5. **Sumisu-san ni aimashita. issho ni tenisu o shimashita.**

III Practice the following patterns by changing the underlined parts as in the examples given.

    A. *ex.* **Kurāku-san wa kyonen no 5-gatsu kara Nihon ni imasu. Soshite rainen no**

      3-gatsu made imasu.

        1. **kotoshi no 1-gatsu, rainen no 8-gatsu**

        2. **senshū, raigetsu no 25-nichi**

    B. *ex.* **[Watashi wa] Shigoto no mae ni shimbun o yomimasu.**

        1. **kaigi**

        2. **shokuji**

    C. *ex.* **[Watashi wa] Shigoto no ato de Tanaka-san ni aimasu.**

        1. **pātī**

        2. **kaimono**

IV Make dialogues by changing the underlined parts as in the examples given.

    A. *ex.* **Q: [Anata wa] Do-yōbi ni donogurai shigoto o shimasu ka.**

      A: 3-jikan dake shimasu.

        1. **benkyō, shimasu, 30-pun**

        2. **hon, yomimasu, 1-jikan**

    B. *ex.* **Q: Kinō shigoto no ato de nani o shimashita ka.**

      A: Tanaka-san ni atte, issho ni ban-gohan o tabemashita.

        1. **hon-ya ni ikimasu. jisho o kaimasu.**

        2. **tenisu o shimasu. uchi ni kaerimasu.**

    C. *ex.* **Q: Nichi-yōbi ni nani o shimashō ka.**

      A: Ginza ni itte, kaimono o shimasen ka.

1. kabuki o mimasu. Ginza de shokuji o shimasu.

2. kōen ni ikimasu. hana o mimasu.

D. *ex.* Q: Howaito-san wa itsu kara Nihon ni imasu ka.

A: <u>Kyonen no 8-gatsu kara</u> imasu.

Q: Itsu made Nihon ni imasu ka.

A: <u>Rainen no 10-gatsu made</u> imasu.

1. 1980-nen, rainen

2. sengetsu no 15-nichi, asatte

Vocabulary

donogurai how long

SHORT DIALOGUES

1. **Yamada:** **Howaito-san wa donogurai Nihon-go no benkyō o shimashita ka.**
   Howaito: **4-shūkan dake shimashita. Mainichi 2-jikan shimashita.**
   Yamada: **Nihon-go no benkyō wa dō deshita ka.**
   Howaito: **Sukoshi muzukashikatta desu ga, omoshirokatta desu.**

   Yamada: How long did you study Japanese?
   White: Only 4 weeks, 2 hours a day.
   Yamada: How did you find Japanese?
   White: It was a little difficult but fun.

2. **Tanaka:** **O-sake wa ikaga desu ka.**
   Hayashi: **Kyō wa kekkō desu.**
   Tanaka: **Dōshite desu ka.**
   Hayashi: **Kuruma de kimashita kara.**

   Tanaka: Will you have some *sake*?
   Hayashi: No, thank you, not today. (*lit.* "As for today, no thank you.")
   Tanaka: Why?
   Hayashi: Because I came by car (and thus I'm driving).

Vocabulary

4-shūkan 4 weeks
  -shūkan (counter)
sukoshi a little

QUIZ

I Read this lesson's opening dialogue and answer the following questions.

1. **Rinda-san wa Sumisu-san no tomodachi desu ka, Hayashi-san no**

      tomodachi desu ka.

2. **Rinda-san wa itsu Nihon ni kimashita ka.**
3. **Rinda-san wa itsu made Nihon ni imasu ka.**
4. **Rinda-san wa donogurai Tōkyō ni imasu ka.**
5. **Rinda-san wa Tōkyō kara doko ni ikimasu ka.**
6. **Rinda-san to Sumisu-san wa Kyōto ya Nara ni itte nani o shimasu ka.**

II Convert the following verbs into their **-te** form.

1. **tabemasu**	4. **kimasu**	7. **imasu**	10. **nomimasu**
2. **ikimasu**	5. **kakimasu**	8. **mimasu**	11. **aimasu**
3. **yomimasu**	6. **kaerimasu**	9. **shimasu**	12. **kikimasu**

III Complete the questions so that they fit the answers.

1. **Tanaka-san wa Amerika ni (   ) kara (   ) made imashita ka.**
   1979-nen no 5-gatsu kara 1982-nen no 3-gatsu made imashita.
2. **Ōsaka ni (   ) imashita ka.**
   1-shūkan imashita.
3. **(   ) Sumisu-san ni aimasu ka.**
   Shigoto no ato de aimasu.

IV Circle the correct words in the parentheses.

1. **Kyonen Nihon ni kimashita. (Soshite, To) rainen kaerimasu.**
2. **Ashita Kyōto ni (ikimasu to, itte), do-yōbi ni Tōkyō ni kaerimasu.**
3. **Tomodachi wa Tōkyō ni (donogurai, dō) imashita ka.**
4. **Kinō tenisu o 1-jikan (goro, gurai) shimashita.**
5. **Sono hon wa (donogurai, dō) desu ka.**
   Omoshiroi desu.
6. **Kaisha ni (nan, dō) de ikimasu ka.**
   Chikatetsu de ikimasu.
   Kaisha made (dō, donogurai) desu ka.
   25-fun (goro, gurai) desu.

V Translate into Japanese.

1. Every morning I listen to the news and then go to the office.
2. I met Mr. Tanaka and had dinner with him. And then I went home.
3. How long do you study Japanese at home?
   Only 30 minutes. (*lit.* "(I) only do it for 30 minutes.")
4. I didn't go anywhere yesterday. I was at home.

LESSON 20   REQUESTS AND ORDERS

Mr. Hayashi telephones a liquor store and orders some beer to be delivered.

はやし：もしもし、はやしですが、ビールを　20ぽん　もってきて
　　　　　ください。

さかや：なんじまでに　とどけましょうか。

はやし：3じまでに　うちに　とどけてください。

さかや：はい、わかりました。ごじゅうしょを　おねがいします。

はやし：あざぶ　2ちょうめ　2の1です。

さかや：すみません、もう　いちど　いってください。

はやし：あざぶ　2ちょうめ　2の1です。

さかや：まいど　ありがとうございます。

■はやしさんは　さかやに　でんわを　しました。さかやは　はやしさ
　んの　じゅうしょを　きいて、はやしさんの　うちに　ビールを
　とどけました。

Hayashi: Moshi moshi, Hayashi desu ga, bīru o 20-pon mottekite kudasai.
Saka-ya: Nanji made ni todokemashō ka.
Hayashi: 3-ji made ni uchi ni todokete kudasai.
Saka-ya: Hai, wakarimashita. Go-jūsho o onegaishimasu.
Hayashi: Azabu 2-chōme 2 no 1 desu.
Saka-ya: Sumimasen, mō ichi-do itte kudasai.
Hayashi: Azabu 2-chōme 2 no 1 desu.
Saka-ya: Maido arigatō gozaimasu.

■ Hayashi-san wa saka-ya ni denwa o shimashita. Saka-ya wa Hayashi-san no jūsho o kiite, Hayashi-san no uchi ni bīru o todokemashita.

Hayashi: Hello, this is Mr. Hayashi. Please bring me 20 bottles of beer.
Clerk: By what time should we deliver it?
Hayashi: Please deliver it to my house by 3:00.
Clerk: Certainly, sir. Please give me your address.

Hayashi: It's 2–1 Azabu 2-*chōme*.
Clerk: Excuse me, would you repeat that, please?
Hayashi: It's 2–1 Azabu 2-*chōme*.
Clerk: Thank you, sir.

■ Mr. Hayashi telephoned the liquor store. The liquor store clerk asked Mr. Hayashi for his address and delivered the beer to his house.

Vocabulary

もってきて　ください	mottekite kudasai	please bring
もってきます（もってくる）	mottekimasu (mottekuru)	bring
なんじまでに	nan-ji made ni	by what time
～までに	made ni	by
とどけましょうか	todokemashō ka	Shall we deliver?
とどけます（とどける）	todokemasu (todokeru)	deliver
とどけて　ください	todokete kudasai	Please deliver . . .
2ちょうめ2の1	2-chōme 2 no 1	2-*chōme* 2–1
2ちょうめ	2-chōme	2-*chōme*
～ちょうめ	-chōme	*chōme*
いちど	ichi-do	once (*lit.* "one time")
～ど	-do	time (counter)
いって　ください	itte kudasai	Please say
いいます（いう）	iimasu (iu)	say
まいどありがとう ございます	maido arigatō gozaimasu	Thank you (for your patronage) each time.
まいど	maido	each time

NOTES

1. **3-ji made ni**

   Do not confuse **3-ji made** and **3-ji made ni**.
   ex. **15-nichi made Tokyo ni ite kudasai.** "Please stay in Tokyo until the 15."
   15-nichi made ni Tokyo ni kite kudasai. "Please come to Tokyo by the 15."

2. **Uchi ni todokete kudasai.**

   Requests are formed by verb **-te** + **kudasai.**

3. **Azabu 2-chōme 2 no 1**

   Japanese city addresses are typically made up of a place name (often combined with **machi** or **chō**, "town, community") + **chōme** + **banchi** + **gō. Chōme** are sections of the **machi.** They may be regular in shape, like a city block, or irregular, their borders being formed by streets or natural features such as rivers. **Chōme** are subdivided into **banchi,** and the **gō** is the individual house or building number. In the address above, 2 **no** 1 is **banchi** number 2, house number 1. The words **banchi** and **gō** are frequently omitted both in speaking and in writing (except in legal documents).

PRACTICE

KEY SENTENCES

1. **Chotto matte kudasai.**
2. **Tsugi no kado o migi ni magatte kudasai.**
3. **Taipu o onegaishimasu.**

1. Just a moment, please.
2. Turn right at the next corner.
3. Please type this.

| Vocabulary |

matte kudasai	please wait	magatte kudasai	please turn
tsugi	next	**magarimasu (magaru)**	turn
kado	corner	**taipu**	typing
migi	right		

EXERCISES

I Verbs: Memorize the following verbs and their **-te** form.

	-masu form	-te form		-masu form	-te form
wait	**machi-masu**	**matte**	deliver	**todoke-masu**	**todokete**
turn	**magari-masu**	**magatte**	show	**mise-masu**	**misete**
bring	**motteki-masu**	**mottekite**	stop, park	**tome-masu**	**tomete**
say	**ii-masu**	**itte**			

II Practice the following pattern by changing the **-masu** form to the **-te** form.

    ex. **Chotto machimasu.** ──────→ **Chotto matte kudasai.**

        1. **Menyū o misemasu.**

        2. **Yukkuri iimasu.**

        3. **Bīru to jūsu o todokemasu.**

III Practice the following patterns by changing the underlined parts as in the examples given.

    A. *ex.* <u>**Taipu**</u> **o onegaishimasu.**

1. kopī
2. kēki
3. sandoitchi to sarada

B. *ex.* <u>Kopī</u> o <u>3-mai</u> onegaishimasu.

    1. kēki, yottsu
    2. bīru, 2-hon

C. *ex.* Tsugi no <u>kado</u> o <u>migi</u> ni magatte kudasai.

    1. shingō, migi
    2. kōsaten, hidari

IV Make dialogues by changing the underlined parts as in the examples given.

A. *ex.* A: <u>Mado</u> o <u>akemashō</u> ka.

    B: Hai, <u>akete</u> kudasai.

    1. doa, shimemasu
    2. terebi, tsukemasu
    3. rajio, keshimasu
    4. jūsho to namae, kakimasu
    5. denwa-bangō, iimasu

B. *ex.* A: Ashita denwa o <u>shite</u> kudasai.

    B: Doko ni <u>denwa o shimashō</u> ka.

    A: Kaisha ni [denwa o] shite kudasai.

    B: Nan-ji ni [denwa o] shimashō ka.

    A: 10-ji made ni onegaishimasu.

    1. hana o todokemasu

Vocabulary

menyū	menu	shingō	traffic light
yukkuri	slowly	kōsaten	intersection
kēki	cake	hidari	left

SHORT DIALOGUE

Ueitoresu:	Irasshaimase.
Yamada:	Kōcha to kēki o onegaishimasu.
Ueitoresu:	Hai, shōshō omachi kudasai.

Waitress:	Good afternoon, madam.
Yamada:	(A cup of) Tea and some cake, please.
Waitress:	Certainly, madam. (Wait) Just a moment, please.

Vocabulary

ueitoresu   waitress

QUIZ

I Read this lesson's opening dialogue and answer the following questions.

1. **Hayashi-san wa doko ni denwa o shimashita ka.**
2. **Saka-ya wa doko ni bīru o todokemasu ka.**
3. **Saka-ya wa bīru o nan-bon todokemasu ka.**
4. **Saka-ya wa nan-ji made ni bīru o todokemasu ka.**
5. **Hayashi-san wa saka-ya ni jūsho o oshiemashita ka.**

II Convert the following verbs into their **-te** form.

1. **iimasu**   4. **kikimasu**   7. **mottekimasu**   10. **aimasu**
2. **imasu**   5. **magarimasu**   8. **ikimasu**   11. **nomimasu**
3. **machimasu**   6. **misemasu**   9. **shimemasu**   12. **shimasu**

III Put the appropriate particles in the parentheses. (If a particle is not required put an X in the parentheses.)

1. **Kore (   ) kudasai.**
2. **Bīru (   ) 5-hon (   ) kudasai.**
3. **Ashita 8-ji han made (   ) kite kudasai.**
4. **Kopī (   ) onegaishimasu.**
5. **Jūsu (   ) 5-hon (   ) bīru (   ) 12-hon uchi (   ) mottekite kudasai.**
6. **Tsugi no kado (   ) hidari (   ) magatte kudasai.**

IV Translate into Japanese.

1. Please show me the menu.
   Certainly. Here you are.
2. Excuse me, but could you please deliver 12 bottles of beer to my house.
   Yes, certainly. It's Mr. Clark, isn't it?
   Yes, that's right.
3. Please give me this small TV set.
   Yes, certainly, sir. Shall I deliver it?
   No, that's all right. (Because) I came by car.

LESSON 21   HAVING THINGS DONE

Giving directions to a taxi driver.

はやし： 　　　とうきょうえきの　ちかくに　いってください。
うんてんしゅ：はい。

はやし： 　　　つぎの　しんごうを　みぎに　まがって、まっすぐ
　　　　　　　　いってください。

はやし： 　　　あの　こうさてんの　てまえで　とめてください。

うんてんしゅ： 1,200えんです。
はやし： 　　　5,000えんで　おねがいします。
うんてんしゅ： 3,800えんの　おつりです。
はやし： 　　　どうも。

Hayashi: Tōkyō Eki no chikaku ni itte kudasai.
Untenshu: Hai.

Hayashi: Tsugi no shingō o migi ni magatte, massugu itte kudasai.

Hayashi: Ano kōsaten no temae de tomete kudasai.

Untenshu: 1,200-en desu.
Hayashi: 5,000-en de onegaishimasu.
Untenshu: 3,800-en no otsuri desu.
Hayashi: Dōmo.

Hayashi: (I want to) go to the neighborhood of Tokyo Station, please.
Driver: Yes, sir.

Hayashi: Please turn right at the next traffic light and go straight ahead.

Hayashi: Please stop just before that crossing.

Driver: That's ¥1,200.
Hayashi: Please take it out of this ¥5,000.
Driver: Here's (your) change, ¥3,800.
Hayashi: Thanks.

うんてんしゅ	**untenshu**	driver
まっすぐ	**massugu**	straight ahead
てまえ	**temae**	just before
とめて　ください	**tomete kudasai**	Please stop.
とめます（とめる）	**tomemasu (tomeru)**	stop
おつり	**otsuri**	change
どうも	**dōmo**	thanks (colloquial)

Making a reservation at a restaurant by telephone.

レストランの　ひと：レストランとうきょうでございます。

はやし：　　　　　　よやくを　おねがいします。

レストランの　ひと：はい、ありがとうございます。いつですか。

はやし：　　　　　　あしたの　ばんです。7じころ　おねがいします。

レストランの　ひと：なんにんさまですか。

はやし：　　　　　　6にんです。

レストランの　ひと：はい、わかりました。おなまえと　おでんわばん
　　　　　　　　　　　ごうを　どうぞ。

Resutoran no hito:	Resutoran Tōkyō de gozaimasu.
Hayashi:	Yoyaku o onegaishimasu.
Resutoran no hito:	Hai, arigatō gozaimasu. Itsu desu ka.
Hayashi:	Ashita no ban desu. 7-ji goro onegaishimasu.
Resutoran no hito:	Nan-nin-sama desu ka.
Hayashi:	6-nin desu.
Resutoran no hito:	Hai, wakarimashita. O-namae to o-denwa-bangō o dōzo.

Restaurant employee:	This is Restaurant Tokyo.
Hayashi:	I'd like to make a reservation.
Restaurant employee:	Thank you. When would you like it for?
Hayashi:	Tomorrow evening, about 7 o'clock.
Restaurant employee:	For how many?
Hayashi:	Six.
Restaurant employee:	Certainly, sir. May I have your name and telephone number, please?

| レストランとうきょう | **Resutoran Tōkyō** | Restaurant Tokyo |

よやく	yoyaku	reservation
なんにんさま	nan-nin-sama	how many people (shopkeeper's expression)
〜さま	-sama	politer form of -san

Having things cleaned.

はやし：　　　　　クリーニングを　おねがいします。いつ　できますか。
クリーニングや：すいようびの　ごご　できます。

■はやしさんは　すいようびの　ごご　クリーニングやに　いきました。

はやし：　　　　　もう　できましたか。
クリーニングや：すみません。まだです。4じころ　できます。
はやし：　　　　　じゃ、また　きます。

Hayashi:　　　　Kurīningu o onegaishimasu. Itsu dekimasu ka.
Kurīningu-ya:　Sui-yōbi no gogo dekimasu.

■**Hayashi-san wa sui-yōbi no gogo kurīningu-ya ni ikimashita.**

Hayashi:　　　　Mō dekimashita ka.
Kurīningu-ya:　Sumimasen. Mada desu. 4-ji goro dekimasu.
Hayashi:　　　　Ja, mata kimasu.

Hayashi:　I'd like to have this (these) cleaned. When will it (they) be done?
Clerk:　　It (they) will be done on Wednesday afternoon.

■Mr. Hayashi went to the cleaner's on Wednesday afternoon.

Hayashi:　Is it (are they) ready?
Clerk:　　I'm sorry, it's (they're) not finished yet. It (they) will be ready about 4:00.
Hayashi:　I'll come back, then.

Vocabulary		
クリーニング	**kurīningu**	dry cleaning
できます（できる）	**dekimasu (dekiru)**	be ready (finished, done)
クリーニングや	**kurīningu-ya**	dry cleaner
まだです	**mada desu**	not yet
まだ	**mada**	yet

LESSON 22 PUBLIC TRANSPORTATION

Mrs. Tanaka went to visit Haruko at the hospital. Mrs. Hayashi is going to visit her tomorrow and is asking how to get to Tokyo Hospital.

たなか：せんしゅう　とうきょうびょういんに　いきました。

はやし：はるこさんは　どうでしたか。

たなか：あまり　げんきでは　ありませんでした。

はやし：どうやって　とうきょうびょういんに　いきましたか。わたし
　　　　も　あした　いきます。

たなか：とうきょうえきで　80ばんの　バスに　のりました。あざぶ
　　　　で　おりて、びょういんまで　5ふんぐらい　あるきました。

はやし：そうですか。とうきょうえきから　あざぶまで　どのぐらい
　　　　かかりますか。

たなか：バスで　30ぷん　かかります。

■たなかさんの　おくさんは　せんしゅう　とうきょうびょういんに
いきました。たなかさんの　おくさんは　とうきょうえきで　バスに
のって、あざぶで　おりました。とうきょうえきから　あざぶまで
30ぷん　かかりました。それから　びょういんまで　5ふんぐらい
あるきました。

Tanaka:	Senshū Tōkyō Byōin ni ikimashita.
Hayashi:	Haruko-san wa dō deshita ka.
Tanaka:	Amari genki dewa arimasendeshita.
Hayashi:	Dōyatte Tōkyō Byōin ni ikimashita ka. Watashi mo ashita iki-masu.
Tanaka:	Tōkyō Eki de 80-ban no basu ni norimashita. Azabu de orite, byōin made 5-fun gurai arukimashita.
Hayashi:	Sō desu ka. Tōkyō Eki kara Azabu made donogurai kakarimasu ka.
Tanaka:	Basu de 30-pun kakarimasu.

■Tanaka-san no okusan wa senshū Tōkyō Byōin ni ikimashita. Tanaka-san no okusan wa Tōkyō Eki de basu ni notte, Azabu de orimashita. Tōkyō Eki kara Azabu made 30-pun kakarimashita. Sorekara byōin made 5-fun gurai arukimashita.

Tanaka: I went to Tokyo Hospital last week.
Hayashi: How was Haruko?
Tanaka: She wasn't feeling very well.
Hayashi: How did you get to Tokyo Hospital? I'm going, too, tomorrow.
Tanaka: I took a No. 80 bus from Tokyo Station. I got off at Azabu and walked about 5 minutes to (get to) the hospital.
Hayashi: I see. How long does it take from Tokyo Station to Azabu?
Tanaka: It takes 30 minutes by bus.

■Mrs. Tanaka went to Tokyo Hospital last week. She took a bus from Tokyo Station and got off at Azabu. It took 30 minutes from Tokyo Station to Azabu. Then she walked about 5 minutes to Tokyo Hospital.

Vocabulary

とうきょうびょういん	**Tōkyō Byōin**	Tokyo Hospital
どうやって	**dōyatte**	how
に	**ni**	on (particle)
のりました	**norimashita**	took, got on
のります（のる）	**norimasu (noru)**	take, get on
おりて	**orite**	get/got off (and)
おります（おりる）	**orimasu (oriru)**	get off
まで	**made**	to, as far as
あるきました	**arukimashita**	walked
あるきます（あるく）	**arukimasu (aruku)**	walk
かかります（かかる）	**kakarimasu (kakaru)**	(it) takes

NOTES

1. **Tōkyō Eki de basu ni norimashita. Azabu de (basu o) orimashita.**

   Note the particles used: **basu NI norimasu,** "take/get on a bus"

   basu O orimasu, "get off the bus"

   Tōkyō Eki DE, "at Tokyo Station"

   Azabu DE, "at Azabu"

2. **5-fun gurai**

   An approximate time period is expressed by the suffix **-gurai.**

   ex. **5-fun gurai,** "about 5 minutes"

   2-jikan gurai, "about 2 hours"

   3-shūkan gurai, "about 3 weeks"

Do not confuse with **goro,** which expresses an approximate specific time. (See Note 5, p. 89.)

3. **Nan-pun, nan-jikan, nan-nichi**

How many minutes, hours, days.

ex. **Nan-jikan kakarimasu ka.** "How long (*lit.* "how many hours") does it take?"

To ask in a more general way, **donogurai,** "how long," may be used.

ex. **Donogurai kakarimasu ka.** "How long does/will it take?"

Donogurai is also used to ask how much something will cost.

ex. **Donogurai/Ikura kakarimasu ka.** "How much will it cost?"

PRACTICE

KEY SENTENCES

1. **Hikōki wa gozen 8-ji 10-pun ni Narita Kūkō o demasu.**
2. **Sumisu-san wa gogo 3-ji ni Narita Kūkō ni tsukimashita.**
3. **Tōkyō Eki de basu ni notte, Ginza de basu o orite kudasai.**
4. **[Watashi no] Uchi kara eki made basu de 10-pun kakarimasu.**

1. The airplane leaves Narita Airport at 8:10 A.M.
2. Mr. Smith arrived at Narita Airport at 3:00 P.M.
3. Take the bus from Tokyo Station and get off at the Ginza.
4. It takes 10 minutes by bus from my house to the station.

| Vocabulary |

o	from (particle)
demasu (deru)	leave
tsukimashita	arrived
tsukimasu (tsuku)	arrive

EXERCISES

I Verbs: Memorize the following verbs and their **-te** form.

	-masu form	**-te** form		**-masu** form	**-te** form
go out, leave	**de-masu**	dete	get off	**ori-masu**	orite
arrive	**tsuki-masu**	tsuite	walk	**aruki-masu**	aruite
take, get on	**nori-masu**	notte	take	**kakari-masu**	kakatte

II Practice the following patterns by changing the underlined parts as in the examples given.

A. *ex.* **[Watashi wa] Densha ni norimasu. Densha o orimasu.**

1. basu
2. takushī

B. *ex.* Tanaka-san wa <u>hiru</u> Ōsaka o demashita. <u>Yūgata</u> Tōkyō ni tsukimashita.

1. 6-ji ni, uchi, 7-ji ni, kaisha
2. asa, Kyōto, 11-ji goro, Tōkyō no uchi

III Make dialogues by changing the underlined parts as in the examples given.

A. *ex.* Q: <u>Hikōki</u> wa nan-ji ni <u>Ōsaka</u> o demasu ka.

A: <u>Gozen 7-ji</u> ni demasu.

Q: [Hikōki wa] Nan-ji ni <u>Tōkyō</u> ni tsukimasu ka.

A: <u>Gozen 8-ji</u> ni tsukimasu.

1. Shinkansen, gogo 1-ji, gogo 4-ji 10-pun
2. Tanaka-san, gozen 10-ji, gogo 1-ji han

B. *ex.* Q: <u>Ueno Eki</u> de nani ni norimashita ka.

A: <u>Densha</u> ni norimashita.

Q: Doko de <u>densha</u> o orimashita ka.

A: <u>Tōkyō Eki</u> de orimashita.

1. basu, kōen no mae
2. takushī, uchi no chikaku

yūgata	late afternoon, early evening
Ueno	Ueno (place name)

SHORT DIALOGUE

Howaito:	Yamada-san wa dōyatte kaisha ni ikimasu ka.
Yamada:	Azabu de basu ni notte, Aoyama 1-chōme de orimasu. Aoyama 1-chōme kara chikatetsu ni notte, Nihombashi de orimasu. Soshite kaisha made 5-fun gurai arukimasu.
Howaito:	O-taku kara kaisha made donogurai kakarimasu ka.
Yamada:	1-jikan gurai kakarimasu.

White:	How do you go to (your) office?
Yamada:	I take a bus from Azabu and get off at Aoyama 1-*chōme*. I take the subway from Aoyama 1-*chōme* and get off at Nihombashi and walk about 5 minutes to my office.
White:	How long does it take from your house to your office?
Yamada:	It takes about one hour.

Aoyama	Aoyama (place name)
Nihombashi	Nihombashi (place name)

QUIZ

I Read this lesson's opening dialogue and answer the following questions.

1. **Tanaka-san no okusan wa itsu Tōkyō Byōin ni ikimashita ka.**
2. **Hayashi-san no okusan wa Tanaka-san no okusan to issho ni Tōkyō Byōin ni ikimashita ka.**
3. **Hayashi-san no okusan wa itsu Tōkyō Byōin ni ikimasu ka.**
4. **Tanaka-san no okusan wa doko de basu o orimashita ka.**
5. **Tōkyō Eki kara Azabu made basu de 1-jikan gurai kakarimashita ka.**

II Complete the questions so that they fit the answers.

1. **Kaisha ni (   ) de ikimasu ka.**
   Chikatetsu de ikimasu.
2. **(   ) de basu o orimasu ka.**
   Tōkyō Eki no mae de orimasu.
3. **(   ) ni norimashō ka.**
   Takushī ni norimasen ka. Tenki ga warui desu kara.
4. **Tōkyō kara Ōsaka made Shinkansen de (   ) kakarimasu ka.**
   3-jikan gurai kakarimasu.
5. **(   ) koko ni kimashita ka.**
   Tōkyō Eki de densha o orite, basu ni norimashita. Soshite kōen no chikaku de orite, aruite kimashita.

III Put the appropriate particles in the parentheses. (If a particle is not required, put an X in the parentheses.)

1. **Tōkyō Eki (   ) basu (   ) notte, Ginza (   ) basu (   ) orite kudasai.**
2. **Asa Kyōto (   ) dete, 5-ji (   ) Tōkyō (   ) tsukimashita. Nan (   ) kimashita ka.**
   Kuruma de kimashita.
3. **Uchi kara eki (   ) basu (   ) 15-fun (   ) kakarimasu.**

IV Translate into Japanese.

1. There was a farewell party for a friend (of mine) at a hotel in the Ginza yesterday.
2. I left the office at 6 o'clock, took a bus, and got off at the Ginza.
3. How long did it take you from the office to the hotel?
   It took about 35 minutes.

LESSON 23 ASKING PERMISSION

Mr. Smith went to an electrical appliance store.

スミス： この　テレビを　つけても　いいですか。

でんきや：はい、どうぞ。つけてください。

スミス： この　テレビの　カタログは　ありますか。

でんきや：はい、その　ケースの　うえに　あります。

スミス： もらっても　いいですか。

でんきや：はい、どうぞ。

スミス： どうも　ありがとう。

■スミスさんは　でんきやで　テレビの　カタログを　もらいました。

Sumisu:	Kono terebi o tsukete mo ii desu ka.
Denki-ya:	Hai, dōzo tsukete kudasai.
Sumisu:	Kono terebi no katarogu wa arimasu ka.
Denki-ya:	Hai, sono kēsu no ue ni arimasu.
Sumisu:	Moratte mo ii desu ka.
Denki-ya:	Hai, dōzo.
Sumisu:	Dōmo arigatō.

■ Sumisu-san wa denki-ya de terebi no katarogu o moraimashita.

Smith:	May I turn this TV set on?
Salesman:	Certainly, sir. (Please turn it on.)
Smith:	Do you have a brochure about this set?
Salesman:	Yes. (They're) On top of that showcase.
Smith:	May I have one?
Salesman:	Certainly, sir.
Smith:	Thank you very much.

■ Mr. Smith got a TV set brochure at an electrical appliance store.

Vocabulary

つけても　いいですか　　**tsukete mo ii desu ka**　　May I turn it on?

でんきや	denki-ya	electrical appliance store or clerk
カタログ	katarogu	catalogue, brochure
ケース	kēsu	showcase

NOTES

1. **Terebi o tsukete mo ii desu ka.**

   (Terebi no katarogu o) Moratte mo ii desu ka.

   Asking permission to do something is done using the following sentence construction.

   Verb **-te** form + **mo ii desu ka**

   Permission is given as follows. The first is politer than the second.
   1. **Hai, dōzo.** "Yes, please (do)."
   2. **Hai, ii desu.** "Yes, you may."

   For refusal of permission, see Note 1, p. 155.

PRACTICE

KEY SENTENCES

1. **Koko de shashin o totte mo ii desu ka.**
2. **Kono heya o tsukatte mo ii desu.**

1. May (I) take a photograph here?
2. You may use this room.

Vocabulary

shashin o totte mo ii desu ka	May (I) take a photograph?
shashin o torimasu (toru)	take a photograph
tsukatte mo ii desu	You may use it.
tsukaimasu (tsukau)	use

EXERCISES

I Verbs: Memorize the following verbs and their **-te** form.

	-masu form	**-te** form
take (a photograph)	**(shashin o) tori-masu**	**totte**
use	**tsukai-masu**	**tsukatte**
go in, enter	**hairi-masu**	**haitte**

II Practice the following patterns.

    A. *ex.* Shashin o torimasu. ────────→ Shashin o totte mo ii desu.

                                 ────────→ Shashin o totte mo ii desu ka.

        1. kono heya o tsukaimasu

        2. kono mizu o nomimasu

        3. rajio o tsukemasu

        4. mado o akemasu

        5. daidokoro ni hairimasu

III Make dialogues by changing the underlined parts as in the examples given.

    A. *ex.* A: **Kono katarogu o moratte** mo ii desu ka.

          B: Hai, dōzo.

        1. kamera no katarogu o moraimasu

        2. kono pen o tsukaimasu

        3. o-tearai o tsukaimasu

        4. koko de shashin o torimasu

        5. kono mizu o nomimasu

        6. daidokoro ni hairimasu

    B. *ex.* A: **Mado** o **akete** mo ii desu ka.

          B: Hai, dōzo. **Akete** kudasai.

        1. rajio, tsukemasu

        2. doa, shimemasu

Vocabulary

pen   pen

SHORT DIALOGUES ─────────────────────────────

1. **Yamada:**   Ashita 2-ji goro denwa o shite mo ii desu ka.
   Hayashi: Sumimasen ga, 2-ji goro uchi ni imasen kara, 6-ji goro onegaishimasu.
   Yamada: Hai, wakarimashita.

   Yamada: May I call you about 2 o'clock tomorrow?
   Hayashi: I'm sorry, but I won't be at home about 2:00, so call me about 6:00.
   Yamada: I see.

2. **Ten'in:**   Go-jūsho to o-namae o onegaishimasu.
   Hayashi: Sumimasen. Pen ga arimasen. Kono pen o tsukatte mo ii desu ka.
   Ten'in: Hai, dōzo.

   Clerk: Your name and address, please.

Hayashi: I'm afraid I don't have a pen. May I use this pen?

Clerk: Certainly. Please do.

3. **Tanaka: Koko wa yūmeina o-tera desu. Naka ni hairimashō.**

   Sumisu: Subarashii niwa desu ne. Kono niwa no shashin o totte mo ii desu ka.

   Tanaka: Sā, wakarimasen. Ano hito ni kikimashō.

Tanaka: This is a famous temple. Let's go inside.

Smith: What a wonderful garden. May I take a picture of this garden?

Tanaka: Well, I don't know. Let's ask that man over there.

Vocabulary

subarashii   wonderful (-i adj.)

sā   well . . .

QUIZ

I Read this lesson's opening dialogue and answer the following questions.

1. **Sumisu-san wa doko de katarogu o moraimashita ka.**
2. **Sumisu-san wa nan no katarogu o moraimashita ka.**
3. **Katarogu wa kēsu no naka ni arimashita ka.**
4. **Katarogu wa doko ni arimashita ka.**

II Convert the following verbs into their **-te** form.

1. **hairimasu**	4. **mimasu**	7. **shimasu**	10. **ikimasu**
2. **kimasu**	5. **tsukaimasu**	8. **torimasu**	11. **imasu**
3. **tabemasu**	6. **nomimasu**	9. **kikimasu**	12. **iimasu**

III Complete the sentences with the appropriate form of the verbs indicated.

1. **Koko de shashin o (   ) mo ii desu ka.**   **(torimasu)**
2. **Issho ni tenisu o (   ) masen ka.**   **(shimasu)**

   Ee, (   ) mashō.   **(shimasu)**
3. **Mado o (   ) mashō ka.**   **(akemasu)**

   Hai, (   ) kudasai.   **(akemasu)**
4. **Kono denwa o (   ) mo ii desu ka.**   **(tsukaimasu)**

   Sumimasen, chotto (   ) kudasai.   **(machimasu)**
5. **Ashita nan-ji ni (   ) mashō ka.**   **(kimasu)**

   8-ji han ni (   ) kudasai.   **(kimasu)**
6. **Kono katarogu o (   ) mo ii desu ka.**   **(moraimasu)**
7. **Hon o (   ), uchi ni kaerimashita.**   **(kaimasu)**

IV Translate into Japanese.

    1. Shall I turn on the light?
       Yes, please.
    2. May I use this telephone?
       Yes, of course. (*lit.* "please.")
    3. Is it O.K. to stay here till 3 o'clock?

LESSON 24 REFUSAL

A man parked his car in a "No Parking" area.

けいかん：　　　もしもし、ここは　ちゅうしゃきんしですから、くるま
　　　　　　　　を　とめないでください。

おとこのひと：すみません。この　ちかくに　ちゅうしゃじょうが
　　　　　　　　ありますか。

けいかん：　　　ええ、つぎの　かどを　ひだりに　まがってください。
　　　　　　　　ひだりがわに　ちゅうしゃじょうが　あります。

おとこのひと：どうも　ありがとう。

■けいかんは　おとこのひとに　ちゅうしゃじょうを　おしえました。

Keikan:	**Moshi moshi, koko wa "Chūsha Kinshi" desu kara, kuruma o tomenaide kudasai.**
Otoko no hito:	**Sumimasen. Kono chikaku ni chūshajō ga arimasu ka.**
Keikan:	**Ee, tsugi no kado o hidari ni magatte kudasai. Hidari-gawa ni chūshajō ga arimasu.**
Otoko no hito:	**Dōmo arigatō.**

■ **Keikan wa otoko no hito ni chūshajō o oshiemashita.**

Policeman:	I say, this is a "No Parking" (area), so don't park (your) car here.
Man:	I'm sorry. Is there a place to park nearby?
Policeman:	Yes. Turn left at the next corner. There's a parking lot on the left-hand side.
Man:	Thank you very much.

■ A policeman directed the man to a parking lot.

Vocabulary

けいかん	**keikan**	policeman
もしもし	**moshi moshi**	I say
ちゅうしゃきんし	**chūsha kinshi**	No Parking
とめないで　ください	**tomenaide kudasai**	Do not park.
とめます（とめる）	**tomemasu (tomeru)**	park

| ちゅうしゃじょう | **chūshajō** | parking lot |
| ひだりがわ | **hidari-gawa** | left-hand side |

NOTE

1. Tomenaide kudasai

The "please do not . . ." construction is formed as follows: verb **nai + de + kudasai**

(For explanation of the **-nai** form, see Grammar IX, p. 130).

For refusal of permission, **Iie, dame desu,** "No, you can't," is sometimes used. **Dame,** "no good, useless, hopeless, out of the question," is a frequently used word in Japanese. Straightforward prohibitive requests such as this are seldom used in politer society. Instead, one says, **Sumimasen, ga,** "Excuse me, but . . ." "I'm sorry, but . . ." and simply gives the reason for not wanting something done,

ex. **O-taku ni kuruma de itte mo ii desu ka.** "Is it all right to go to your house by car?"

Sumimasen ga, chūshajō ga arimasen kara . . . "I'm sorry, but there's no parking place."

PRACTICE

KEY SENTENCES

1. Koko de tabako o suwanaide kudasai.
2. Koko wa "Chūsha Kinshi" desu kara, kuruma o tomenaide kudasai.

1. Please don't smoke here.
2. This is a "No Parking" (area), so don't park (your) car here.

Vocabulary

tabako	tobacco, cigarette
suwanaide kudasai	Do not smoke.
suimasu (suu)	smoke, inhale

EXERCISES

I Verbs: Memorize the following verbs and their **-nai** form.

	-masu form	**-te** form	**-nai** form
inhale	**sui-masu**	sutte	**suwanai**
stop, park	**tome-masu**	tomete	**tomenai**

take (a photograph)	(shashin o) tori-masu	totte	toranai
use	tsukai-masu	tsukatte	tsukawanai
open	ake-masu	akete	akenai
close	shime-masu	shimete	shimenai

II Practice the following pattern.

ex. tabako o suimasu ⟶ Tabako o suwanaide kudasai.

1. kuruma o tomemasu
2. shashin o torimasu
3. kono heya o tsukaimasu
4. mado o akemasu
5. doa o shimemasu

III Make dialogues by changing the underlined part as in the examples given.

A. ex. A: Doa o shimete mo ii desu ka.

B: Iie, shimenaide kudasai. Atsui desu kara.

1. mado
2. kono doa

B. ex. A: Koko wa iriguchi desu kara, kuruma o tomenaide kudasai.

B: Dōmo sumimasen.

1. deguchi
2. mise no mae

Vocabulary

deguchi exit

SHORT DIALOGUES

1. **Otoko no hito:** Koko de tabako o sutte mo ii desu ka.
   Sumisu: Sumimasen ga, suwanaide kudasai.

   Man: May I smoke here?
   Smith: I'm afraid not. (*lit.* "I'm sorry, please don't.")

2. **Onna no hito:** Denki o keshimashō ka.
   Tanaka: Iie, ima kara kono heya o tsukaimasu kara, kesanaide kudasai.

   Woman: Shall I turn off the light?
   Tanaka: No, we are going to use this room (from now), so don't turn it off.

QUIZ

I Read this lesson's opening dialogue and answer the following questions.

1. **Dare ga otoko no hito ni chūshajō o oshiemashita ka.**
2. **Otoko no hito wa doko o hidari ni magarimasu ka.**
3. **Otoko no hito wa tsugi no kado o hidari ni magatte, doko ni ikimasu ka.**

II Convert the following verbs into their **-nai** form.

1. **tabemasu**	6. **yomimasu**	11. **keshimasu**
2. **mimasu**	7. **shimasu**	12. **tsukemasu**
3. **ikimasu**	8. **suimasu**	13. **tsukaimasu**
4. **kimasu**	9. **akemasu**	14. **shimemasu**
5. **iimasu**	10. **magarimasu**	15. **torimasu**

III Complete the sentences with the appropriate form of the verbs indicated.

1. **Koko de tabako o (   ) mo ii desu ka.**   (suimasu)
   Iie, sumimasen ga, (   ) kudasai.   (suimasu)
2. **Mado o (   ) mo ii desu ka.**   (akemasu)
   Hai, (   ) mo ii desu.   (akemasu)
3. **Ashita o-taku ni (   ) mo ii desu ka.**   (ikimasu)
   Hai, dōzo (   ) kudasai.   (kimasu)
4. **Doa o (   ) mashō ka.**   (shimemasu)
   Iie, (   ) kudasai. Atsui desu kara.   (shimemasu)

IV Put the appropriate particles in the parentheses. (If a particle is not required, put an X in the parentheses.)

1. **Koko (   ) "Chūsha Kinshi" desu (   ), kuruma (   ) tome-naide kudasai.**
2. **Tsugi no kado (   ) hidari (   ) magatte kudasai.**
3. **Densha (   ) tabako (   ) suwanaide kudasai.**
4. **Kinō no asa 8-ji goro uchi (   ) dete, yoru 10-ji (   ) kaerimashita.**

V Translate into Japanese.

1. Please do not go into that room now.
2. Please do not smoke here.
3. Turn right at the next traffic light.

LESSON 25 NOW IN PROGRESS

Mr. Hayashi is looking for Mr. Smith. He knocks on the door.

はやし : すみません、スミスさんは　いますか。

ひしょ : いいえ、いません。3がいの　かいぎしつに　います。

はやし : かいぎを　していますか。

ひしょ : いいえ、スライドを　みています。

はやし : どうも。

■ スミスさんは　かいぎしつで　スライドを　みています。

Hayashi: Sumimasen, Sumisu-san wa imasu ka.
Hisho: Iie, imasen. 3-gai no kaigi-shitsu ni imasu.
Hayashi: Kaigi o shite imasu ka.
Hisho: Iie, suraido o mite imasu.
Hayashi: Dōmo.

■ Sumisu-san wa kaigi-shitsu de suraido o mite imasu.

Hayashi: Excuse me, is Mr. Smith here?
Secretary: No, he isn't. He's in the conference room on the third floor.
Hayashi: Is he in conference?
Secretary: No. He's looking at (some) slides.
Hayashi: Thanks.

■ Mr. Smith is looking at slides in the conference room.

Vocabulary

かいぎしつ	**kaigi-shitsu**	conference room
〜しつ	**-shitsu**	room
かいぎを　して　います	**kaigi o shite imasu**	is in conference
（して　いる）	**(shite iru)**	
スライド	**suraido**	slide
みて　います（みて　いる）	**mite imasu (mite iru)**	is looking

NOTES

1. **Kaigi o shite imasu.**
   Suraido o mite imasu.
   The present progressive is expressed as follows: verb **-te** + **imasu**.
   This construction expresses either action that is presently going on or action that regularly takes place.
   ex. **Sumisu-san wa maishū Taimu o yonde imasu.** "Mr. Smith reads *Time* every week."
   There is also the past progressive.
   ex. **Kinō no gogo nani o shite imashita ka.** "What were you doing yesterday afternoon?"

2. **Dōmo**
   A colloquial shortening of **dōmo arigatō,** "Thank you so much." It is also widely used as an abbreviation of **dōmo sumimasen,** "I'm sorry." It is not especially polite.

PRACTICE

KEY SENTENCES

1. **Yamada-san wa ima denwa o shite imasu.**
2. **Howaito-san wa ima shigoto o shite imasu.**

1. Mr. Yamada is making a telephone call now.
2. Miss White is working now.

| Vocabulary |

denwa o shite imasu   is telephoning
shigoto o shite imasu is working

EXERCISES

I Verbs: Memorize the following **-te imasu** forms.

		Present Progressive	
		aff.	*neg.*
	-masu form	-te imasu	-te imasen
talk	hanashi o shi-masu	hanashi o shite imasu	hanashi o shite imasen
read	yomi-masu	yonde imasu	yonde imasen
listen	kiki-masu	kiite imasu	kiite imasen
write	kaki-masu	kaite imasu	kaite imasen

Past Progressive		
	aff.	*neg.*
	-te imashita	**-te imasendeshita**
talk	**hanashi o shite imashita**	**hanashi o shite imasendeshita**
read	**yonde imashita**	**yonde imasendeshita**
listen	**kiite imashita**	**kiite imasendeshita**
write	**kaite imashita**	**kaite imasendeshita**

II Practice the following pattern.

   ex. **hon o yomimasu** ⟶ **Tanaka-san wa hon o yonde imasu.**

     1. **rajio o kikimasu**   **Tanaka-san wa**

     2. **tegami o kakimasu**   **Tanaka-san wa**

     3. **tomodachi to hanashi o shimasu**   **Tanaka-san wa**

III Make dialogues by changing the underlined parts as in the examples given.

   A. *ex.* **Q: Ima hon o yonde imasu ka.**

       A*a*: Hai, yonde imasu.

       A*n*: Iie, yonde imasen.

       1. **kōhī, nomimasu**

       2. **tegami, kakimasu**

       3. **shigoto, shimasu**

   B. *ex.* **Q: Dare ga denwa o shite imasu ka.**

       A: Howaito-san ga [denwa o] shite imasu.

       1. **terebi o mimasu, Yamada-san**

       2. **tegami o kakimasu, Sumisu-san**

   C. *ex.* **Q: Yamada-san wa nani o shite imasu ka.**

       A: Shimbun o yonde imasu.

       1. **Howaito-san, denwa o shimasu**

       2. **Ichirō-san, terebi o mimasu**

       3. **Tanaka-san, biru o nomimasu**

   D. *ex.* **Q: Yamada-san wa doko de shashin o totte imasu ka.**

       A: Niwa de [shashin o] totte imasu.

       1. **denwa o shimasu, tonari no heya**

       2. **hon o yomimasu, ima**

   E. *ex.* **Q: Yamada-san wa ima kōhī o nonde imasu ka.**

       A: Iie, shimbun o yonde imasu.

       1. **denwa o shimasu, tegami o kakimasu**

       2. **kaigi o shimasu, shokuji o shimasu**

       3. **shashin o torimasu, Howaito-san to hanashi o shimasu**

Vocabulary

hanashi o shimasu (suru)   talk
Ichirō   a given name (male)

SHORT DIALOGUE

Hayashi: Yamada-san wa ima doko ni imasu ka.
Howaito: Tonari no heya ni imasu.
Hayashi: [Yamada-san wa] Ima nani o shite imasu ka.
Howaito: Okyaku-san to hanashi o shite imasu.

Hayashi: Where is Miss Yamada now?
White: [She's] In the next room.
Hayashi: What's she doing now?
White: [She's] Talking with a client.

Vocabulary

o-kyaku-san   client

QUIZ ▩▩▩▩▩▩

I Read this lesson's opening dialogue and answer the following questions.

1. **Sumisu-san wa 2-kai ni imasu ka, 3-gai ni imasu ka.**

2. **Sumisu-san wa 3-gai no doko ni imasu ka.**

3. **Sumisu-san wa nani o shite imasu ka.**

II Complete the questions so that they fit the answers.

1. **Tanaka-san wa ima (   ) ni imasu ka.**
   2-kai ni imasu.
   2-kai de (   ) o shite imasu ka.
   Tegami o kaite imasu.

2. **Hayashi-san wa (   ) de shashin o totte imasu ka.**
   Asoko de totte imasu.

3. **Sumisu-san wa (   ) to hanashi o shite imasu ka.**
   Sumisu-san no hisho to hanashi o shite imasu.

4. **Howaito-san wa (   ) ni denwa o shite imasu ka.**
   Kaisha ni shite imasu.

III Translate into Japanese.

1. Mr. Hayashi will telephone Mr. Smith.

2. Mr. Hayashi is telephoning Mr. Smith.
3. What is that girl over there doing?
   She is waiting for a friend.
4. Miss White is not working now.

LESSON 26 READING REVIEW

■すずきさんが ブラウンさんの うちに でんわを しました。すず
　きさんは ブラウンさんの ともだちです。

すずき：　もしもし、すずきですが、ブラウンさんの おたくですか。
ブラウン：あ、すずきさん、こんばんは。
すずき：　ブラウンさん、らいしゅうの どようびの ばん、わたしの
　　　　　うちで パーティーを します。わたしの たんじょうびの
　　　　　パーティーです。おくさんと いっしょに きませんか。
ブラウン：どうも ありがとうございます。よろこんで いきます。
すずき：　では、どようびに。
ブラウン：おでんわ どうも ありがとうございました。

■きょうは パーティーの ひです。
　ブラウンさんと おくさんが すずきさんの うちに つきました。

すずき：　よく いらっしゃいました。こちらへ どうぞ。
ブラウン：おまねき ありがとうございます。これを どうぞ。
すずき：　きれいな はなですね。どうも ありがとうございます。
ブラウン：この ワインも どうぞ。
すずき：　みなさんに ごしょうかい しますから、どうぞ こちらへ。

■とても にぎやかな パーティーです。

■12じです。みんなは かえります。

すずきさんの ともだち：ブラウンさん、くるまで きましたか。
ブラウン：　　　　　　　いいえ、でんしゃで きました。

すずきさんの　ともだち：おそいですから　わたしの　くるまで　かえ
　　　　　　　　　　　　りませんか。

ブラウン：　　　　　　　そうですか。ありがとうございます。おねが
　　　　　　　　　　　　いします。

みんな：　　　　　　　　とても　たのしかったです。きょうは　どう
　　　　　　　　　　　　も　ありがとうございました。

すずき：　　　　　　　　どういたしまして。わたしも　たのしかった
　　　　　　　　　　　　です。また　きてください。

すずきさんの　おくさん：どうぞ　きをつけて。

みんな：　　　　　　　　おやすみなさい。

すずき：　　　　　　　　おやすみなさい。

■ Suzuki-san ga Buraun-san no uchi ni denwa o shimashita. Suzuki-san wa
Buraun-san no tomodachi desu.

Suzuki:　Moshi moshi, Suzuki desu ga, Buraun-san no o-taku desu ka.
Buraun:　A, Suzuki-san, kombanwa.
Suzuki:　Buraun-san, raishū no do-yōbi no ban, watashi no uchi de pātī o
　　　　　shimasu. Watashi no tanjōbi no pātī desu. Okusan to issho ni ki-
　　　　　masen ka.
Buraun:　Dōmo arigatō gozaimasu. Yorokonde ikimasu.
Suzuki:　Dewa, do-yōbi ni.
Buraun:　O-denwa dōmo arigatō gozaimashita.

■ Kyō wa pātī no hi desu. Buraun-san to okusan ga Suzuki-san no uchi ni
tsukimashita.

Suzuki:　Yoku irasshaimashita. Kochira e dōzo.
Buraun:　Omaneki arigatō gozaimasu. Kore o dōzo.
Suzuki:　Kireina hana desu ne. Dōmo arigatō gozaimasu.
Buraun:　Kono wain mo dōzo.
Suzuki:　Mina-san ni go-shōkai shimasu kara, dōzo kochira e.

■ Totemo nigiyakana pātī desu.

■ 12-ji desu. Minna wa kaerimasu.

Suzuki-san no tomodachi:　Buraun-san, kuruma de kimashita ka.
Buraun:　　　　　　　　　Iie, densha de kimashita.
Suzuki-san no tomodachi:　Osoi desu kara, watashi no kuruma de kaeri-
　　　　　　　　　　　　masen ka.

Buraun:	Sō desu ka. Arigatō gozaimasu. Onegaishimasu.
Minna:	Totemo tanoshikatta desu. Kyō wa dōmo arigatō gozaimashita.
Suzuki:	Dō itashimashite. Watashi mo tanoshikatta desu. Mata kite kudasai.
Suzuki-san no okusan:	Dōzo ki o tsukete.
Minna:	Oyasumi nasai.
Suzuki:	Oyasumi nasai.

■ Mr. Suzuki telephoned the Browns' house. Mr. Suzuki is a friend of Mr. Brown's.

Suzuki:	Hello. This is Suzuki. Is this the Browns' residence?
Brown:	Ah, Mr. Suzuki! Good evening.
Suzuki:	Mr. Brown, we're having a party at my house next Saturday evening. It's my birthday party. Won't you come, together with Mrs. Brown?
Brown:	Thank you very much. We'll be happy to come.
Suzuki:	Well then, (see you) on Saturday.
Brown:	Thank you for your telephone call.

■ Today is the day of the party. Mr. and Mrs. Brown have arrived at Mr. Suzuki's house.

Suzuki:	How nice of you to come. This way, please.
Brown:	Thank you for your invitation. These are for you.
Suzuki:	What lovely flowers! Thank you very much.
Brown:	This wine is for you, too.
Suzuki:	Come this way and I'll introduce you to everybody.

■ It is a very lively party.

■ (Now) It is 12 o'clock. Everyone is leaving.

Mr. Suzuki's friend:	Mr. Brown, did you come by car?
Brown:	No, we came by train.
Mr. Suzuki's friend:	Since it's late, can't I drive you home? (*lit.* "Won't you go home in my car?")
Brown:	Oh, would you (do that)? Thank you. (*lit.* "I'm happy to accept your offer.")
All:	It was very enjoyable. Thank you very much for today.
Suzuki:	You're welcome. I enjoyed it too. Please come again.
Mrs. Suzuki:	Please be careful (on your way home).
All:	Good-night!
The Suzukis:	Good-night!

| Vocabulary |

| すずき | **Suzuki** | a surname |

よろこんで	**yorokonde**	(I'd) be happy to.
ひ	**hi**	day
おまねき　ありがとう　ございます	**omaneki arigatō gozaimasu**	Thank you for your invitation.
ワイン	**wain**	wine
みなさん	**mina-san**	everyone (excluding the speaker and his or her group)
みんな	**minna**	everyone
おそい	**osoi**	late (**-i** adj.)
きを　つけて	**ki o tsukete**	take care, be careful

LESSON 27 PRESENT CONDITION

Mr. Smith tells Mr. Hayashi that his brother has arrived in Japan.

スミス：せんしゅう　あにが　アメリカから　にほんに　きました。

はやし：おにいさんは　おくさんと　いっしょに　きましたか。

スミス：いいえ、しごとですから　ひとりで　きました。いま　きょう
　　　　とに　いっています。あには　りょこうがいしゃに　つとめて
　　　　います。

はやし：おにいさんは　いつまで　きょうとに　いますか。

スミス：こんしゅうの　すいようびまで　います。それから　ホンコン
　　　　に　いって、アメリカに　かえります。

はやし：アメリカの　どこに　すんでいますか。

スミス：ニューヨークに　すんでいます。

■スミスさんの　おにいさんは　りょこうがいしゃに　つとめています。
　せんしゅう　にほんに　きました。いま　きょうとに　いっています。

Sumisu:　　Senshū ani ga Amerika kara Nihon ni kimashita.
Hayashi:　 O-niisan wa okusan to issho ni kimashita ka.
Sumisu:　　Iie, shigoto desu kara, hitori de kimashita. Ima Kyōto ni itte i-masu. Ani wa ryokō-gaisha ni tsutomete imasu.
Hayashi:　 O-niisan wa itsu made Kyōto ni imasu ka.
Sumisu:　　Konshū no sui-yōbi made imasu. Sorekara Honkon ni itte, Ame-rika ni kaerimasu.
Hayashi:　 Amerika no doko ni sunde imasu ka.
Sumisu:　　Nyū Yōku ni sunde imasu.

■Sumisu-san no o-niisan wa ryokō-gaisha ni tsutomete imasu. Senshū Nihon ni kimashita. Ima Kyōto ni itte imasu.

Smith:　　　My (older) brother came to Japan from America last week.
Hayashi:　 Did your brother come with his wife?

Smith:	No, he came on business, so he came alone. He's in Kyoto now. My brother works for a travel agency.
Hayashi:	How long will your brother be in Kyoto?
Smith:	He'll be there until this week Wednesday. After that he'll go to Hong Kong, then return to America.
Hayashi:	Where does he live in America?
Smith:	He lives in New York (City).

■ Mr. Smith's (older) brother works for a travel agency. He came to Japan last week. Now he is in Kyoto.

Vocabulary

あに	**ani**	(my) older brother
おにいさん	**o-niisan**	(your) older brother
りょこうがいしゃ	**ryokō-gaisha**	travel agency
つとめて います	**tsutomete imasu**	be employed, work for
つとめます（つとめる）	**tsutomemasu (tsutomeru)**	serve, hold a post
ホンコン	**Honkon**	Hong Kong
すんで います	**sunde imasu**	live (*lit.* "is living")
すみます（すむ）	**sumimasu (sumu)**	live
ニューヨーク	**Nyū Yōku**	New York

NOTES

1. Ima Kyōto ni itte imasu.

Verb **-te imasu** is used here. The sentence literally means, "Having gone to Kyoto, he is there now." Other common examples of this usage are, **Tanaka-san wa kekkon shite imasu.** "Mr. Tanaka is married." (*lit.* "Mr. Tanaka, having got married, is married.") And **Bengoshi wa mō kimashita ka.** "Has the lawyer come yet?" **Hai, kite imasu.** "Yes, he has."

2. Ani wa ryokō-gaisha ni tsutomete imasu.

The particle used with the verb **tsutomeru** is **ni**. Here again the verb **-te** form is used.

When asked what kind of work they do, Japanese usually reply by giving their place of work rather than the type of work. Note also that in Japanese siblings are always referred to as older or younger brothers or sisters, for which there are separate words. I.e., **ani**, "my older brother," **otōto**, "my younger brother," **o-nii-san**, "your older brother," **otōto-san**, "your younger brother," etc. Note the following terms for one's own and for other person's relatives.

	Related to the Speaker	Related to Others
family	kazoku	go-kazoku
husband	shujin	go-shujin
wife	kanai	okusan *pronounced ok-san*
child	kodomo	kodomo-san/okosan
son	musuko	musuko-san/botchan
daughter ——————→	musume	musume-san/ojō-san
parents	ryōshin	go-ryōshin
father	chichi	o-tōsan
mother	haha	o-kāsan
grandfather	sofu	oji-san
grandmother	sobo	obā-san
brothers and sisters	kyōdai	go-kyōdai
older brother	ani	o-nii-san
older sister	ane	o-nē-san
younger brother	otōto	otōto-san
younger sister	imōto	imōto-san
grandchild	mago	o-mago-san
uncle	oji	oji-san
aunt	oba	oba-san
nephew	oi	oigo-san
niece	mei	meigo-san
cousin	itoko	o-itoko-san

3. **Nyū Yōku ni sunde imasu.**

In describing where people live, the verb **-te** form is used. **Uru**, the verb meaning "sell" and **shiru**, "know," similarly use the **-te** form.

PRACTICE

KEY SENTENCES

1. **Sumisu-san no o-niisan wa ima Nihon ni kite imasu.**
2. **Kurāku-san wa Tōkyō ni sunde imasu.**
3. **Hayashi-san wa Nihon Ginkō ni tsutomete imasu.**
4. **Watashi wa Tanaka-san o yoku shitte imasu.**
5. **Chika 1-kai de niku ya sakana o utte imasu.**

1. Mr. Smith's older brother is in Japan now.
2. Mr. Clark lives in Tokyo.
3. Mr. Hayashi works for the Bank of Japan.
4. I know Mr. Tanaka well.
5. They sell meat, fish (and other things) in the first basement.

shitte imasu (shiru)	know
chika 1-kai	first basement
chika	basement (*lit.* "underground")
utte imasu	sell (*lit.* "is selling")
urimasu (uru)	sell

EXERCISES

I Verbs: Memorize the following verbs and their **-te imasu** forms.

	-masu form	**-te imasu** form	
		aff.	*neg.*
live	**sumi-masu**	sunde imasu	sunde imasen
work for	**tsutome-masu**	tsutomete imasu	tsutomete imasen
know	*	shitte imasu	shirimasen**
sell	**uri-masu**	utte imasu	utte imasen

*The form **shirimasu** is never used; **shitte imasu** replaces it.

The negative of **shitte imasu is the irregular **shirimasen**.

II Practice the following pattern by changing the underlined part as in the example given.

ex. [Watashi wa] Tōkyō ni sunde imasu.

1. Tōkyō no Azabu
2. kaisha no chikaku

III Make dialogues by changing the underlined parts as in the examples given.

A ex. Q: Howaito-san wa ima Nihon ni kite imasu ka.

A*a*: Hai, kite imasu. Sengetsu [Nihon ni] kimashita.

A*n*: Iie, kite imasen. Raigetsu [Nihon ni] kimasu.

1. Tōkyō, kimasu
2. gaikoku, ikimasu

B. ex. Q: Tanaka-san o shitte imasu ka.

A*a*: Hai, shitte imasu.

A*n*: Iie, shirimasen.

1. Howaito-san
2. Yamada-san no jūsho
3. Hayashi-san no atarashii denwa-bangō
4. ii niku-ya

C. *ex.* Q: Tanaka-san no tomodachi wa doko ni tsutomete imasu ka.

A: <u>Taishikan</u> ni tsutomete imasu.

1. depāto
2. gakkō
3. ryokō-gaisha

D. *ex.* Q: <u>Kasa</u> wa doko de utte imasu ka.

A: <u>1-kai</u> de utte imasu.

1. sētā, 4-kai
2. kutsu, 6-kai
3. kitte, ano mise

Vocabulary

gaikoku	foreign country
sētā	sweater

SHORT DIALOGUE

Suzuki: Sumisu-san wa doko ni tsutomete imasu ka.
Sumisu: ABC ni tsutomete imasu.
Suzuki: Jā, Kyōto shisha no Satō-san o shitte imasu ka.
Sumisu: Ee, shitte imasu.

Suzuki: Where do you work, Mr. Smith?
Smith: I work for ABC.
Suzuki: Then, do you know Mr. Satō in the Kyoto branch?
Smith: Yes, I do.

Vocabulary

Satō	a surname

QUIZ

I Read this lesson's opening dialogue and answer the following questions.

1. **Dare to dare ga hanashi o shite imasu ka.**
2. **Senshū dare ga Amerika kara Nihon ni kimashita ka.**
3. **Sumisu-san no o-niisan wa ima Tōkyō ni imasu ka.**
4. **Sumisu-san no o-niisan wa doko ni tsutomete imasu ka.**
5. **Sumisu-san no o-niisan wa doko ni sunde imasu ka.**

II Complete the questions so that they fit the answers.

1. (   ) de kitte o utte imasu ka.
   Ano mise de utte imasu.
2. **Ano hito wa (   ) ni tsutomete imasu ka.**
   Depāto ni tsutomete imasu.
3. (   ) **ga Hayashi-san no atarashii denwa-bangō o shitte imasu ka.**
   Hayashi-san no hisho ga shitte imasu.
4. **Howaito-san wa ima (   ) ni itte imasu ka.**
   Ginkō ni itte imasu.

III Put the appropriate particles in the parentheses. (If a particle is not required, put an X in the parentheses.)

1. **Kochira wa Tōkyō Denki (   ) Tanaka-san desu.**
2. **Tanaka-san wa doko (   ) tsutomete imasu ka.**
   Tōkyō Denki (   ) tsutomete imasu.
3. **Sumisu-san wa ima Tōkyō (   ) shigoto o shite imasu.**
4. **Buraun-san wa doko (   ) sunde imasu ka.**
   Ueno Eki (   ) chikaku (   ) sunde imasu.
5. **Doko (   ) Ei-go (   ) shimbun (   ) utte imasu ka.**
   Asoko (   ) utte imasu.

IV Translate into Japanese.

1. Do you know Mr. Tanaka?
   No, I don't know (him).
2. I live near (my) office. It's a 15-minute walk.
3. Mr. Smith works for ABC.

LESSON 28 EXPRESSING PREFERENCES

Mr. Smith wants to buy some antique furniture. He is asking Miss Yamada where to find some.

スミス：わたしは　にほんの　ふるい　かぐが　すきです。せんげつ
　　　　たんすを　かいました。つぎは　つくえを　かいたいです。
　　　　いい　みせを　しっていますか。

やまだ：さあ、しりません。はやしさんは　いろいろな　ことを　よく
　　　　しっていますから　はやしさんに　きいてください。

■スミスさんは　ふるい　かぐが　すきです。スミスさんは　やまださ
んに　ふるい　かぐの　みせについて　ききました。

Sumisu:　**Watashi wa Nihon no furui kagu ga suki desu. Sengetsu tansu o kaimashita. Tsugi wa tsukue o kaitai desu. Ii mise o shitte imasu ka.**

Yamada:　**Sā, shirimasen. Hayashi-san wa iroirona koto o yoku shitte imasu kara Hayashi-san ni kiite kudasai.**

■**Sumisu-san wa furui kagu ga suki desu. Sumisu-san wa Yamada-san ni furui kagu no mise ni tsuite kikimashita.**

Smith:　I like antique Japanese furniture. Last month I bought a *tansu*. Next, I want to buy a table. Do you know a good store?

Yamada:　Let me see . . . No, I don't. Mr. Hayashi knows a lot about various things, so ask him.

■ Mr. Smith likes antique furniture. Mr. Smith asked Miss Yamda about stores that sell antique furniture.

WATASHI WA NIHON NO FURUI KAGU
GA SUKI DESU....

かぐ	**kagu**	furniture
たんす	**tansu**	*tansu* (chest of drawers)
つくえ	**tsukue**	table
いろいろな　こと	**iroirona koto**	various things
いろいろな	**iroirona**	various (**-na** adj.)
こと	**koto**	thing
みせに　ついて	**mise ni tsuite**	about stores
〜に　ついて	**ni tsuite**	about, concerning

GRAMMAR X

Desire, Preference, Like and Dislike

1. person WA noun GA SUKI **desu**
2. person WA noun GA II **desu**
   (person WA) noun WA noun GA II **desu**
3. Watashi wa verb -TAI **desu**

- Particle **ga** is used with
  suki desu (**-na** adj.)
  ii desu (**-i** adj.)

- In "I like bananas," "like" is a verb and "bananas" is the object, but in Japanese, "bananas" takes the particle **ga**, and they are described as being "likable," using an adjective rather than a verb.
  ex. **Banana ga suki desu.** "I like bananas." (*lit.* "Bananas are likable.")
  Anata ga suki desu. "I love you." (*lit.* "You are lovable.")

- The same construction is used with the adjective **ii**, "good, preferable," etc.
  ex. **Kōhī ga ii desu.** "I'd like coffee." (*lit.* "Coffee is preferable.") Note the following constructions, all of which mean "I'd like coffee."
  1. **Watashi wa kōhī ga ii desu.** "I'd like coffee." (*lit.* "As for me, coffee is preferable.")
  2. **Nomimono wa kōhī ga ii desu.** "I'd like coffee." (*lit.* "As for something to drink, coffee is my choice.")
  3. **Watashi wa nomimono wa kōhī ga ii desu.** "I'd like coffee." (*lit.* "As for me, regarding something to drink, coffee is my choice.")
  In this last sentence, the speaker first talks about himself, "**watashi**," then he chooses the category of drinks, "**nomimono**," and talks about it.

- The verb **wakarimasu** also takes **ga** (see Note 2, p. 104.), as does the verb **dekimasu,** expressing possibility, ability, etc.
  ex. **Watashi wa taipu ga dekimasu.** "I can type." (*lit.* "As far as I'm concerned, typing (is something) I can do.")
  Note: **Dekimasu** also has the meaning "be done" or "be ready." (See Lesson 21.)

- Verb **-tai desu**

  Constructions expressing desire can be made from the **-masu** form as follows:
  iki-masu   **iki-tai**
  tabe-masu   **tabe-tai**
  The verb **-tai** form is inflected like an **-i** adjective.
  ex. **Ikitai desu.** "(I) want to go."
      Ikitakunai desu. "(I) don't want to go."
      Ikitakatta desu. "(I) wanted to go."
      Ikitakunakatta desu. "(I) didn't want to go."

- Verb **-tai** expresses the speaker's desire.
  ex. **Takushī de ikitai desu.** "(I) want to go by taxi."
  It can be made into a question by adding the question marker **ka**.
  But asking a person, especially someone senior, what he wishes to do in this form is often considered not polite, and simple questions are preferable.
  ex. **Takushī de ikimasu ka.** "Do you (want to) go by taxi?"
  This form cannot be used to refer to a third person.
  The particle **ga** is sometimes used instead of **o**.
  Suraido o/ga mitai desu. "(I) want to see the slides."

NOTES

1. **Shitte imasu**, "(I) know," always takes the verb **-te** form. The reply is irregular:
   A*a*: **Hai, shitte imasu.** "Yes, (I) know."
   A*n*: **Iie, shirimasen.** "No, (I) don't know."

2. **Sā, shirimasen.**
   Sā . . . ("Let me see . . .") is an expression often used in Japanese when thinking about an answer.

PRACTICE

KEY SENTENCES

1. **Tanaka-san wa gorufu ga jōzu desu.**
2. **[Watashi wa] Ringo ga suki desu.**
3. **[Watashi wa] Taipu ga dekimasu.**
4. **[Watashi wa] Atama ga itai desu.**
5. **[Watashi wa] Yōroppa ni ikitai desu.**
6. **[Watashi wa] Ima nani mo tabetakunai desu.**

1. Mr. Tanaka is good at golf.
2. I like apples.
3. I can type.
4. I have a headache.

5. I'd like to go to Europe.

6. I don't want to eat anything now.

Vocabulary

jōzuna	good at (**-na** adj.)	**atama**	head
dekimasu	can (do)	**itai**	aching (**-i** adj.)
(dekiru)		**Yōroppa**	Europe

EXERCISES

I Memorize the following adjectives and verb.

		Present Form		Past Form	
		aff.	*neg.*	*aff.*	*neg.*
-na adj.	skilled in	**jōzu desu**	**jōzu dewa arimasen**	**jōzu deshita**	**jōzu dewa arimasendeshita**
	like, love	**suki desu**	**suki dewa arimasen**	**suki deshita**	**suki dewa arimasendeshita**
verb	be able to (do)	**dekimasu**	**dekimasen**	**dekimashita**	**dekimasen deshita**
-i adj.	be painful	**itai desu**	**itakunai desu**	**itakatta desu**	**itakunakatta desu**

II Practice the following patterns by changing the underlined part as in the examples given.

    A. *ex.* **Tanaka-san wa <u>gorufu</u> ga jōzu desu.**

        1. **Doitsu-go**

        2. **ryōri**

    B. *ex.* **[Watashi wa] <u>Atama</u> ga itai desu.**

        1. **nodo**

        2. **onaka**

        3. **ha**

III Make dialogues by changing the underlined parts as in the examples given.

    A. *ex.* **Q: [Anata wa] <u>Kudamono</u> ga suki desu ka.**

        A*a*: Hai, totemo suki desu.

        A*n*: Iie, amari suki dewa arimasen.

        1. **eiga**

        2. **ryokō**

        3. **Haruko-san**

B. *ex.* **Q:** [Anata wa] <u>Nihon-go</u> ga dekimasu ka.

     A*a*: Hai, sukoshi dekimasu.

     A*n*: Iie, zenzen dekimasen.

     1. Furansu-go

     2. taipu

C. *ex.* **Q:** [Anata wa] <u>Atama</u> ga itai desu ka.

     A*a*: Hai, itai desu.

     A*n*: Iie, itakunai desu.

     1. nodo

     2. onaka

     3. ha

D. *ex.* **Q:** [Anata wa] Donna <u>kudamono</u> ga suki desu ka.

     A: <u>Ringo</u> ga suki desu.

     1. yasai, tomato

     2. ryōri, niku no ryōri

IV Memorize the following **-tai desu** form.

	Present Form		Past Form	
	aff.	*neg.*	*aff.*	*neg.*
want to go	ikitai desu	ikitakunai desu	ikitakatta desu	ikitakunakatta desu
want to send	okuritai desu	okuritakunai desu	okuritakatta desu	okuritakunakatta desu

V Practice the following **-tai desu** form.

    1. eiga ni ikimasu

       [Watashi wa] Eiga ni ikitai desu.

                            ikitakunai desu.

                            ikitakatta desu.

                            ikitakunakatta desu.

    2. terebi o mimasu

       [Watashi wa] Terebi o mitai desu.

                            mitakunai desu.

                            mitakatta desu.

                            mitakunakatta desu.

    3. Tanaka-san ni aimasu

       [Watashi wa] Tanaka-san ni aitai desu.

                                  aitakunai desu.

                                aitakatta desu.

                                aitakunakatta desu.

VI Practice the following pattern by changing the underlined part as in the example given.

   A. *ex.* [Watashi wa] <u>Yama</u> ni ikitai desu.

      1. toshokan
      2. onsen
      3. Kyōto no matsuri

   B. *ex.* [Watashi wa] Ima <u>terebi</u> o mitakunai desu.

      1. eiga
      2. suraido

VII Make dialogues by changing the underlined parts as in the examples given.

   A. *ex.* **Q:** [Anata wa] Doko ni ikitai desu ka.

      A: <u>Yama</u> ni ikitai desu.

      1. umi
      2. onsen

   B. *ex.* **Q:** [Anata wa] Nani o kaitai desu ka.

      A: <u>Kagu</u> o kaitai desu.

      1. nekutai
      2. kutsushita
      3. tsukue

   C. *ex.* **Q:** [Anata wa] Ima nani o shitai desu ka.

      A: <u>Tenisu o shitai</u> desu.

      1. hon o yomimasu
      2. eiga ni ikimasu
      3. ryokō o shimasu

   D. *ex.* **Q:** [Anata wa] Nani o <u>shitai</u> desu ka.

      A: Nani mo <u>shitakunai</u> desu.

      1. tabemasu
      2. nomimasu
      3. kaimasu

   E. *ex.* **Q:** [Anata wa] <u>Doko ni ikitai</u> desu ka.

      A: <u>Doko ni mo ikitakunai</u> desu.

      1. dare ni, aimasu

Vocabulary			
Doitsu-go	German language	**okuritai**	want to send
nodo	throat	**okurimasu (okuru)**	send
onaka	stomach	**yama**	mountain
ha	tooth	**toshokan**	library

kudamono	fruit	**onsen**	hot spring
Furansu-go	French language	**matsuri**	festival
tomato	tomato	**kutsushita**	socks

SHORT DIALOGUES

1. **Tanaka:** Kono ryōri wa totemo oishii desu.
   Howaito: Sō desu ka. Mō sukoshi ikaga desu ka.
   Tanaka: Arigatō gozaimasu. Itadakimasu. Howaito-san wa ryōri ga jōzu desu ne.

   Tanaka: This dish is very good.
   White: Is it? Would you like some more?
   Tanaka: Thank you. I'd love some more. You're a good cook.

2. **Isha:** Dō shimashita ka.
   Yamada: Kinō kara kibun ga warui desu.
   Isha: Netsu ga arimasu ka.
   Yamada: Ee, 39-do arimasu. Atama mo itai desu.
   Isha: Nodo mo itai desu ka.
   Yamada: Hai, itai desu.
   Isha: Kusuri o agemasu kara shokuji no ato de nonde kudasai. Dōzo o-daiji ni.

   Doctor: What's the matter?
   Yamada: I haven't felt well since yesterday.
   Doctor: Do you have a fever?
   Yamada: Yes. My temperature is 39 degrees (C.). I have a headache.
   Doctor: Do you have a sore throat too?
   Yamada: Yes, I do.
   Doctor: (*After the examination.*) I'll give you some medicine. Take it after meals.
   Look after yourself.
   (Note: Parts of the body are given in Appendix F.)

3. **Tanaka:** Tsugi no nichi-yōbi ni nani o shitai desu ka.
   Hayashi: Tenisu o shitai desu. Hon mo yomitai desu. Tanaka-san wa nani o shitai desu ka.
   Tanaka: [Watashi wa] Eiga ni ikitai desu.

   Tanaka: What would you like to do next Sunday?
   Hayashi: I'd like to play tennis. I'd like to read a book, too. What would you like to do?
   Tanaka: I'd like to go to a movie.

4. **Howaito:** Kono nimotsu o Amerika ni okuritai desu. Donogurai kaka-rimasu ka.
   Yūbinkyoku no hito: Kōkūbin desu ka, funabin desu ka.
   Howaito: Funabin de onegaishimasu.

Yūbinkyoku no hito: Sō desu ne. Ikkagetsu gurai kakarimasu.

White:	I'd like to send this parcel to the United States. How long will it take?
Post office clerk:	By airmail or sea mail?
White:	By sea mail, please.
Post office clerk:	Let me see . . . It'll take about one month.

5. **Hayashi:** **Senshū no nichi-yōbi ni haikingu ni ikimashita ka.**
   Tanaka: **Iie, ikitakatta desu ga, atama ga itakatta desu kara ikimasen deshita.**

   Hayashi: Did you go hiking last week Sunday?
   Tanaka: No. I wanted to, but I had a headache, so I didn't go.

Vocabulary

isha	doctor	**nimotsu**	parcel
dō shimashita ka	What's the matter?	**kōkūbin**	airmail
kibun	feeling	**funabin**	sea mail
netsu	fever	**sō desu ne**	Let me see . . .
39-do	39 degrees (Centigrade)	**ikkagetsu**	(for) one month
-do	degree	**-kagetsu**	month (see Appendix
dōzo o-daiji ni	Look after yourself.		G.)

QUIZ

I Read this lesson's opening dialogue and answer the following questions.

1. **Sumisu-san wa donna kagu ga suki desu ka.**
2. **Sumisu-san wa mō tansu o kaimashita ka.**
3. **Yamada-san wa Nihon no furui kagu no ii mise o shitte imasu ka.**
4. **Sumisu-san wa Hayashi-san ni nani ni tsuite kikimasu ka.**

II Complete the questions so that they fit the answers.

1. **Shūmatsu ni (   ) o shitai desu ka.**
   Eiga o mitai desu.
2. **Tsugi no nichi-yōbi ni (   ) ni ikitai desu ka.**
   Doko ni mo ikitakunai desu. Uchi ni itai desu.
3. **(   ) kudamono ga suki desu ka.**
   Ringo ga suki desu.
4. **Issho ni shokuji ni ikimasen ka.**
   Zannen desu ga, [watashi wa] ima (   ) mo tabetakunai desu.

III Put the appropriate particles in the parentheses. (If a particle is not required, put an X in the parentheses.)

1. Kurāku-san (   ) tenisu (   ) jōzu desu (   ), watashi (   ) jōzu dewa arimasen.

2. Ano hito (   ) Nihon-go (   ) dekimasu. Totemo jōzu desu.

3. Kinō kara nodo (   ) itai desu kara, hiru-yasumi (   ) byōin (   ) ikitai desu.

4. Ima nani (   ) nomitakunai desu.

5. Kyō doko ni (   ) ikitakunai desu. Uchi (   ) itai desu. Uchi (   ) hon (   ) yomitai desu.

IV Translate into Japanese.

1. Miss White likes apples.

2. Can you ski?
   Yes, I can.

3. I want to meet a friend tomorrow and play tennis (together).

4. I wanted to write a letter yesterday, but there wasn't time.

5. My throat is sore, so I don't want to eat anything.

LESSON 29 DINING OUT

Mr. Tanaka has invited Mr. Brown to a meal. They are in a restaurant looking at the menu and conversing.

たなか： すみません、メニューを みせてください。

ウェイトレス：はい、どうぞ。

たなか： のみものは なにが いいですか。

ブラウン： ビールが いいです。

たなか： りょうりは すきやきが いいですか、しゃぶしゃぶが いいですか。

ブラウン： すきやきは せんしゅう たべましたから、しゃぶしゃぶが いいです。

たなか： しょくじの あとで コーヒーは いかがですか。

ブラウン： はい、いただきます。

たなか： ビールを 2ほんと しゃぶしゃぶを おねがいします。デザートは メロンが いいです。

ウェイトレス：はい、わかりました。

■たなかさんと ブラウンさんは レストランで しょくじを しました。ビールを のんで、しゃぶしゃぶを たべました。しょくじの あとで コーヒーを のみました。

Tanaka:	Sumimasen, menyū o misete kudasai.
Ueitoresu:	Hai, dōzo.
Tanaka:	Nomimono wa nani ga ii desu ka.
Buraun:	Bīru ga ii desu.
Tanaka:	Ryōri wa sukiyaki ga ii desu ka, shabushabu ga ii desu ka.
Buraun:	Sukiyaki wa senshū tabemashita kara, shabushabu ga ii desu.
Tanaka:	Shokuji no ato de kōhī wa ikaga desu ka.
Buraun:	Hai, itadakimasu.
Tanaka:	Bīru o 2-hon to shabushabu o onegaishimasu. Dezāto wa meron ga ii desu.

Ueitoresu: Hai, wakarimashita.

■ **Tanaka-san to Buraun-san wa resutoran de shokuji o shimashita. Bīru o nonde shabushabu o tabemashita. Shokuji no ato de kōhī o nomimashita.**

Tanaka:	Excuse me, could we see the menu, please? (*lit.* "Please show us the menu.")
Waitress:	Certainly, sir. Here you are.
Tanaka:	What would you like to drink?
Brown:	I'd like some beer.
Tanaka:	As for dinner, would you like sukiyaki or (would you like) *shabushabu*?
Brown:	I had sukiyaki last week, so I'd like *shabushabu*.
Tanaka:	After the meal, how about some coffee?
Brown:	Yes, I'd love some.
Tanaka:	Two bottles of beer and some *shabushabu*, please. For dessert, we'd like some melon.
Waitress:	I see.

■ Mr. Tanaka and Mr. Brown had a meal in a restaurant. They drank beer and ate *shabushabu*. After the meal they had coffee.

Vocabulary

のみもの	**nomimono**	beverage
すきやき	**sukiyaki**	sukiyaki
しゃぶしゃぶ	**shabushabu**	*shabushabu*
デザート	**dezāto**	dessert
メロン	**meron**	melon

NOTES

1. **Nomimono wa nani ga ii desu ka.**
   Bīru ga ii desu.
   See Grammar X (p. 174) for replies when a choice is offered.

2. **Ryōri wa sukiyaki ga ii desu ka, shabushabu ga ii desu ka.**
   When offering a choice between two possibilities, the key word is replaced and the predicate is repeated. Note the difference between this and the usual English construction.
   ex. **Kyōto ni ikimasu ka, Ōsaka ni ikimasu ka.** "Are you going to Kyoto or (are you going to) Osaka?"

3. **Sukiyaki wa senshū tabemashita kara**
   Although **sukiyaki** is the object, it is also the topic and therefore takes the particle **wa**.

PRACTICE

KEY SENTENCES

1. Watashi wa jūsu ga ii desu.
2. Nomimono wa jūsu ga ii desu.

1. I'll have fruit juice.
2. (As for something) to drink, I'll have fruit juice.

EXERCISES

I Practice the following pattern by changing the underlined part as in the example given.

   ex. [Watashi wa] Ryokō wa Kyōto ga ii desu.

     1. getsu-yōbi
     2. raigetsu
     3. onsen

II Make dialogues by changing the underlined parts as in the examples given.

  A. *ex.* A: Bīru ga ii desu ka, wain ga ii desu ka.

       B: Bīru ga ii desu.

     1. kōhī, kōcha
     2. niku no ryōri, sakana no ryōri
     3. yama, umi
     4. do-yōbi, nichi-yōbi

  B. *ex.* A: Nomimono wa kōhī ga ii desu ka, kōcha ga ii desu ka.

       B: Kōcha ga ii desu.

     1. dezāto, o-kashi, kudamono
     2. doraibu, konshū, raishū
     3. kaigi, 9-ji kara, 10-ji kara

  C. *ex.* A: Dezāto wa nani ga ii desu ka.

       B: Aisukurīmu ga ii desu.

     1. ryōri, sukiyaki
     2. hiru-gohan, sandoitchi

Vocabulary

aisukurīmu   ice cream

SHORT DIALOGUES

1. Hayashi: Ryōri wa niku ga ii desu ka, sakana ga ii desu ka.
   Howaito: Niku ga ii desu.

Hayashi:	Dewa, sukiyaki wa ikaga desu ka.
Howaito:	Ee, sukiyaki o onegaishimasu.

Hayashi:	(As for the meal) Would you like meat or fish?
White:	I'd like meat.
Hayashi:	Then how about sukiyaki?
White:	Yes, sukiyaki please.

2.
Tanaka:	Shokuji wa nan-ji goro ga ii desu ka.
Howaito:	6-ji ga ii desu.
Tanaka:	Dewa, shokuji no mae ni niwa de shashin o torimasen ka.
Howaito:	Ee, torimashō.

Tanaka:	What time would you like to eat? (*lit.* "What time would you like the meal?")
White:	Six o'clock would be nice.
Tanaka:	Well then, wouldn't you like to take some pictures in the garden before dinner?
White:	Yes, let's take some.

3.
Hayashi:	Shūmatsu ni doraibu ni ikimasen ka.
Howaito:	Ee, ii desu ne.
Hayashi:	Do-yōbi ga ii desu ka, nichi-yōbi ga ii desu ka.
Howaito:	Do-yōbi ga ii desu.
Hayashi:	Doko ni ikimashō ka. Umi wa dō desu ka.
Howaito:	Ee, watashi wa umi ga suki desu. Umi ni ikitai desu.

Hayashi:	Wouldn't you (like to) go for a drive this weekend?
White:	Yes. How nice.
Hayashi:	Would you like to go on Saturday or (would you prefer) Sunday?
White:	Saturday would be fine.
Hayashi:	Where shall we go? What about the seaside?
White:	Yes. I like the sea. I'd like to go to the seaside.

QUIZ ▰▰▰▰▰▰

I Read this lesson's opening dialogue and answer the following questions.

1. **Tanaka-san to Buraun-san wa ima doko ni imasu ka.**
2. **Tanaka-san to Buraun-san wa nani o nomimasu ka.**
3. **Tanaka-san to Buraun-san wa sukiyaki o tabemasu ka, shabushabu o tabemasu ka.**

II Complete the questions so that they fit the answers.

1. **Nomimono wa (   ) ga ii desu ka.**
   Kōhī ga ii desu.

2. Ryōri wa sakana ga ii desu ka, (   ) ga ii desu ka.
   Niku ga ii desu.
3. Shokuji wa (   ) kara ga ii desu ka.
   11-ji kara ga ii desu.
4. Ryokō wa (   ) ga ii desu ka.
   Kyōto ga ii desu.

III Put the appropriate particles in the parentheses. (If a particle is not required, put an X in the parentheses.)

1. Raigetsu no yasumi ni Kyōto (   ) ikitai desu. Anata (   )?
   Watashi (   ) Ōsaka (   ) ii desu.
2. Dezāto (   ) kudamono (   ) ii desu (   ), aisukurīmu (   ) ii desu (   ).
   Aisukurīmu (   ) ii desu.
3. Shokuji (   ) ato de, kudamono (   ) onegaishimasu.
4. Kaigi (   ) mae (   ), watashi (   ) heya (   ) kite kudasai.

IV Translate into Japanese.

1. What would you like for dessert?
   Some fruit, please.
2. I wanted to drink some coffee before the meeting, but there wasn't time, so I drank some after the meeting.

LESSON 30 READING REVIEW

■ブラウンさんと　おくさんは　アメリカで　にほんごの　べんきょう
　を　していました。そして　きょう　ブラウンさんは　アメリカの
　さとうせんせいに　にほんごで　てがみを　かきました。

さとうせんせい、おげんきですか。
　とうきょうは　とても　あついですが、わたしたちは　げんきです。
わたしは　まいにち　ちかてつで　かいしゃに　いきます。うちから
かいしゃまで　20ぷんぐらいです。とうきょうの　ちかてつは　べんり
ですが、あさ　8じころから　9じころまでと　ごご　5じごろから　6じは
んごろまで、とても　こんでいます。しゅうまつには　ドライブを
したいですが、わたしたちは　くるまが　ありませんから、でんしゃで
おもしろい　ところに　いきます。
　しごとは　とても　いそがしいです。せんしゅう　おおさかと
きょうとの　ししゃに　いきました。きょうとの　かいぎの　あとで
ちいさい　おてらに　いきました。しずかでした。にわが　きれい
でした。ほかの　おてらも　みたかったですが、じかんが　ありません
でした。ざんねんでした。
　かないは　にほんじんの　ともだちや　アメリカじんの　ともだちと
ちいさい　べんきょうの　グループを　つくりました。グループの
ひとは　まいつき　15にちに　あって、にほんと　アメリカの
しゃかいや　ぶんかや　かんがえかたや　けいざいや　せいじについて
はなしを　します。
　かないは　じかんが　ありますから、いろいろな　べんきょうを
しています。そして　にほんじんの　ともだちが　たくさん　あります。
かないは　にほんごが　じょうずです。かんじも　よみます。さいきん
かないは　まいあさ　にほんごの　べんきょうを　しています。わたし
は　かようびにだけ　にほんごの　べんきょうを　しています。

らいげつから　きんようびにも　したいです。いまの　テキストは
もうすぐ　おわりますから、らいげつから　あたらしいのを　つかいま
す。わたしは　あたらしい　テキストを　たのしみに　しています。
　では　また　てがみを　かきます。
　みなさまに　どうぞ　よろしく。おげんきで。さようなら。

　8がつ　いつか

　　　　　　　　　　　　　　ジョン・ブラウン

■ Buraun-san to okusan wa Amerika de Nihon-go no benkyō o shite imashita. Soshite kyō Buraun-san wa Amerika no Satō-sensei ni Nihon-go de
tegami o kakimashita.

Satō-sensei, o-genki desu ka.
　Tōkyō wa totemo atsui desu ga, watashi-tachi wa genki desu. Watashi
wa mainichi chikatetsu de kaisha ni ikimasu. Uchi kara kaisha made
20-pun gurai desu. Tōkyō no chikatetsu wa benri desu ga, asa 8-ji goro
kara 9-ji goro made to gogo 5-ji goro kara 6-ji han goro made, totemo
konde imasu. Shūmatsu ni wa doraibu o shitai desu ga, watashi-tachi wa
kuruma ga arimasen kara, densha de omoshiroi tokoro ni ikimasu.
　Shigoto wa totemo isogashii desu. Senshū Ōsaka to Kyōto no shisha ni
ikimashita. Kyōto no kaigi no ato de chiisai o-tera ni ikimashita. Shizuka
deshita. Niwa ga kirei deshita. Hoka no o-tera mo mitakatta desu ga, jikan
ga arimasendeshita. Zannen deshita.
　Kanai wa Nihon-jin no tomodachi ya Amerika-jin no tomodachi to
chiisai benkyō no gurūpu o tsukurimashita. Gurupu no hito wa maitsuki
15-nichi ni atte, Nihon to Amerika no shakai ya bunka ya kangaekata ya
keizai ya seiji ni tsuite hanashi o shimasu.
　Kanai wa jikan ga arimasu kara, iroirona benkyō o shite imasu. Soshite
Nihon-jin no tomodachi ga takusan arimasu. Kanai wa Nihon-go ga jōzu
desu. Kanji mo yomimasu. Saikin kanai wa maiasa Nihon-go no benkyō o
shite imasu. Watashi wa ka-yōbi ni dake Nihon-go no benkyō o shite i-
masu. Raigetsu kara kin-yōbi ni mo shitai desu. Ima no tekisuto wa mō
sugu owarimasu kara, raigetsu kara atarashii no o tsukaimasu. Watashi wa atarashii tekisuto o tanoshimi ni shite imasu.
　Dewa mata tegami o kakimasu.
　Mina-sama ni dōzo yoroshiku. O-genki de. Sayōnara.

8-gatsu itsuka

　　　　　　　　　　　　　　　　Jon Buraun

■Mr. and Mrs. Brown studied Japanese in America. And today Mr. Brown wrote a letter in Japanese to their teacher in America, Satō Sensei.

Dear Satō Sensei,

How are you? It is very hot in Tokyo, but we are well.

I go to my office every day by subway. It takes (*lit.* is) about 20 minutes from my house to the office. Tokyo subways are convenient, but they are very crowded from about 8:00 in the morning till about 9:00 and from about 5:00 in the afternoon till about 6:30. On weekends, we'd like to go driving, but since we don't have a car, we visit interesting places by train.

I'm very busy with work. I visited our Osaka and Kyoto branches last week. After a meeting in Kyoto I went to a small temple. It was quiet, and the garden was beautiful. I wanted to see other temples but, sorry to say, did not have time.

My wife has formed a small study group with Japanese and American friends. The people in the group meet on the 15 of each month and talk about Japanese and American community life and social conditions, culture, ways of thinking, economy, politics, etc.

My wife has time, so she is studying various things. And she has many Japanese friends. My wife's Japanese is good. She reads *kanji,* too. Nowadays my wife has a Japanese lesson every morning. I have a Japanese lesson only on Tuesday. From next month, I want to have one on Friday, too. I'll soon finish my present textbook, so I will use a new one from next month. I am looking forward to the new textbook. I'll write a letter again (soon).

Please give my best regards to everyone. Take care of yourself.

Good-bye,

August 5

John Brown

Vocabulary

さとうせんせい	**Satō-sensei**	Professor Satō
せんせい	**sensei**	(term of respect for professors, doctors, lawyers, etc.)
こんで います	**konde imasu**	be crowded
こみます（こむ）	**komimasu (komu)**	be crowded
ところ	**tokoro**	place
ほか	**hoka**	other
グループ	**gurūpu**	group
つくりました	**tsukurimashita**	formed
つくります（つくる）	**tsukurimasu (tsukuru)**	form
まいつき	**maitsuki**	every month
しゃかい	**shakai**	society, social conditions
ぶんか	**bunka**	culture
かんがえかた	**kangaekata**	way of thinking
けいざい	**keizai**	economy
せいじ	**seiji**	politics

さいきん	saikin	nowadays
テキスト	tekisuto	text
もう すぐ	mō sugu	very soon
おわります（おわる）	owarimasu (owaru)	finish
あたらしいの	atarashii no	new one
の	no	one
たのしみに して います	tanoshimi ni shite imasu	be looking forward to
みなさまに どうぞ よろしく	mina-sama ni dōzo yoroshiku	Best regards to everyone.
みなさま	mina-sama	everyone (politer than **minna-san**)
〜に よろしく	ni yoroshiku	Best regards to . . .
おげんきで	o-genki de	Take care of yourself. (*lit.* "(Keep) well.")
ジョン	Jon	John

APPENDICES

A. Particles

Particles	Examples	Lesson
wa	1. Watashi <u>wa</u> Sumisu desu.	1
	2. Hayashi-san <u>wa</u> Kyōto ni ikimasu.	6
	3. Ōsaka ni <u>wa</u> ikimasen.	6
	4. Kinō <u>wa</u> Sumisu-san no uchi ni ikimashita.	11
	5. Sukiyaki <u>wa</u> senshū tabemashita.	29
no	1. Tōkyō Denki <u>no</u> Tanaka desu.	1
	2. Watashi <u>no</u> meishi desu.	2
	3. Watashi <u>no</u> desu.	2
	4. Atarashii <u>no</u> o tsukaimasu.	30
	5. Nihon <u>no</u> kuruma desu.	5
	6. 100-en <u>no</u> kitte o kudasai.	5
	7. Kyōto <u>no</u> shisha ni ikimashita.	6
	8. Tēburu no ue ni hana to shimbun ga arimasu.	8
	9. Kyonen <u>no</u> 5-gatsu 18-nichi ni ikimashita.	7
	10. Shokuji <u>no</u> ato de shimbun o yomimasu.	19
	11. Tsugi <u>no</u> shingō o migi ni magatte kudasai.	20
	12. Tomodachi <u>no</u> Kurāku-san ni moraimashita.	15
	13. Watashi <u>no</u> sukina iro desu.	15
ka	1. Sumisu-san desu <u>ka</u>.	1
	2. Bengoshi desu <u>ka</u>, kaishain desu <u>ka</u>.	1
	3. Donata desu <u>ka</u>.	1
	4. Sō desu <u>ka</u>.	12
kara	1. 10-ji <u>kara</u> desu.	3
	2. 10-ji <u>kara</u> 6-ji made desu.	3
	3. Amerika <u>kara</u> kimashita.	6
	4. Tōkyō eki <u>kara</u> Azabu made 30-pun kakarimashita.	22
	5. Kyō wa do-yōbi desu <u>kara</u>, byōin wa 12-ji made desu.	9
made	1. 6-ji <u>made</u> desu.	3
	2. 10-ji kara 6-ji <u>made</u> desu.	3
	3. Byōin <u>made</u> 5-fun gurai arukimashita.	22
	4. Tōkyō eki kara Azabu <u>made</u> 30-pun kakarimashita.	22
o	1. Sore <u>o</u> kudasai.	4
	2. Kabuki <u>o</u> mimasu.	10

	3. Nihongo no benkyō o shimasu.	10
	4. Tsugi no shingō o migi ni magatte kudasai.	21
	5. Hikōki wa nanji ni Ōsaka o demasu ka.	22
mo	1. Kore mo 3,000-en desu.	4
	2. Ōsaka ni mo ikimasu ka.	6
	3. Hon mo yomitai desu.	28
	4. Dare mo imasen.	8
de	1. Hitori de ikimasu.	6
	2. 5,000-en de onegaishimasu.	21
	3. Takushī de kimashita.	7
	4. Ginza no pureigaido de kaimashita.	10
	5. Taishikan de pātī ga arimasu.	18
	6. Shigoto no ato de tomodachi to shokuji o shimashita.	19
to	1. Kaisha no hito to ikimasu.	6
	2. Tēburu no ue ni hana to shimbun ga arimasu.	8
ga	1. Dono densha ga ikimasu ka.	6
	2. Tomodachi no Rinda-san ga kimashita.	19
	3. Ikkai ni ima ga arimasu.	8
	4. Maiasa kōhī o nomimasu ga, nani mo tabemasen.	11
	5. Katō desu ga, go-shujin wa irasshaimasu ka.	12
ni	1. Ōsaka no shisha ni/e ikimasu.	6
	2. Sumisu-san wa gogo 3-ji ni kūkō ni tsukimashita.	22
	3. Nichi-yōbi ni ikimashita.	7
	4. Ima ni isu ya tēburu ga arimasu.	8
	5. Bengoshi ni aimasu.	12
	6. Tomodachi ni tegami o kakimasu.	12
	7. Kurāku-san wa Tanaka-san ni kabin o agemashita.	15
	8. Tanaka-san wa Kurāku-san ni/kara kabin o moraimashita.	15
	9. Nikkō ni/e sukī ni ikimasu.	16
	10. Ryokō-gaisha ni tsutomete imasu.	27
	11. Nyū Yōku ni sunde imasu.	27
ya	1. Ima ni isu ya tēburu ga arimasu.	8
ne	1. Asoko ni uketsuke ga arimasu ne.	8
yo	1. Ee, arimasu yo.	9

made ni	1. 3-ji <u>made ni</u> todokete kudasai.	20
. . . wa . . . ga	1. Watashi <u>wa</u> eiga no kippu <u>ga</u> 2-mai arimasu.	18
	2. Watashi <u>wa</u> taipu <u>ga</u> dekimasu.	28
	3. Sumisu-san <u>wa</u> Nihon no furui kagu <u>ga</u> suki desu.	28
	4. Watashi <u>wa</u> atama <u>ga</u> itai desu.	28
	5. Watashi <u>wa</u> suraido o/<u>ga</u> mitai desu.	28
	6. Watashi <u>wa</u> jūsu <u>ga</u> ii desu.	29
	7. (Watashi <u>wa</u>) nomimono <u>wa</u> bīru <u>ga</u> ii desu.	29

B. Interrogatives

Interrogatives	Examples	Lesson
donata/dare	Kochira wa <u>donata/dare</u> desu ka.	1, 5
donata/dare no	Kore wa <u>donata/dare</u> no hon desu ka.	2
dare to	Sumisu-san wa <u>dare to</u> Narita Kūkō ni ikimasu ka.	6
dare ga	<u>Dare ga</u> kyō taishikan ni ikimasu ka.	6
	Niwa ni <u>dare ga</u> imasu ka.	8
dare ni	<u>Dare ni</u> denwa o shimasu ka.	12
	<u>Dare ni</u> aimasu ka.	12
nan	Kore wa <u>nan</u> desu ka.	2
nan-ji	Ima <u>nan-ji</u> desu ka.	3
nan de	Sumisu-san wa Tanaka-san no uchi ni <u>nan de</u> ikimashita ka.	7
	Sumisu-san wa <u>nan de</u> Ei-go no setsumei o kikimashita ka.	14
nani ga	Ima ni <u>nani ga</u> arimasu ka.	8
	Konban taishikan de <u>nani ga</u> arimasu ka.	18
	Ryōri wa <u>nani ga</u> ii desu ka.	29
nani o	Shūmatsu ni <u>nani o</u> shimasu ka.	10
itsu	Tanjōbi wa <u>itsu</u> desu ka.	3
	<u>Itsu</u> Nihon ni kimashita ka.	6
itsu ga	Kaigi wa <u>itsu ga</u> ii desu ka.	29
ikura	Sore wa <u>ikura</u> desu ka.	4
ikutsu	Tēburu no ue ni ringo ga <u>ikutsu</u> arimasu ka.	9
doko	Basu noriba wa <u>doko</u> desu ka.	9
doko no	Kore wa <u>doko no</u> kamera desu ka.	9
doko ni	Tanaka-san wa kinō <u>doko ni</u> ikimashita ka.	6
	Tanaka-san wa <u>doko ni</u> imasu ka.	9
	Kuruma no kagi wa <u>doko ni</u> arimasu ka.	9
	<u>Doko ni</u> denwa o shimasu ka.	12
	Sumisu-san no o-niisan wa <u>doko ni</u> sunde imasu ka.	27
doko de	Kyō <u>doko de</u> hiru-gohan o tabemasu ka.	10
	Pātī wa <u>doko de</u> arimasu ka.	18
doko ga	Resutoran wa <u>doko ga</u> ii desu ka.	29

dono	<u>Dono</u> densha ga ikimasu ka.	6
dore	Ano kasa wa ikura desu ka. <u>Dore</u> desu ka.	5
dōshite	<u>Dōshite</u> Sumisu-san wa kūkō ni ikimasu ka.	9
donna	Tōkyō Hoteru wa <u>donna</u> hoteru desu ka.	13
	<u>Donna</u> kagu ga suki desu ka.	28
ikaga/dō	Kabuki wa <u>ikaga/dō</u> deshita ka.	13, 14
	<u>Dō</u> shimashita ka.	28
donogurai	Do-yōbi ni <u>donogurai</u> shigoto o shimasu ka.	19
	<u>Donogurai</u> kakarimasu ka.	22
dōyatte	<u>Dōyatte</u> Tōkyō Byōin ni ikimashita ka.	22

C. Sentence Patterns

Sentence patterns	Sample Sentences	Lesson
1. . . . wa . . . desu	1. Watashi wa Tanaka desu.	1
	2. Kore wa kaisha no denwa-bangō desu.	2
	3. Ginkō wa 9-ji kara 3-ji made desu.	3
	4. Kono ringo wa totemo oishii desu.	13
	5. Kyō wa ii tenki desu ne.	13
	6. Kabuki wa totemo omoshirokatta desu.	14
2. . . . wa . . . ga . . . desu	1. Watashi wa ringo ga suki desu.	28
	2. Watashi wa atama ga itai desu.	28
	3. Nomimono wa jūsu ga ii desu.	29
	4. Watashi wa sui-yōbi ga ii desu.	29
3. -tai desu	1. Nihon no furui kagu o kaitai desu.	28
4. . . . ni . . . ga arimasu/imasu	1. Ikkai ni ima ga arimasu.	8
	2. Niwa ni Tanaka-san ga imasu.	8
5. . . . wa . . . ni arimasu/imasu	1. Tanaka-san wa tonari no heya ni imasu.	9
	2. Takushī noriba wa eki no mae ni arimasu.	9
6. . . . o onegaishimasu	1. Sandoitchi to sarada o onegaishimasu.	20
7. . . . o kudasai	1. Kore o kudasai.	4
	2. 100-en no kitte o 10-mai kudasai.	5
8. . . . ni/e -masu	1. Watashi wa ashita ginkō ni ikimasu.	6

9. ... de ... o -masu	1. Watashi wa raishū Ginza de kabuki o mimasu.	10
10. ... ni ... o -masu	1. Watashi wa tomodachi ni tegami o kakimasu.	12
	2. Sumisu-san wa Hayashi-san ni hon o moraimashita.	15
11. ... wa ... ga -masu	1. Watashi wa eiga no kippu ga 2-mai arimasu.	18
	2. Watashi wa taipu ga dekimasu.	28
12. ... de ... ga arimasu	1. Do-yōbi ni taishikan de pātī ga arimasu.	18
13. ... ni -masu	1. Watashi wa 9-ji ni kaisha ni tsukimasu.	22
14. ... o -masu	1. Watashi wa 5-ji ni kaisha o demasu.	22
15. -masen ka	1. Issho ni sukī ni ikimasen ka.	16
	2. Raishū no do-yōbi ni uchi ni kimasen ka.	17
16. -mashō ka	1. Nanji ni aimashō ka.	16
	2. Chizu o kakimashō ka.	17
17. -te, -masu	1. Watashi wa kinō shigoto no ato de, shoku-ji o shite, 9-ji goro uchi ni kaerimashita.	19
18. -te imasu	1. Yamada-san wa ima denwa o shite imasu.	25
	2. Kurāku-san wa Tōkyō ni sunde imasu.	27
	3. Watashi wa Tanaka-san o yoku shitte imasu.	27
19. -te kudasai	1. Chotto matte kudasai.	20
20. -te mo ii desu ka	1. Kono heya o tsukatte mo ii desu ka.	23
21. -naide kudasai	1. Koko de tabako o suwanaide kudasai.	24

D. Adjectives

Included in the following list of adjectives are some which do not appear in the text.

-i adjectives

abunai, dangerous	**karai**, hot, spicy	**semai**, narrow
akarui, bright	**karui**, light	**shiokarai**, salty
amai, sweet	**kitanai**, dirty	**sukunai**, few, a little

atarashii, new, fresh	**kurai**, dark	**suppai**, sour
atatakai, warm		**suzushii**, cool
atsui, hot	**mijikai**, short	
	muzukashii, difficult	**tadashii**, correct
chiisai, samll		**takai**, high, expensive
chikai, near	**nagai**, long	**tanoshii**, pleasant
		tōi, far
furui, old	**ōi**, many, much	**tsumaranai**, boring
	oishii, delicious	**tsumetai**, cold
hayai, fast, early	**ōkii**, large	
hikui, low	**omoi**, heavy	**wakai**, young
hiroi, wide	**omoshiroi**, interesting	**warui**, bad
ii, good	**osoi**, slow, late	**yasashii**, easy
isogashii, busy		**yasui**, cheap
itai, painful	**samui**, cold	

-na adjectives

anzenna, safe	**hetana**, unskillful	**shinsetsuna**, kind
	himana, free	**shitsureina**, rude
benrina, convenient		**shizukana**, quiet
	iroirona, various	**sukina**, likeable
daijina, important		
damena, no good	**jōzuna**, skillful	**teineina**, polite
fubenna, inconvenient	**kiraina**, unlikeable	**yūmeina**, famous
fushinsetsuna, unkind.	**kireina**, clean, pretty	
genkina, well, healthy	**nigiyakana**, lively	

Color words

akai, red	**kuroi**, black
aoi, green, blue	
	midoriiro no,* green
chairoi, chairo no,* brown	**murasaki no**,* purple
kiiroi, kiiro no,* yellow	
	shiroi, white

*Note that these words are nouns and are followed by the particle **no**.

E. Verb Conjugation

The following are the **-masu**, **-te**, **-nai**, plain dictionary and **-ta** forms of Regular I, Regular II and Irregular verbs. (See also Model Verb Conjugation in Lesson 19.)

Regular I					
-masu	**-te**	**-nai**	dictionary	**-ta**	
aimasu	atte	awanai	au	atta	meet
arimasu	atte	nai	aru	atta	be, have
arukimasu	aruite	arukanai	aruku	aruita	walk
chigaimasu	chigatte	chigawanai	chigau	chigatta	be wrong
gambarimasu	gambatte	gambaranai	gambaru	gambatta	do one's best
hairimasu	haitte	hairanai	hairu	haitta	enter
iimasu	itte	iwanai	iu	itta	say
ikimasu	itte	ikanai	iku	itta	go
irasshaimasu	irasshatte	irassharanai	irassharu	irasshatta	go, be
itadakimasu	itadaite	itadakanai	itadaku	itadaita	accept
kaerimasu	kaette	kaeranai	kaeru	kaetta	return
kaimasu	katta	kawanai	kau	katta	buy
kakarimasu	kakatte	kakaranai	kakaru	kakatta	(it) takes
kakimasu	kaite	kakanai	kaku	kaita	write
keshimasu	keshite	kesanai	kesu	keshita	turn off
kikimasu	kiite	kikanai	kiku	kiita	listen
komimasu	konde	komanai	komu	konda	be crowded
machimasu	matte	matanai	matsu	matta	wait
magarimasu	magatte	magaranai	magaru	magatta	turn
mochimasu	motte	motanai	motsu	motta	have, hold
moraimasu	moratte	morawanai	morau	moratte	receive
nomimasu	nonde	nomanai	nomu	nonda	drink
norimasu	notte	noranai	noru	notta	ride, get on
okurimasu	okutte	okuranai	okuru	okutta	send
oshimasu	oshite	osanai	osu	oshita	push
owarimasu	owatte	owaranai	owaru	owatta	finish
shitteimasu	shitte	shiranai	shiru	shitta	know
suimasu	sutte	suwarai	suu	sutta	smoke (cigarettes)
sumimasu	sunde	sumanai	sumu	sunda	live
torimasu	totte	toranai	toru	totta	take (a picture)

tsukaimasu	tsukatte	tsukawanai	tsukau	tsukatta	use
tsukimasu	tsuite	tsukanai	tsuku	tsuita	arrive
tsukurimasu	tsukutte	tsukuranai	tsukuru	tsukutta	make
urimasu	utte	uranai	uru	utta	sell
wakarimasu	wakatte	wakaranai	wakaru	wakatta	understand
yomimasu	yonde	yomanai	yomu	yonda	read

Regular II					
-masu	**-te**	**-nai**	dictionary	**-ta**	
agemasu	agete	agenai	ageru	ageta	give
akemasu	akete	akenai	akeru	aketa	open
dekimasu	dekite	dekinai	dekiru	dekita	be able
demasu	dete	denai	deru	deta	leave
imasu	ite	inai	iru	ita	be
kakemasu	kakete	kakenai	kakeru	kaketa	sit down
mimasu	mite	minai	miru	mita	see
misemasu	misete	misenai	miseru	miseta	show
orimasu	orite	orinai	oriru	orita	get off
oshiemasu	oshiete	oshienai	oshieru	oshieta	tell
shimemasu	shimete	shimenai	shimeru	shimeta	close
tabemasu	tabete	tabenai	taberu	tabeta	eat
todokemasu	todokete	todokenai	todokeru	todoketa	deliver
tomemasu	tomete	tomenai	tomeru	tometa	stop, park
tsukemasu	tsukete	tsukenai	tsukeru	tsuketa	turn on
(ki o)					
tsukemasu	tsukete	tsukenai	tsukeru	tsuketa	be careful
tsutomemasu	tsutomete	tsutomenai	tsutomeru	tsutometa	work for

Irregular					
-masu	**-te**	**-nai**	dictionary	**-ta**	
kimasu	kite	konai	kuru	kita	come
mottekimasu	mottekite	mottekonai	mottekuru	mottekita	bring

shimasu	shite	shinai	suru	shita	do
onegai- shimasu	onegaishite	onegaishinai	onegaisuru	onegaishita	beg a favor
shitsurei- shimasu	shitsureishite	shitsurei- shinai	shitsureisuru	shitsureishita	be rude
(benkyō o) shimasu	shite	shinai	suru	shita	study

The following is a selection of compounds that are formed with **suru** and are conjugated in the same way as **benkyō o shimasu**.

denwa o shimasu, telephone
doraibu o shimasu, go for a drive/ driving

gorufu o shimasu, play golf

hanashi o shimasu, talk

kaigi o shimasu, have a meeting
kaimono o shimasu, shop
kopī o shimasu, make a copy
kurīningu o shimasu, dry clean

pātī o shimasu, give a party

ryokō o shimasu, take a trip

setsumei o shimasu, explain
shigoto o shimasu, work
shōkai o shimasu, introduce
shutchō o shimasu, go on a business trip
sōbetsukai o shimasu, give a farewell party
sukī o shimasu, ski

taipu o shimasu, type
tenisu o shimasu, play tennis

unten o shimasu, drive

yoyaku o shimasu, make a reservation

F. Ko-so-a-do

	ko- words	**so-** words	**a-** words	**do-** words
direction	**kochira** here, this way	**sochira** there, that way	**achira** over there	**dochira** where
people	**kochira** this person	**sochira** that person	**achira** that person over there	**donata, dare** who
thing	**kore** this	**sore** that	**are** that over there	**dore** which
place	**koko** here	**soko** there	**asoko** over there	**doko** where
demonstrative	**kono kamera** this camera	**sono kamera** that camera	**ano kamera** that camera over there	**dono kamera** which camera

G. Country, Nationality, Language

	Country	Nationality	Language
Australia	Ōsutoraria	Ōsutoraria-jin	Ei-go
Brazil	Burajiru	Burajiru-jin	Porutogaru-go
Canada	Kanada	Kanada-jin	Ei-go/Furansu-go
China	Chūgoku	Chūgoku-jin	Chūgoku-go
Egypt	Ejiputo	Ejiputo-jin	Arabia-go
France	Furansu	Furansu-jin	Furansu-go
Germany	Doitsu	Doitsu-jin	Doitsu-go
Indonesia	Indoneshia	Indoneshia-jin	Indoneshia-go
Italy	Itaria	Itaria-jin	Itaria-go
Japan	Nihon	Nihon-jin	Nihon-go
New Zealand	Nyūjīrando	Nyūjīrando-jin	Ei-go
Russia	Roshia	Roshia-jin	Roshia-go
Spain	Supein	Supein-jin	Supein-go
Switzerland	Suisu	Suisu-jin	Doitsu-go/Furansu-go/ Itaria-go
Thailand	Tai	Tai-jin	Tai-go
United Kingdom	Igirisu	Igirisu-jin	Ei-go
United States	Amerika	Amerika-jin	Ei-go

The question words are: **Doko no kuni**, belonging to or coming from "What country." (This is often shortened to **doko?**) **Nani-go**, "What language," and **nani-jin**, "What nationality."

H. Common Japanese Names (Source: Nippon Univac Kaisha, Ltd., 1975.)

Family Names	Male Given Names	Female Given Names
1. Katō	1. Hiroshi	1. Yoshiko
2. Suzuki	2. Toshio	2. Keiko
3. Watanabe	3. Yoshio	3. Kazuko
4. Tanaka	4. Kazuo	4. Hiroko
5. Itō	5. Akira	5. Yōko

I. Counters

The abstract numbers (**ichi, ni, san**) are given on p. 28 (0–20), p. 33 (20, 30, . . .) and p. 41 (100, 200, . . .). The **hitotsu, futatsu, mittsu** system is given on p. 48. Two counters (**-mai** and **-hon**) appear on p. 45. Below are other counters used in this book.

1. Floors of a house or building: **-kai**. Which/how many floors, **nan-kai/nan-gai**.

ikkai, 1st floor	**go-kai**, 5th floor	**kyū-kai**, 9th floor
ni-kai, 2nd floor	**rokkai**, 6th floor	**jukkai**, 10th floor
san-gai, 3rd floor	**nana-kai**, 7th floor	**jūikkai**, 11th floor
yon-kai, 4th floor	**hachi-kai**, 8th floor	**jūni-kai**, 12th floor

Also: **chika ikkai**, (1st) basement, **chika ni-kai**, 2nd basement, etc.

2. Liquid measure (cupful, glassful): **-hai, -bai, -pai**. How many, **nam-bai**.

ippai, 1 cupful   **go-hai**, 5 cupfuls   **kyū-hai**, 9 cupfuls
ni-hai, 2 cupfuls   **roppai**, 6 cupfuls   **juppai**, 10 cupfuls
san-bai, 3 cupfuls   **nana-hai**, 7 cupfuls   **jūippai**, 11 cupfuls
yon-hai, 4 cupfuls   **happai**, 8 cupfuls   **jūni-hai**, 12 cupfuls

3. People: **-nin**. How many people, **nan-nin**.

hitori, 1 person   **roku-nin**, 6 people   **ku-nin**, 9 people
futari, 2 people   **shichi-nin**, 7 people   **jū-nin**, 10 people
san-nin, 3 people   **nana-nin**, 〃 〃   **jūichi-nin**, 11 people
yo-nin, 4 people   **hachi-nin**, 8 people   **jūni-nin**, 12 people
go-nin, 5 people   **kyū-nin**, 9 people

4. Times: **-kai, -do**. Generally speaking, these two counters may be used inter-changeably. How many times, **nan-kai**. How many times/degrees, **nan-do**.

ikkai, ichi-do, once   **nana-kai, nana-do**, 7 times
ni-kai, ni-do, twice   **hachi-kai, hachi-do**, 8 times
san-kai, san-do, 3 times   **kyū-kai, kyū-do**, 9 times
yon-kai, yon-do, 4 times   **jukkai, jū-do**, 10 times
go-kai, go-do, 5 times   **jūikkai, jūichi-do**, 11 times
rokkai, roku-do, 6 times   **jūni-kai, jūni-do**, 12 times

J. Extent, Frequency, Quantity

1. Extent

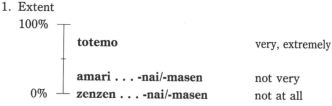

100%		
	totemo	very, extremely
	amari . . . -nai/-masen	not very
0%	**zenzen . . . -nai/-masen**	not at all

ex. **Kono nomimono wa <u>totemo</u> oishii desu**. "This drink is very good."
Kono nomimono wa <u>amari</u> oishiku<u>nai</u> desu. "This drink is not very good."
Kono nomimono wa <u>zenzen</u> oishiku<u>nai</u> desu. "This drink is not good at all."

2. Frequency

100%	**itsumo**	always
	yoku	often
	tokidoki	sometimes
	tamani	occasionally
	amari . . . -masen	not very often
0%	**zenzen . . . -masen**	never

ex. **Ban-gohan no ato de <u>itsumo</u> terebi o mimasu**. "(I) always watch TV after supper."
Ban-gohan no ato de <u>yoku</u> terebi o mimasu. "(I) often watch TV after supper."
Ban-gohan no ato de <u>tokidoki</u> terebi o mimasu. "(I) sometimes watch TV after supper."

Ban-gohan no ato de <u>tamani</u> terebi o <u>mi</u>masu. "(I) occasionally watch TV after supper."

Ban-gohan no ato de <u>amari</u> terebi o <u>mi</u>masen. "(I) don't often watch TV after supper."

Ban-gohan no ato de <u>zenzen</u> terebi o <u>mi</u>masen. "(I) never watch TV after supper."

3. Quantity

100%		
	takusan	a lot, many
	sukoshi	few, a little
0%	**zenzen . . . -masen**	none at all

ex. **Mise ga <u>takusan</u> arimasu.** "There are a lot of stores."
Mise ga <u>sukoshi</u> arimasu. "There are a few stores."
Mise ga <u>zenzen</u> ari<u>ma</u>sen. "There are no stores."

K. Time Expressions

1. Every, **mai-**

   mai-nichi, every day   **mai-shū**, every week
   mai-ban, every evening, every night   **mai-tsuki/mai-getsu**, every month
   mai-asa, every morning   **mai-nen/mai-toshi**, every year

2. Period of Time

   Minutes, **-fun, -pun**. How many minutes, **nam-pun (kan)**.

   ippun (kan), (for) 1 minute   **happun (kan)**, (for) 8 minutes
   ni-fun (kan), (for) 2 minutes   **hachi-fun (kan)**, 〃 〃 〃
   sam-pun (kan), (for) 3 minutes   **kyū-fun (kan)**, (for) 9 minutes
   yom-pun (kan), (for) 4 minutes   **juppun (kan)**, (for) 10 minutes
   go-fun (kan), (for) 5 minutes   **jūippun (kan)**, (for) 11 minutes
   roppun (kan), (for) 6 minutes   **jūni-fun (kan)**, (for) 12 minutes
   nana-fun (kan), (for) 7 minutes

   Hours, **-jikan**. How many hours, **nan-jikan**.

   ichi-jikan, (for) 1 hour   **shichi-jikan**, (for) 7 hours
   ni-jikan, (for) 2 hours   **hachi-jikan**, (for) 8 hours
   san-jikan, (for) 3 hours   **ku-jikan**, (for) 9 hours
   yo-jikan, (for) 4 hours   **ju-jikan**, (for) 10 hours
   go-jikan, (for) 5 hours   **jūichi-jikan**, (for) 11 hours
   roku-jikan, (for) 6 hours   **jūni-jikan**, (for) 12 hours
   nana-jikan, (for) 7 hours

   Days, **-nichi (kan)**. How many days, **nan-nichi (kan)**.

   ichinichi (kan), (for) 1 day   **nanoka (kan)**, (for) 7 days
   futsuka (kan), (for) 2 days   **yōka (kan)**, (for) 8 days
   mikka (kan), (for) 3 days   **kokonoka (kan)**, (for) 9 days
   yokka (kan), (for) 4 days   **tōka (kan)**, (for) 10 days

itsuka (kan), (for) 5 days

muika (kan), (for) 6 days

jūichi-nichi (kan), (for) 11 days

jūni-nichi (kan), (for) 12 days

Weeks, -shūkan. How many weeks, nan-shūkan.

isshūkan, (for) 1 week

ni-shūkan, (for) 2 weeks

san-shūkan, (for) 3 weeks

yon-shūkan, (for) 4 weeks

go-shūkan, (for) 5 weeks

roku-shūkan, (for) 6 weeks

nana-shūkan, (for) 7 weeks

hasshūkan, (for) 8 weeks

kyū-shūkan, (for) 9 weeks

jusshūkan, (for) 10 weeks

jūisshūkan, (for) 11 weeks

jūni-shūkan, (for) 12 weeks

Months, -kagetsu (kan). How many months, nan-kagetsu (kan).

ikkagetsu (kan), (for) 1 month

ni-kagetsu (kan), (for) 2 months

san-kagetsu (kan), (for) 3 months

yon-kagetsu (kan), (for) 4 months

go-kagetsu (kan), (for) 5 months

rokkagetsu (kan), (for) 6 months

nana-kagetsu (kan), (for) 7 months

shichi-kagetsu (kan), (for) 7 months

hakkagetsu (kan), (for) 8 months

kyū-kagetsu (kan), (for) 9 months

jukkagetsu (kan), (for) 10 months

jūikkagetsu (kan), (for) 11 months

jūni-kagetsu (kan), (for) 12 months

Years, -nen (kan). How many years, nan-nen (kan).

ichi-nen (kan), (for) 1 year

ni-nen (kan), (for) 2 years

san-nen (kan), (for) 3 years

yo-nen (kan), (for) 4 years

go-nen (kan), (for) 5 years

roku-nen (kan), (for) 6 years

nana-nen (kan), (for) 7 years

shichi-nen (kan), (for) 7 years

hachi-nen (kan), (for) 8 years

kyū-nen (kan), (for) 9 years

jū-nen (kan), (for) 10 years

jūichi-nen (kan), (for) 11 years

jūni-nen (kan), 12 years

Note: Except for -jikan and -shūkan the suffix kan may be considered optional and need be added only when specificity is called for.

3. Relative Time

Day

ototoi, day before yesterday

kinō, yesterday

kyō, today

ashita, tomorrow

asatte, day after tomorrow

Week

sensen-shū, week before last

sen-shū, last week

kon-shū, this week

rai-shū, next week

sarai-shū, week after next

Morning

ototoi no asa, morning before last

kinō no asa, yesterday morning

kesa, this morning

ashita no asa, tomorrow morning

asatte no asa, morning of the day
            after tomorrow

Month

sensen-getsu, month before last

sen-getsu, last month

kon-getsu, this month

rai-getsu, next month

sarai-getsu, month after next

<table>
<tr><td>Evening</td><td>Year</td></tr>
</table>

Evening

ototoi no ban/yoru, evening/night before last

kinō no ban/yoru, yesterday evening/ night

komban, this evening

ashita no ban/yoru, tomorrow evening/night

asatte no ban/yoru, evening/night of the day after tomorrow

Year

ototoshi, year before last

kyonen, last year

kotoshi, this year

rai-nen, next year

sarai-nen, year after next

4. Seasons

haru, spring   **natsu**, summer   **aki**, autumn   **fuyu**, winter

L. Parts of the Face and Body

1. Face, **kao**, and head, **atama**

ago, chin, jaw   **kami**, hair   **mayu/mayuge**, eyebrow

ha, tooth   **kuchi**, mouth   **me**, eye

hana, nose   **kuchibiru**, lip   **mimi**, ear

hitai, forehead   **mabuta**, eyelid   **shita**, tongue

hoho, cheek   **matsuge**, eyelash

2. Body, **karada**

ashi, foot, leg   **mune**, chest   **te**, hand

hifu, skin   **nodo**, throat   **tsume**, nail

kata, shoulder   **onaka**, stomach, abdomen   **ude**, arm

koshi, hip   **oshiri**, buttock   **yubi**, finger, toe

kubi, neck   **senaka**, back

M. Kanji

Each **kanji** conveys an idea, and most of them have at least two readings. The numbers in parentheses indicate the number of strokes.

Counters, Day of the Week, Date

四
し、よん

四 │ ㄇ ㄇ 四 四 (5)

百
ひゃく

百 一 ㄒ ㄒ 万 百 百 (6)

五
ご

五 一 ㄱ 万 五 (4)

千
せん

千 ノ ニ 千 (3)

六
ろく

六 ` 亠 宀 六 (4)

万
まん

万 一 ㄱ 万 (3)

七
しち、なな

七 一 七 (2)

一つ	二つ	三つ	四つ	五つ
ひと	ふた	みっ	よっ	いっ
六つ	七つ	八つ	九つ	十
むっ	なな	やっ	ここの	とお

日 曜 日
にちようび

日 │ ㄇ 日 日 (4)

月 曜 日
げつようび

月 ノ 冂 月 月 (4)

火 曜 日
かようび

火 ` ` ⺌ 火 (4)

水 曜 日
すいようび

水 │ ⺆ 才 水 (4)

木 曜 日
もくようび

木 一 十 才 木 (4)

金 曜 日
きんようび

金 ノ 八 亼 今 仐 全 釒 金 (8)

土 曜 日
どようび

土 一 十 土 (3)

一月一日
いちがつついたち

四月六日
し　がつむいか

七月七日
しちがつなのか

九月八日
く　がつようか

十月十一日
じゅうがつじゅういちにち

十二月二十日
じゅうにがつはつか

QUIZ ANSWERS ■■■■||||||||||

Lesson 1

I 1. Sumisu desu. 2. Iie, Nihon-jin dewa arimasen. 3. Bengoshi desu.
II 1. Sumisu-san 2. Doitsu-jin 3. bengoshi 4. donata
III 1. wa 2. ka, ka 3. no
IV 1. Sumisu desu. 2. Hajimemashite. Dōzo yoroshiku. 3. Yamada-san, kochira wa Tōkyō Denki no Tanaka-san desu. 4. Sumisu-san wa Amerika-jin desu ka, Doitsu-jin desu ka.

Lesson 2

I 1. Meishi desu. 2. Hai, kaisha no namae desu. 3. Kaisha no [jūsho] desu. 4. Iie, uchi no denwa-bangō dewa arimasen. 5. Zero-san no san-yon-zero-zero no kyū-zero-san-ichi desu.
II 1. kaisha 2. dare/donata 3. nan 4. nan-ban
III 1. wa 2. wa, ka, no, wa, no 3. wa, no, no
IV 1. Kochira wa Tanaka-san desu. 2. Kore wa Tanaka-san no meishi desu. 3. Kore wa Tanaka-san no uchi no denwa-bangō dewa arimasen. Kaisha no desu. 4. [Anata no] Kaisha no denwa-bangō wa nan-ban desu ka.

Lesson 3

I 1. Iie, 10-ji dewa arimasen. 2. 10-ji kara desu. 3. Iie, 7-ji made dewa arimasen.
II 1. nan-ji 2. nan-yōbi 3. nan-nichi
III 1. wa 2. no, wa 3. wa, kara, made
IV 1. Dōmo arigatō. 2. Dō itashimashite. 3. Sumimasen. Yūbinkyoku wa nan-ji made desu ka. 4. Kyō wa 15-nichi desu. Ashita wa 16-nichi desu. 5. Kyō wa moku-yōbi desu. Kinō wa sui-yōbi deshita.

Lesson 4

I 1. Iie, [kore wa] tokei dewa arimasen. 2. [Are wa] Terebi desu. 3. [Are wa] 50,000-en desu. 4. Iie, [sore wa] 50,000-en dewa arimasen. 5. [Sore wa] 5,000-en desu. 6. Hai, [kore mo] 5,000-en desu.
II 1. nan 2. ikura 3. donata 4. Are
III 1. o 2. wa, mo, mo, mo, wa, wa
IV 1. Sore o misete kudasai. 2. Kore o kudasai. 3. Kore wa ikura desu ka. 4. Irasshaimase.

Lesson 5

I 1. [Sono Doitsu no kamera wa/Sore wa] 50,000-en desu. 2. Iie, [kono kamera wa/kore wa] Doitsu no dewa arimasen. 3. [Kono kamera wa/Kore wa] 35,000-en desu. 4. [Ano chiisai rajio wa/Are wa] Nihon no desu.
II 1. ikura 2. Are 3. Igirisu, Doko
III 1. wa, no, mo, no 2. o 3. o, x 4. wa 5. x, wa, x
IV 1. Kore wa ikura desu ka. 2. Kono rajio wa ikura desu ka. 3. Watashi no tokei wa Nihon no dewa arimasen. Amerika no desu. 4. Sono chiisai tēpurekōdā o misete kudasai. 5. Fuirumu o mittsu kudasai. Dono fuirumu desu ka. Sono fuirumu desu.

Lesson 6

I 1. Kyōto no shisha ni/e ikimasu. 2. Kaisha no hito to ikimasu. 3. Asatte kaerimasu.
II 1. Ginkō, Yūbinkyoku 2. Itsu 3. Doko, Dare/Donata

III 1. x, ni/e 2. to, ni/e 3. wa, x 4. de 5. ni/e, mo, wa 6. ga
IV 1. Sumimasen, kono basu wa Tōkyō Eki ni/e ikimasu ka. 2. Tanaka-san wa kinō kaisha no hito to Ōsaka ni/e ikimashita. Soshite asatte Tōkyō ni/e kaerimasu. 3. Sumisu-san wa kyonen hitori de Nihon ni/e kimashita. 4. Dare/Donata ga kūkō ni/e ikimashita ka. Tanaka-san no hisho ga ikimashita.

Lesson 7

I 1. Sumisu-san ga ikimashita. 2. Nichi-yōbi ni ikimashita. 3. Iie, densha de ikimasen deshita. 4. Takushī de ikimashita.
II 1. doko 2. itsu 3. nan-nichi, Nan, Dare/Donata
III 1. de, ni/e, mo 2. x, ni
IV 1. Konnichiwa. 2. Yoku irasshaimashita. 3. Dōzo okake kudasai.
V 1. Dōzo kochira ni/e. 2. Dōzo ohairi kudasai. 3. Tanaka-san wa kinō takushī de uchi ni/e kaerimashita. 4. Howaito-san wa kin-yōbi ni Ōsaka no shisha ni/e ikimasu.

Lesson 8

I 1. Ima ni arimasu. 2. Shimbun to hana ga arimasu. 3. Tanaka-san no okusan ga imasu. 4. Dare mo imasen.
II 1. dare/donata 2. nani 3. dare/donata 4. nani
III 1. arimasu 2. imasu 3. imasen 4. arimasen
IV 1. no, ni, ga 2. no, to, ga 3. ya, ga 4. ga, mo
V 1. Ima ni isu ya tēburu ga arimasu. 2. Niwa ni Tanaka-san to otoko no ko ga imasu. 3. Daidokoro ni dare ga imasu ka. Dare mo imasen. 4. Isu no ue ni nani mo arimasen.

Lesson 9

I 1. Yūbinkyoku ni ikimasu. 2. Iie, sūpā no mae dewa arimasen.
II 1. doko 2. nani 3. doko 4. Dōshite 5. ikutsu 6. nan-nin
III 1. wa, x, no, ni 2. ni, x, x 3. ni/e, kara 4. wa, ni
IV 1. Saka-ya wa yaoya no tonari desu./Saka-ya wa yaoya no tonari ni arimasu. 2. Sumimasen, o-tearai wa doko desu ka./Sumimasen, o-tearai wa doko ni arimasu ka. Asoko desu./Asoko ni arimasu. 3. Howaito-san wa Ōsaka ni/e ikimashita kara, kyō kaisha ni imasen. 4. Dōshite kyō byōin wa 12-ji made desu ka. Do-yōbi desu kara. 5. Hon-ya no mae ni kodomo ga 5-nin imasu.

Lesson 10

I 1. Kabuki o mimasu. 2. Iie, hitori de mimasen. 3. Senshū kaimashita. 4. Ginza no pureigaido de kaimashita.
II 1. Nan-yōbi 2. doko 3. nani 4. nani
III 1. ni 2. de, ni/e 3. de, o 4. de, mo 5. o 6. x, de, o
IV 1. Nichi-yōbi ni depāto de kamera o kaimashita. 45,000-en deshita. 2. Kinō nani o shimashita ka. Asa, uchi de Nihon-go no tēpu o kikimashita. Gogo Ginza ni/e ikimashita. Soshite, Ginza de kamera o kaimashita. 3. Howaito-san wa asa nani mo tabemasen.

Lesson 12

I 1. Katō-san ga shimashita. 2. Imasen deshita. 3. 9-ji goro kaerimasu. 4. Hai, shimasu.
II 1. nani, Dare/Donata 2. dare/donata 3. Dare/Donata
III 1. Iie, kimasen 2. mimasu, Iie, mimasen 3. yoku 4. yomimasu, yomimasen
IV 1. ni 2. ni 3. x, to 4. ni, o 5. ga, wa
V 1. Moshi-moshi, Tanaka-san no o-taku desu ka. 2. Tōkyō Denki no Tanaka desu. Hayashi-san wa irasshaimasu ka. 3. Mata ato de denwa o shimasu. 4. Kurāku-san ni

kaisha no denwa-bangō o kikimashita.   5. Kurāku-san wa amari tomodachi ni tegami o kakimasen ga, Howaito-san wa yoku kakimasu.

Lesson 13

I   1. Hai, tabemashita.   2. Nihon no o-kashi o tabemashita.   3. O-cha o nomimashita.
II   1. genki   2. omoshiroi   3. donata/dare   4. donna
III   1. oishikunai desu   2. kireina   3. omoshirokunai desu   4. yokunai desu   5. yūmeina 6. chikai desu
IV   1. Kōhī wa ikaga desu ka. Arigatō gozaimasu. Itadakimasu.   2. Kōhī o mō ippai ikaga desu ka. Iie, mō kekkō desu.   3. Watashi-tachi wa yūmeina resutoran de ban-gohan o tabemashita.   4. Ano kissaten wa kirei desu ga, shizuka dewa arimasen.   5. [Watashi wa] Kyō isogashii desu.

Lesson 14

I   1. Kabuki o mimashita.   2. Omoshirokatta desu.   3. Iyahōn de kikimashita.
II   1. yasashii   2. chikai   3. tsumaranai   4. ōkii   5. takai   6. isogashii   7. atsui 8. shizukana   9. furui   10. warui
III   1. nani, dō, yokatta   2. Dōshite   3. donna
IV   1. yokatta desu   2. dō   3. nigiyaka deshita   4. kirei dewa arimasen   5. omoshiroku-nakatta desu   6. genki deshita
V   1. Kinō no kaigi wa dō deshita ka.   2. Kinō no tenki wa yokatta desu.   3. Ano resutoran no ryōri wa amari oishikunakatta desu.

Lesson 15

I   1. Tanjōbi ni moraimashita.   2. Kurāku-san ni/kara moraimashita.   3. Kurāku-san ga agemashita.   4. Tanaka-san ni agemashita.
II   1. dare/donata   2. dare/donata   3. nani
III   1. ni/kara   2. ga, o   3. ni, o   4. ni, o, mo
IV   1. Tanaka-san wa Kurāku-san ni kireina kabin o moraimashita.   2. Hayashi-san wa Sumisu-san ni Kyōto no chizu o agemashita.   3. Ano hito ni meishi o agemashita ka. Hai, agemashita.

Lesson 16

I   1. Nikkō ni ikimasu.   2. Iie, hitori de ikimasen.   3. Tōkyō Eki (no kaisatsuguchi) de aimasu.   4. 7-ji ni aimasu.   5. Densha de ikimasu.
II   1. Doko, Nan-ji   2. Dare/Donata
III   1. ni, o   2. ni, ni   3. ni, ni   4. ni, de
IV   1. Do-yōbi ni depāto ni/e kaimono ni ikimashita.   2. Issho ni shokuji o shimasen ka. Ee, shimashō. Doko ni/e ikimashō ka. Eki no chikaku no atarashii resutoran ni/e ikimasen ka. Ee, sō shimashō.

Lesson 17

I   1. Do-yōbi [no ban] desu.   2. Ikimasu.   3. Tanaka-san no uchi de shimasu.   4. Azabu ni arimasu.   5. Hai, kakimasu.
II   1. ni, ni, ni/e, ni, o   2. ni, ga, ga   3. o
III   1. Nichi-yōbi ni uchi ni/e kimasen ka.   2. Kin-yōbi ni uchi de Kurāku-san no sōbetsukai o shimasu. Kimasen ka. Ee, zehi.   3. Issho ni shokuji o shimasen ka.   4. Samui desu ne. Mado o shimemashō ka. Hai, onegaishimasu.   5. Chizu o kakimashō ka.

Lesson 18

  I   1. Eiga no kippu ga arimasu.   2. 2-mai arimasu.   3. Pātī ni ikimasu.   4. Pātī ga arimasu.   5. Iie, ikimasen.   6. Ashita Sumisu-san to ikimasu.

  II   1. nan-nin   2. itsu   3. nani   4. doko

  III   1. ga   2. ni   3. de   4. ga, x   5. de, ga   6. no, ga, x, x, ga

  IV   1. Watashi wa imōto ga 3-nin arimasu. Imōto wa Tōkyō to Ōsaka ni imasu.   2. Tanaka-san, 8-gatsu ni yasumi ga arimasu ka. Iie, arimasen. 9-gatsu ni arimasu.   3. Raishū, Kyōto no shisha de kaigi ga arimasu.

Lesson 19

  I   1. Sumisu-san no tomodachi desu.   2. Kinō kimashita.   3. Raishū no moku-yōbi made imasu.   4. Mikka(kan) imasu.   5. Kyōto ya Nara ni/e ikimasu.   6. Furui o-tera ya niwa o mimasu.

  II   1. tabete   4. kite   7. ite   10. nonde
       2. itte   5. kaite   8. mite   11. atte
       3. yonde   6. kaette   9. shite   12. kiite

  III   1. itsu/nan-nen no nan-gatsu, itsu/nan-nen no nan-gatsu   2. donogurai/nan-nichi(kan) gurai/nan-shūkan gurai   3. Itsu

  IV   1. Soshite   2. itte   3. donogurai   4. gurai   5. dō   6. nan, donogurai, gurai

  V   1. Maiasa nyūsu o kiite, kaisha ni/e ikimasu.   2. Tanaka-san ni atte, issho ni ban-gohan o tabemashita. Soshite uchi ni kaerimashita.   3. Donogurai uchi de Nihon-go no benkyō o shimasu ka. 30-pun dake shimasu.   4. Kinō doko ni/e mo ikimasen deshita. Uchi ni imashita.

Lesson 20

  I   1. Sakaya ni (denwa o) shimashita.   2. Hayashi-san no uchi ni todokemasu.   3. 20-pon todokemasu.   4. 3-ji made ni todokemasu.   5. Hai, oshiemashita.

  II   1. itte   4. kiite   7. mottekite   10. atte
       2. ite   5. magatte   8. itte   11. nonde
       3. matte   6. misete   9. shimete   12. shite

  III   1. o   2. o, x   3. ni   4. o   5. o, to, o, ni/e   6. o, ni/e

  IV   1. Menyū o misete kudasai. Hai, dōzo.   2. Sumimasen ga, uchi ni bīru o 12-hon todokete kudasai. Hai, wakarimashita. Kurāku-san desu ne. Ee, sō desu.   3. Kono chiisai terebi o kudasai. Hai, wakarimashita. Todokemashō ka. Iie, kekkō desu. Kuruma de kimashita kara.

Lesson 22

  I   1. Senshū ikimashita.   2. Iie, (issho ni) ikimasen deshita.   3. Ashita ikimasu.   4. Azabu de orimashita.   5. Iie, kakarimasen deshita.

  II   1. nan   2. Doko   3. Nani   4. donogurai/nan-jikan gurai   5. Dōyatte

  III   1. de, ni, de, o   2. o, ni, ni, de   3. made, de, x

  IV   1. Kinō Ginza no hoteru de tomodachi no sōbetsukai ga arimashita.   2. Kaisha o 6-ji ni dete, basu ni notte, Ginza de orimashita.   3. Kaisha kara hoteru made donogurai kakarimashita ka. 35-fun gurai kakarimashita.

Lesson 23

  I   1. Denki-ya de moraimashita.   2. Terebi no katarogu o moraimashita.   3. Iie, kēsu no naka ni arimasen deshita.   4. Kēsu no ue ni arimashita.

  II   1. haitte   4. mite   7. shite   10. itte
       2. kite   5. tsukatte   8. totte   11. ite

3. tabete　6. nonde　9. kiite　12. itte

III　1. totte　2. shi, shi　3. ake, akete　4. tsukatte, matte　5. ki, kite　6. moratte　7. katte

IV　1. Denki o tsukemashō ka. Hai, onegaishimasu.　2. Kono denwa o tsukatte mo ii desu ka. Hai, dōzo.　3. 3-ji made koko ni ite mo ii desu ka.

Lesson 24

I　1. Keikan ga oshiemashita.　2. Tsugi no kado o hidari ni magarimasu. 3.　Chūshajō ni/e ikimasu.

II　1. tabenai　5. iwanai　9. akenai　13. tsukawanai
　　2. minai　6. yomanai　10. magaranai　14. shimenai
　　3. ikanai　7. shinai　11. kesanai　15. toranai
　　4. konai　8. suwanai　12. tsukenai

III　1. sutte, suwanaide　2. akete, akete　3. itte, kite　4. shime, shimenaide

IV　1. wa, kara, o　2. o, ni/e　3. de, o　4. o, ni

V　1. Ima ano heya ni hairanaide kudasai.　2. Koko de tabako o suwanaide kudasai.
　　3. Tsugi no shingō o migi ni/e magatte kudasai.

Lesson 25

I　1. 3-gai ni imasu.　2. Kaigishitsu ni imasu.　3. Suraido o mite imasu.

II　1. doko/nan-gai, nani　2. doko　3. dare/donata　4. doko

III　1. Hayashi-san wa Sumisu-san ni denwa o shimasu.　2. Hayashi-san wa Sumisu-san ni denwa o shite imasu.　3. Ano onna no ko wa nani o shite imasu ka. Tomodachi o matte imasu.　4. Howaito-san wa ima shigoto o shite imasen.

Lesson 27

I　1. Sumisu-san to Hayashi-san ga hanashi o shite imasu.　2. Sumisu-san no o-niisan ga kimashita.　3. Iie, imasen.　4. Ryokō-gaisha ni tsutomete imasu.　5. Nyū Yōku ni sunde imasu./Amerika ni sunde imasu.

II　1. Doko　2. doko　3. Dare/Donata　4. doko

III　1. no　2. ni, ni　3. de　4. ni, no, ni　5. de, no, o, de

IV　1. Tanaka-san o shitte imasu ka. Iie, shirimasen.　2. Watashi wa kaisha no chikaku ni sunde imasu. Aruite 15-fun desu.　3. Sumisu-san wa ABC ni tsutomete imasu.

Lesson 28

I　1. Nihon no furui kagu ga suki desu.　2. Hai, mō kaimashita.　3. Iie, shirimasen.
　　4. Furui kagu no mise ni tsuite kikimasu.

II　1. nani　2. doko　3. Donna　4. nani

III　1. wa, ga, ga, wa　2. wa, ga　3. ga, ni, ni/e　4. mo　5. mo, ni, de, o/ga

IV　1. Howaito-san wa ringo ga suki desu.　2. Sukī ga dekimasu ka. Hai, dekimasu.
　　3. Ashita tomodachi ni atte, issho ni tenisu o/ga shitai desu.　4. Kinō tegami o/ga kaki-takatta desu ga, jikan ga arimasen deshita.　5. [Watashi wa] Nodo ga itai desu kara, nani mo tabetakunai desu.

Lesson 29

I　1. Resutoran ni imasu.　2. Bīru o nomimasu.　3. Shabushabu o tabemasu.

II　1. nani　2. niku　3. nan-ji　4. doko

III　1. ni/e, wa, wa, ga　2. wa, ga, ka, ga, ka, ga　3. no, o　4. no, ni, no, ni/e

IV　1. Dezāto wa nani ga ii desu ka. Kudamono o onegaishimasu.　2. Kaigi no mae ni kōhī o/ga nomitakatta desu ga, jikan ga arimasen deshita kara, kaigi no ato de nomimashita.

JAPANESE-ENGLISH GLOSSARY

a, Ah, 53
achira, over there, that person over there, 199
agemashita, gave; *agemasu, ageru*, give, 109
aimashō ka, shall (we) meet, 114; *aimasu, au*, meet, 89
aisukurīmu, ice cream, 184
akachan, baby, 117
akai, red, 48
akemashō ka, shall (I) open; *akemasu, akeru*, open, 120
amari . . . -masen, does not . . . often, 89
amari . . .-nai/-masen, not very . . . , 97
Amerika, America, 23
Amerika-jin, an American, 23
Amerika Taishikan, American Embassy, 23
anata, you, 21, 23
ane, older sister, 110, 169
ani, older brother, 168, 169
ano, that (over there), 46, 48
aoi, blue, 50
are, that (one) over there, 40, 46
arigatō gozaimasu, (I am) grateful, 26
arimasen, do/does not have, 20
arimasendeshita, was/were not, 33
arimasu, aru, is/are (inanimate), 20, 66
arimasu, aru, have, 124
arukimashita, walked; *arukimasu, aruku*, walk, 145
asa, morning, 83
asa-gohan, breakfast, morning meal, 83
asatte, the day after tomorrow, 53
ashita, tomorrow, 33
asoko, over there, that place (over there), 70
atama, head, 176
atarashii, new, fresh, 100
ato de, afterwards, later, 88
atsukunakatta, was not hot; *atsui*, hot, 104

ban, evening, 83
-ban, number, 29
banana, banana, 20
banchi (part of a block in an address), 137
bangō, number, 26
ban-gohan, dinner, evening meal, 83
basu, bus, 57
basu-noriba, bus terminal, 76
bengoshi, lawyer, 19
benkyō o shimasu (suru), study, 80
benri(na), convenient, 100
bideo, video, 121
biru, building, 70
bīru, beer, 49
botchan, son, 169

bun, part, 41
bunka, culture, 189
byōin, hospital, 74

cha, tea, 83
chichi, father, 110
chigaimasu, chigau, That's/It's wrong/different, 92
chiisai, small, 44
chika, basement, underground, 170
chikai, near, close to, 98
chika 1-ikai (ikkai), first basement, 170
chikaku, neighborhood, vicinity; *no chikaku ni/e*, near, close to, 68
chikatetsu, subway, underground railway, 57
chizu, map, 83
chō, town, community, 137
-chōme (block in an address), 137
chotto, a little, 127
Chūgoku, China, 23
Chūgoku-jin, a Chinese, 23
chūshajō, parking lot, 155
chūsha kinshi, no parking, 154

daidokoro, kitchen, 66
dake, only, 130
dame, no good, useless, hopeless, out of the question, 155; *dame(na)*, 191
dare, who, 21
dare mo . . . -masen, nobody is, 66
dare no, whose, 29
de, at, 79
de, by, 61
de gozaimasu, This is . . . , 92
deguchi, exit, 156
dekimasu, dekiru, be able to, can (do), be ready/finished/done, 143, 174, 176
demasu, deru, leave, start, 146
demo, but, 121
denchi, battery, 46
denki, (electric) light, 121
denki-ya, electrical appliance store/clerk, 150
densha, (electric) train, 56
denwa, telephone, 26
denwa-bangō, telephone number, 26
denwa o shimasu (suru), make a phone call, telephone, 79, 89
depāto, department store, 32
deshita, was/were, 20, 33
desu, is/are, 19, 54, 67
dewa, well then, 39, 42
dewa arimasen, is/are not, 21
dezāto, dessert, 183

dō, how, 103
-do, times, 137
-do, degree, 180
doa, door, 121
dochira, where, 119
dō deshita ka, How was it, 103, 104
dō desu ka, How is it, 96
dō itashimashite, Don't mention it, You're welcome, 32
Doitsu, Germany, 23
Doitsu-go, German language, 178
Doitsu-jin, a German, 23
doko, where, belonging to or coming from what place, 48, 80
doko ni mo, nowhere, 67
dōmo, very much, 26
dōmo, thanks, 142, 159
dōmo arigatō gozaimasu, Thank you very much, 26
donata, who, 21, 23
donna, what kind of, 96, 100
dono, which, 50
donogurai, how long, 134; how much, 146
doraibu, driving, a drive, 116
dore, which one, 44
dō shimashita ka, What's the matter, 180
dōshite, why, 73, 76
dōyatte, how, 145
do-yōbi, Saturday, 35
dōzo, please (accept, do), 26, 96
dōzo o-daiji ni, Look after yourself, 180
dōzo yoroshiku, Please favor me, 19, 21

e, picture, 83
e, to (particle), 53
ee, yes, 26
eiga, movie, film, 36
Ei-go, English language, 104
eki, station, 56
en, yen, 39

fuirumu, film, 39, 45
-fun (-pun), minute, 32
funabin, sea mail, 61, 180
Furansu, France, 48
Furansu-go, French language, 179
furui, old, not fresh, 100
futari, 2 people, 76
futatsu, two, 48
futsuka, 2nd day of the month, 35

ga (subject marker, particle), 57
ga, but (particle), 86
ga (particle), 88
gaikoku, foreign country, 171
gakkō, school, 29
gakusei, student, 23

-gatsu, month, 33
genkan, entrance hall, 68
genki(na), well, healthy, 100
getsu-yōbi, Monday, 35
ginkō, bank, 23
go, five, 28
-go, language, 48
go- (honorific), 88
gō, number, 137
gochisōsama, Thank you for a lovely meal, 96
gogo, p.m., afternoon, 32
gohan, meal, 80
gojuppun, gojippun, 50 minutes, 32
5(go)-nin, 5 people, 74
goro, about, 86, 89
gorufu, golf, 106
go-ryōshin, parents, 169
go-shōkai shimasu, Let me introduce you, 23
go-shujin, husband, 88
gozen, a.m., morning, 33
gurai, about, approximately, 101, 145
gurūpu, group, 189
gyū-niku, beef, 100

ha, tooth, 178
hachi, eight, 28
hagaki, postcard, 45, 68
haha, mother, 91, 169
hai, yes, certainly, 20, 23
-hai, measureful (counter), 95
haikingu, hiking, 117
hairimasu, hairu, enter, go/come in, 61, 150
haizara, ashtray, 42
hajimemashite, How do you do, 19, 21; *hajimeru*, begin, 21
hako, box, 68
han, half, 30 minutes after the hour, 33
hana, flower, 66
hanashi o shimasu (suru), talk, 161
hana-ya, flower shop, florist, 45
hatsuka, 20th day of the month, 35
heya, room, 76
hi, day, 166
hidari, left, 139
hidari-gawa, left-hand side, 155
higashi, east, 54
hikōki, airplane, 76
hima(na), free, 100
hiragana (Japanese script), 111
hirakimasu, hiraku, open, 32
hiru, noon, daytime, 33
hiru-gohan, lunch, noon meal, 80
hiru-yasumi, lunch time, noon recess, 33
hisho, secretary, 23
hītā, heater, 121
hito, person, 32
hitori, 1 person, 76

hitori de, alone, 53
hitotsu, one, 46
hoka, other, 189
hon, book, 29
-hon (counter), 45, 49
hontō ni, really, truly, 101
hon-ya, book store/seller, 45, 74
hoteru, hotel, 91
hyaku, one hundred, 33, 41

ichi, one, 28
ichi-do, once, one time, 137
1(ichi)-ji han, half past one, 33
ichiman, ten thousand, 41
ichioku, one hundred million, 41
Igirisu, United Kingdom, 48
ii, good, 79
ii desu ne, It's/That's nice/good/all right, 79
iie, no, 20, 23
iie, dame desu, No, you can't, 155
iie, mō kekkō desu, No, (thank you). That was enough, 95
iimasu, iu, say, speak, 137
ikaga, how, 95
ikaga desu ka, How is it, 95, 96
ikimasu, iku, go, is going, will go, 53
ikkagetsu, (for) one month, 180
1-kai (ikkai), first floor, ground floor, 68
ikura, how much, 39, 146
ikutsu, how many, 46, 76
ima, living room, 66
ima, now, 32
imasu, iru, is/are (animate), 66
imasu, iru, stay, 130
imōto, imōto-san, younger sister, 126, 169
ippai, 1 cupful/glassful/bottleful, 95
irasshaimase, Come in, Welcome, 39
irasshaimashita, came, 61; *irasshaimasu, irassharu*, is/are, 61, 88
iriguchi, entrance, 76
iro, color, 108
iroiro(na), various, 174
isha, doctor, 180
isogashii, busy, 100
issho ni, together (with), 114
isu, chair, 66
itadakimasu, itadaku, eat, 95, 96
itai, aching, painful, 176
Itaria, Italy, 48
itoko, cousin, 169
itsu, when, 32, 36
itsuka, 5th day of the month, 35
itsutsu, five, 49
itte kudasai, Please say/speak, 137
iyahōn, earphones, 61, 104

ja, well then, 39

-ji, o'clock, 32
jikan, time, 124
-jikan, (for) . . . hours, 133
-jin, person (suffix), 23
jisho, dictionary, 110
jogingu o shimasu (suru), jog, 92
jōzu(na), good at, skillful, 176
jū, ten, 28
jugyō, class, lesson, 126
18(jūhachi)-nichi, 18th day of the month, 33, 35
11(jūichi)-nichi, 11th day of the month, 35
10(jū)-ji, 10 o'clock, 32
10(jū)-mai, 10 sheets, 49
12(jūni)-hon, 12 bottles, 49
jūsho, address, 29
jūsu, juice, 83
jūyokka, 14th day of the month, 35

ka (question marker, particle), 20, 23
kabin, vase, 108
kabuki, kabuki (Japanese theater), 78
kado, corner, 138
kaerimasu, kaeru, return, come/go back, 53
-kagetsu, (for) . . . month(s), 180
kagi, key, 29
kagu, furniture, 174
-kai, floor (counter), 68
kaigi, conference, meeting, 36
kaigi o shimasu (suru), hold a meeting/conference, 86; *kaigi o shite imasu*, be holding a meeting, be in conference, 158, 159
kaigi-shitsu, conference/meeting room, 158
kaimashita, bought; *kaimasu, kau*, buy, 79
kaimono, shopping, 83
kaimono o shimasu (suru), shop, 81
kaisatsuguchi, ticket gate, 76
kaisha, company, 26
kaishain, company employee, 23
kakarimasu, kakaru, (it) takes/costs, 145, 146
kakemasu, kakeru, sit, 61
kakimasu, kaku, write, draw, 89
kamera, camera, 44
kamera-ya, camera store/clerk, camera seller, 44
-kan, for (a period of time), 132
Kanada, Canada, 62
kanai, wife, 111, 169
kangaekata, way of thinking, 189
kangeikai, welcome party, 121
kanji (Chinese characters), 111
kanrinin, superintendent, 73
kara, from (particle), 32, 56
kara, so, because (particle), 73
kasa, umbrella, 39, 42
katarogu, catalogue, 150
ka-yōbi, Tuesday, 35

kazoku, family, 83, 169
keikan, policeman, 154
keizai, economy, 189
kēki, cake, 139
kekkon, marriage, 126; *kekkon shite imasu*, be married, 168
kekkon-shiki, wedding, 126
keshimasu, kesu, turn/switch off, 121
kēsu, showcase, 150
ki, tree, 101
kibun, feeling, 180
kikimasu, kiku, listen, hear, 83; ask, 90, 91
kimashita, came, 54, 56; *kimasu, kuru*, come, 56
kinō, yesterday, 33
kin-yōbi, Friday, 33, 35
ki o tsukete, Take care, Be careful, 166
kippu, ticket, 76
kippu-uriba, ticket office, 76
kirei(na), pretty, clean, 95
kiro, kilogram, 49
kissaten, coffee shop, café, 83
kitte, postage stamp, 49
ko, child, 66
kōban, police box, 76
kōcha, black tea, 83
kochira, this one, this person, 19, 21; *kochira*, here, this way, this direction, 61
kodomo, child, 69, 169
kōen, park, 95, 100
kōhī, coffee, 83
kōkanshu, switchboard/telephone operator, 92
koko, here, this place, 76
kokonoka, 9th day of the month, 35
kokonotsu, nine, 48
kōkūbin, airmail, 180
komban, this evening, tonight, 83
konde imasu, komimasu, komu, be crowded, 189
kongetsu, this month, 126
kono, this, 46, 47
konshū, this week, 130
kopī, photocopy, 121; *kopī o shimasu (suru)*, 120
koppu, mug, glass, cup, 117
kore, this (one), 26, 39, 46
kōsaten, intersection, 139
koto, thing, 174
kotoshi, this year, 86
ku, nine, 28
kudamono, fruit, 179
kudasai, Please give (me) . . . , 39
9(ku)-ji, 9 o'clock, 32
kukkī, cookie, 96
kūkō, airport, 57
kurai, dark, 121
kuremasu, kureru, give, 109

kurīningu, dry cleaning; *kurīningu-ya*, dry cleaner, 143
kurisumasu kādo, Christmas card, 91
kuroi, black, 50
kuruma, car, vehicle, 29
kusuri, medicine, 76
kusuri-ya, pharmacy, drug store, 76
kutsu, shoes, 83
kutsushita, socks, 179
kyō, today, 33
kyōdai, brothers, sisters, siblings, 126, 169
kyonen, last year, 54, 56
kyū, nine, 28

machi, town, street, community, 106, 137
machimasu, matsu, wait, 92
mada desu, not yet, 143
made, to, as far as (particle), 145
made, until (particle), 32
made ni, by (particle), 137
mado, window, 68
mae, in front of, before, 68
magatte kudasai, Please turn; *magarimasu, magaru*, turn, 138
mago, grandchild, 169
-mai (counter), 45, 49
mai-, every, 80
maiasa, every morning, 83
maiban, every evening/night, 83
maido, each (every) time; *maido arigatō gozaimasu*, Thank you (for your patronage) each time, 137
mainen, every year, 91
mainichi, every day, 54, 80
maishū, every week, 83
maitsuki, every month, 189
massugu, straight, straight ahead, 142
mata, again, 88
matsuri, festival, 179
matte kudasai, Please wait; *machimasu, matsu*, wait, 130, 138
megane, (eye)glasses, 76
mei, meigo-san, niece, 169
meishi, business card, name card, 26
menyū, menu, 139
meron, melon, 183
meshiagatte kudasai, Please eat/have (some), 95
migi, right, 138
mikan, tangerine, 49
mikka, 3rd day of the month, 35
mikka, (for) 3 days, 130
mimasu, miru, see, watch, look at, 78, 130
mina-sama, everyone, 190
mina-sama ni dōzo yoroshiku, Best regards to everyone, 190
minna, mina-san, everyone, 166

miruku, milk, 83

mise, store, shop, 91

misete kudasai, Please show me; *misemasu, miseru*, show, 39

mite imasu (iru), is looking, is watching, 158

mittsu, three, 45

mizu, water, 42

mo, too (particle), 39

mō, already, 79, 96

mō, more (another), 95

moku-yōbi, Thursday, 33, 35

moraimashita, received; *moraimasu, morau*, receive, 108, 109

moshi moshi, hello, 88; I say, 154

mō sugu, very soon, 190

mottekite kudasai, Please bring; *mottekimasu, mottekuru*, bring, 137

muika, 6th day of the month, 35

musuko, musuko-san, son, 127, 169

musume, musume-san, daughter, 127, 169

muttsu, six, 48

muzukashii, difficult, hard, 100

naisen-bangō, extension number, 91

naka, inside, 68

namae, name, 26

nana, seven, 28

nanatsu, seven, 48

nan-ban, what number, 27, 29

nan-bon, how many bottles, 76

nangatsu, which month, 32

nani/nan, what, 27, 29; *nani/nan de*, how, by what means, 62, 63

nani mo, nothing; *nani mo . . . -masen*, nothing is, 69

nan-ji, what time, 32

nan-jikan, how many hours, 146

nanji made ni, by what time, 137

nan-mai, how many sheets, 76

nan-nen, what year, 63

nan-nichi, which day of the month, how many days, 32, 36, 146

nan-nin, how many people, 76

nanoka, 7th day of the month, 35

nan-pun, how many minutes, 146

nan-sai, how old, 127

nan-yōbi, which day of the week, 32, 36

natsu, summer, 37

natsu-yasumi, summer vacation, 37

ne, Isn't it/Aren't there, 70, 73

nekutai, necktie, 110

-nen, year, 63

nengajō, New Year's card, 91

netsu, fever, 180

ni, in, at (particle), 66

ni, on (particle), 61, 145

ni, to (particle), 53, 114, 115

ni, to, from (particle), 79, 88, 108, 109

ni, two, 28

-nichi, day, 33

nichi-yōbi, Sunday, 35

ni chōme ni no ichi, 2-chōme 2-1 (address), 137

nigiyaka(na), lively, 99, 104

Nihon, Japan, 23

Nihon Ginkō, Bank of Japan, 23

Nihon-go, Japanese language, 48

Nihon-jin, a Japanese, 23

2(ni)-jikan, 2 hours, 133

nijū, twenty, 28

20(niju)ppun gurai, (for) about 20 minutes, 101

nijūyokka, 24th day of the month, 35

2(ni)-kiro, 2 kilograms, 48

niku, meat, 76

niku-ya, meat store, butcher, 76

nimotsu, parcel, 180

-nin, person/people (counter), 74

ni tsuite, concerning, about, 174

niwa, garden, 66

ni yoroshiku, Best regards to, 21, 190

no (possessive particle), 19, 21

no ato de, after, 132

nodo, throat, 178

no mae ni, before, in front of, 68, 133

nomimasu, nomu, drink, take (medicine), 81, 83

nomimono, beverage, drink, 174, 183

-noriba, boarding place, 74

norimashita, got on; *norimasu, noru*, get on, ride, take, 145

nyūsu, news, 83

o, from, out of (particle), 146

o (object marker, particle), 39, 79

o- (honorific), 69

oba, oba-san, aunt, 169

obā-san, grandmother, 169

o-cha, tea, 83

o-genki de, Take care of yourself, 190

ohairi kudasai, Do come in, 61

oi, oigo-san, nephew, 169

oishii, good, tasty, delicious, 95

o-itoko-san, cousin, 169

oji, oji-san, uncle, 169

ojī-san, grandfather, 169

ojō-san, daughter, 127, 169

okake kudasai, Do sit down, 61

o-kane, money, 126

okāsan, mother, 91, 169

o-kashi, cake, 95

ōkii, big, large, 48

okosan, child, 127

okurimasu, okuru, send, 178

okusan, wife, 66, 169

o-kyaku-san, client, customer, guest, 161

omachi kudasai, Please wait, 92

omaneki arigatō gozamiasu, Thank you for your invitation, 166

omoshiroi, entertaining, interesting, 100

onaka, stomach, abdomen, 178

onegaishimasu, Please (do) . . . , 88

o-nē-san, older sister, 169

ongaku, music, 83

o-nii-san, older brother, 168, 169

onna, woman, female; *onna no hito*, woman, 32

onna no ko, girl, 68

onsen, hot spring, spa, 179

orite, get off (and); *orimasu, oriru*, get off, 130, 145

o-sake, Japanese rice wine, 83

oshiemasu, oshieru, tell, show, teach, 90, 91

oshimasu, osu, push, 130

osoi, late, slow, 166

o-taku, residence, 88

o-tearai, lavatory, toilet, 69

o-tera, temple, 130

otoko, man, male; *otoko no hito*, man, 58

otoko no ko, boy, 66

otōsan, father, 91, 169

otōto, otōto-san , younger brother, 169

ototoi, the day before yesterday, 63

otsuri, change, 142

owarimasu, owaru, finish, end, 190

pan, bread, 76

pan-ya, bread store, bakery, 76

pātī, party, 36

pen, pen, 61, 151

posuto, mail box, post box, 73

pureigaido, theater booking agency, 79

raigetsu, next month, 63

rainen, next year, 56

raishū, next week, 63

rajio, radio, 42

rei, zero, 28

rekishi, history, 110

rekōdo, record, 83

reshīto, receipt, 42

resutoran, restaurant, 80

ringo, apple, 42

roku, six, 28

6(roku)-gatsu, June, 33

6(roku)-ji, 6 o'clock, 32

ryokō, trip, travel, 106; *ryokō o shimasu (suru)*, take a trip, travel, 129, 198

ryokō-gaisha, travel agency, 168

ryōri, food, cooking, cuisine, 106

ryōshin, parents, 169

sā, well, let me see, 152, 175

-sai, . . . years old (counter), 127

saikin, nowadays, recently, 190

sakana, fish, 76

sakana-ya, fish shop/seller, 45, 76

saka-ya, liquor store, 76

sake, Japanese rice wine, 83

-sama, Mr., Mrs., Ms., Miss, 143

sampo, a walk; *sampo o shimasu (suru)*, take a walk, 116

samukatta, was cold; *samui*, cold, 104

san, three, 28

-san, Mr., Mrs., Ms., Miss, 19

sandoitchi, sandwich, 83

39(sanjūku)-do, 39 degrees, 180

san-nin, 3 people, 54

sanzen-en, 3, 000 yen, 39

sarada, salad, 83

seiji, politics, 189

sen, one thousand, 41

sengetsu, last month, 57

sensei, teacher, professor, 91, 189

senshū, last week, 54, 56

sētā, sweater, 171

setsumei, explanation, 104

shakai, society, community life, social conditions, 189

shashin, photograph, 68; *shashin o torimasu (toru)*, take a photograph, 150; *shashin o totte mo ii desu ka*, May I take a photograph, 150

shi, four, 28

shichi, seven, 28

shīdī, CD, compact disc, 83

shigoto, work, 36; *shigoto o shimasu (suru)*, work, 81

shiki, ceremony, 126

shimasu, suru, do, 78

shimbun, newspaper, 29

shimemasu, shimeru, close, shut, 121

shingō, traffic light, 139

Shinkansen, Shinkansen, New Trunk Line, 63

shinsetsu(na), kind, helpful, 100

shisha, branch office, 53

shita, under, beneath, 69

shite imasu (iru), be doing, 158, 168

shitsu, room, 158

shitsurei, rudeness, 61; *shitsurei shimasu*, May I, Excuse me, I'm sorry, Good-bye, 61, 88

shitte imasu (shiru), know, 170

shizuka(na), quiet, calm, 97

shokudō, dining room, cafeteria, lunch room, restaurant, 69, 86

shokuji, meal; *shokuji o shimasu (suru)*, have a meal, eat, 100

shōshō, a moment, 92

shujin, husband, 169

-shūkan, weeks (counter), 134

shūmatsu, weekend, 78

shutchō, business trip, 53; *shutchō desu ka*, Is it a business trip (you're going on), 53

sōbetsukai, farewell party, 119

sobo, grandmother, 169

sochira, there, that way, that person, 199

sō desu, That's right, 26

sō desu ka, I see, 88

sō desu nē, Let me see, 180

sofu, grandfather, 169

soko, there, that place, 76

sono, that, 44, 46

sore, that (one), 39, 46

sorekara, and, and then, after that, 45, 130

soshite, and then, 53

subarashii, wonderful, 152

suimasu, suu, smoke, inhale, 155

sui-yōbi, Wednesday, 35

sukī, skiing, 114

suki(na), like, likeable, favorite, 109

sukiyaki, sukiyaki, 183

sukoshi, a little, 134

sukunai, a little, 191

sumimasen, Excuse me, I'm sorry, 32, 155

sunde imasu, live, is living; *sumimasu, sumu*, live, 168

sūpā, supermarket, 73

sūpu, soup, 83

supūn, spoon, 117

suraido, slide, 158

suwanaide kudasai, Do not smoke, 155

tabako, tobacco, cigarette, 155

tabemashita, ate; *tabemasu, taberu*, eat, 80

-tachi, (plural suffix for people), 100

taipu, typing, 89, 138; *taipu o shimasu (suru)*, 198

taishikan, embassy, 23

takai, expensive, high, 100

takusan, many, lots of, 74

takushī, taxi, 61

takushī-noriba, taxi stand, 74

tamago, egg, 100

tana, shelf, 68

tanjōbi, birthday, 33

tanoshii, enjoyable, 106

tanoshimi ni shite imasu (iru), be looking forward to, 190

tansu, chest of drawers, 174

tatemono, building, 74

tēburu, table, 66

tegami, letter, 83

tekisuto, text, 190

temae, just before, this side of, 142

ten, (decimal) point, 41

ten'in, store clerk, 39

tenisu, tennis, 83; *tenisu o shimasu (suru)*, play tennis, 81, 198

tenki, weather, 101

tēpu, tape, 48

tēpurekōdā, tape recorder, 42

terebi, television, TV set, 42

to, and (particle), 66

to, with (particle), 53

tō, ten, 45

todana, closet, cabinet, cupboard, 68

todokemashō ka, Shall we deliver; *todokemasu, todokeru*, deliver, 137

tōi, far, 97

tōka, 10th day of the month, 35

tokei, clock, watch, 27

tokidoki, sometimes, 86

tokoro, place, 189

tomato, tomato, 179

tomete kudasai, Please stop, 142; *tomemasu, tomeru*, park, stop, 138, 154; *tomenaide kudasai*, Do not park, 154

tomodachi, friend, 57

tonari, next to, 73

torimasu, toru, take, 150

tori-niku, chicken meat, 100

toshokan, library, 178

totemo, very, 95

tsugi, next, 138

tsugō, condition, 117; *tsugō ga warui desu*, conditions are unfavorable, 114, 117

tsuitachi, 1st day of the month, 35

tsukatte mo ii desu, You may use it; *tsukaimasu, tsukau*, use, 150

tsukete mo ii desu ka, May I turn (it) on, 149; *tsukemasu, tsukeru*, switch/turn on, 121

tsukimashita, arrived; *tsukimasu, tsuku*, arrive, 146

tsukue, desk, table, 174

tsukurimashita, made, formed; *tsukurimasu, tsukuru*, form, make, build, 189

tsumaranai, boring, uninteresting, 98

tsumetai, cold, 191

tsutomete imasu, be employed, work for; *tsutomemasu, tsutomeru*, serve, work for, 168

uchi, home, house, 26, 88

ue, top, 66

ueitoresu, waitress, 139

uketsuke, reception, 70

umi, sea, ocean, 117

untenshu, driver, 142

-uriba, selling place, 76

urusai, noisy, 121

utte imasu, sell, is selling; *urimasu, uru*, sell, 170

wa (topic marker, particle), 19
wain, wine, 166
wakarimashita, Sure, Certainly, I see, 89, 114
wakarimashita, understood; *wakarimasu, wakaru*, understand, 73, 104, 174
warui, bad, 97
watashi, I, 19
watashi no, my, 26
watashi-tachi, we, 100

-ya, store, shop, clerk, seller, 44
ya, and (etc.), 66
yama, mountain, 178
yaoya, vegetable store, greengrocer, 76
yasai, vegetable, 100
yasashii, easy, 100
yasui, inexpensive, cheap, 100
yasumi, rest (period), vacation, holiday, day off, closing day, 33, 76, 126
yattsu, eight, 48
yo, I tell you (particle), 73
-yōbi, day of the week, 33
yobimasu, yobu, call, 130
yoi, good, 98
yōka, 8th day of the month, 35
yokka, 4th day of the month, 35

yoku, well, 61
yoku, often, 89
yoku irasshaimashita, How nice of you to come, 61
yokunai, not good, 97
yomimasu, yomu, read, 79, 83
yon, four, 28
4(yon)-shūkan, 4 weeks, 134
yorokonde (yorokobu), (I'd) love/be happy to, gladly, with pleasure, 114, 166
Yōroppa, Europe, 176
yoroshiku, regards, 21, 190
yottsu, four, 48
yoyaku, reservation, 143
yūbinkyoku, post office, 36
yūgata, late afternoon, early evening, 147
yukkuri, slowly, 139
yūmei(na), famous, well known, 95, 100

zannen(na), regrettable; *zannen desu ga*, I'm sorry, but . . . , 114, 116
zasshi, magazine, 83
zehi, by all means, 114, 119
zenzen . . . -masen, never (do), 91
zenzen . . . -masen, not at all, 104
zero, zero, 26, 28

ENGLISH-JAPANESE GLOSSARY

Note: Idiomatic expressions have been omitted, as well as counters, particles that have no independent meaning and words listed in some appendices. Since equivalents differ in nuance, refer to the pages listed to check context and usage.

about, *goro*, 86, 89; *gurai*, 101, 145
about (concerning), *ni tsuite*, 174
aching, *itai*, 176
address, *jūsho*, 29
after, *(no) ato de*, 132
afternoon (p.m.), *gogo*, 32
after that, *sorekara*, 130
afterwards, *ato de*, 88
again, *mata*, 88
airmail, *kōkūbin*, 180
airplane, *hikōki*, 76
airport, *kūkō*, 57
a little, *chotto*, 127; *sukoshi*, 134; *sukunai*, 191
alone, *hitori de*, 53
already, *mō*, 79, 96
and, *to*, 66; and (etc.), *ya*, 66
and then, *sorekara*, 45; *soshite*, 53
apple, *ringo*, 42
approximately, *gurai*, 101, 145
arm, *ude*, 193
arrive, *tsukimasu (tsuku)*, 146
as far as, *made*, 145
ashtray, *haizara*, 42
ask, *kikimasu (kiku)*, 90, 91
at, *ni*, 66; *de*, 79
aunt, *oba, oba-san*, 169

baby, *akachan*, 117
back, *senaka*, 193
bad, *warui*, 97
bakery, *pan-ya*, 76
banana, *banana*, 20
bank, *ginkō*, 23
basement, *chika*, 170
battery, *denchi*, 46
be able, *dekimasu (dekiru)*, 174, 176
because, *kara*, 73
beef, *gyū-niku*, 100
beer, *bīru*, 49
before, *mae*, 68; *(no) mae ni*, 133
begin, *hajimeru*, 25
be married, *kekkon shite iru*, 168
beneath, *shita*, 69
beverage, *nomimono*, 174, 183
big, *ōkii*, 48
birthday, *tanjōbi*, 33

black, *kuroi*, 50
black tea, *kōcha*, 83
blue, *aoi*, 50
body, *karada*, 193
book, *hon*, 29
book store/seller, *hon-ya*, 45, 74
boring, *tsumaranai*, 98
box, *hako*, 68
boy, *otoko no ko*, 66
branch office, *shisha*, 53
bread, *pan*, 76
breakfast, *asa-gohan*, 83
bright, *akarui*, 191
bring, *mottekimasu (mottekuru)*, 137
brothers/sisters, *kyōdai*, 126, 169
brown, *chairoi, chairo no*, 191
build, *tsukurimasu (tsukuru)*, 189
building, *biru*, 70; *tatemono*, 74
bus, *basu*, 57
business card, *meishi*, 26
business trip, *shutchō*, 53
bus terminal, *basu-noriba*, 76
busy, *isogashii*, 100
but, *ga*, 86; *demo*, 121
butcher, *niku-ya*, 76
buy, *kaimasu (kau)*, 79
by, *de*, 61; *made ni*, 137
by all means, *zehi*, 114, 119

cabinet, *todana*, 68
café, *kissaten*, 83
cafeteria, *shokudō*, 86
cake, *kēki*, 139; *o-kashi*, 95
call, *yobimasu (yobu)*, 130
calm, *shizuka(na)*, 97
camera, *kamera*, 44
camera store/clerk, *kamera-ya*, 44
can, *dekimasu (dekiru)*, 174, 176
car, *kuruma*, 29
catalogue, *katarogu*, 150
CD (compact disk), *shīdī*, 83
ceremony, *shiki*, 126
chair, *isu*, 66
change, *otsuri*, 142
cheap, *yasui*, 100
cheek, *hoho*, 193
chest, *mune*, 193
chest of drawers, *tansu*, 174
chicken (meat), *tori-niku*, 100
child, *ko*, 66; *kodomo*, 69, 169; *okosan*, 127
chin, *ago*, 193
Christmas card, *kurisumasu kado*, 91
cigarette, *tabako*, 155

class, *jugyō*, 126
clean, *kirei(na)*, 95
client, *o-kyaku-san*, 161
clock, *tokei*, 27
close, *shimeru*, 121
close, *chikai*, 98
close (to), *(no) chikaku ni/de*, 68
closet, *todana*, 68
coffee, *kōhī*, 83
coffee shop, *kissaten*, 83
cold, *samui*, 104; *tsumetai*, 191
color, *iro*, 108
come, *kimasu (kuru)*, 56
come back, *kaerimasu (kaeru)*, 53
come in, *hairimasu (hairu)*, 61, 150
company, *kaisha*, 26
concerning, *ni tsuite*, 174
condition, *tsugō*, 117
conference, *kaigi*, 36
conference room, *kaigi-shitsu*, 158
convenient, *benri(na)*, 100
cookie, *kukkī*, 96
cooking, *ryōri*, 106
cool, *suzushii*, 191
corner, *kado*, 138
correct, *tadashii*, 191
cost, *kakarimasu (kakaru)*, 145, 146
cousin, *itoko, o-itoko-san*, 169
crowded (be), *komimasu (komu)*, 189
cuisine, *ryōri*, 106
culture, *bunka*, 189
cup, *koppu*, 117
cupboard, *todana*, 68
customer, *o-kyaku-san*, 161

dangerous, *abunai*, 191
dark, *kurai*, 121
daughter, *musume, musume-san*, 127, 169; *ojo-san*, 127, 169
day, *hi*, 166; *-nichi*, 33
day after tomorrow, *asatte*, 53
day before yesterday, *ototoi*, 63
day off, *yasumi*, 126
daytime, *hiru*, 33
decimal point, *ten*, 41
degree, *-do*, 180
delicious, *oishii*, 95
deliver, *todokemasu (todokeru)*, 137
department store, *depāto*, 32
desk, *tsukue*, 174
dessert, *dezāto*, 183
dictionary, *jisho*, 110
difficult, *muzukashii*, 100
dining room, *shokudō*, 69
dinner, *ban-gohan*, 83
dirty, *kitanai*, 191
do, *shimasu (suru)*, 78

doctor, *isha*, 180
door, *doa*, 121
draw, *kakimasu (kaku)*, 89
drink, *nomimasu (nomu)*, 81, 83
drink, *nomimono*, 174, 183
drive, *unten o shimasu (suru)*, 198
drive, driving, *doraibu*, 116
driver, *untenshu*, 142
drug store, *kusuri-ya*, 76
dry clean, *kurīningu o shimasu (suru)* 198
dry cleaner, *kurīningu-ya*, 143
dry cleaning, *kurīningu*, 143

ear, *mimi*, 193
early, *hayai*, 191
earphones, *iyahōn*, 61, 104
east, *higashi*, 53
easy, *yasashii*, 100
eat, *itadakimasu (itadaku)*, 95, 96; *tabemasu (taberu)*, 80
economy, *keizai*, 189
egg, *tamago*, 100
eight, *hachi*, 28; *yattsu*, 48
electrical appliance store/clerk, *denki-ya*, 150
embassy, *taishikan*, 22
employed (be), *tsutomemasu (tsutomeru)*, 168
employee (company), *kaishain*, 23
end, *owarimasu (owaru)*, 190
English, *Ei-go*, 104
enjoyable, *tanoshii*, 106
enter, *hairimasu (hairu)*, 61, 150
entertaining, *omoshiroi*, 100
entrance, *iriguchi*, 76
entrance hall, *genkan*, 68
Europe, *Yōroppa*, 176
evening (early), *yugata*, 147
evening meal, *ban-gohan*, 83
everyone, *mina-sama*, 190; *minna, mina-san*, 166
exit, *deguchi*, 156
expensive, *takai*, 100
explain, *setsumei o shimasu (suru)*, 198
explanation, *setsumei*, 104
extension number, *naisen-bangō*, 91
eye, *me*, 193
eyebrow, *mayu, mayuge*, 93
eyeglasses, *megane*, 76
eyelash, *matsuge*, 193
eyelid, *mabuta*, 193

family, *kazoku*, 83
famous, *yūmei(na)*, 95, 100
far, *tōi*, 97
farewell party, *sōbetsukai*, 119
fast, *hayai*, 191
father, *chichi*, 110; *otōsan*, 91, 169
favorite, *suki(na)*, 109

feeling, *kibun*, 180
festival, *matsuri*, 179
fever, *netsu*, 180
few, *sukunai*, 191
film, *fuirumu*, 39, 45
film (movie), *eiga*, 36
finger, *yubi*, 193
finish, *owarimasu (owaru)*, 190
finished (be), *dekimasu (dekiru)*, 143
fish, *sakana*, 76
fish shop/seller, *sakana-ya*, 45, 76
five, *go*, 28; *itsutsu*, 49
florist, *hana-ya*, 45
flower, *hana*, 66
flower shop, *hana-ya*, 45
foot, *ashi*, 193
forehead, *hitai*, 193
foreign country, *gaikoku*, 171
four, *shi*, *yon*, 28; *yottsu*, 48
free, *hima(na)*, 100
fresh, *atarashii*, 100
Friday, *kin-yōbi*, 33, 35
friend, *tomodachi*, 57
from, *kara*, 32, 56
fruit, *kudamono*, 179
furniture, *kagu*, 174

garden, *niwa*, 66
get off, *orimasu (oriru)*, 130, 145
get on, *norimasu (noru)*, 145
girl, *onna no ko*, 68
give, *agemasu (ageru)*, 109; *kuremasu (kureru)*, 109
give a party, *patī o shimasu (suru)*, 198
glass, *koppu*, 117
glasses (eyeglasses), *megane*, 76
go, *ikimasu (iku)*, 53
go back, *kaerimasu (kaeru)*, 53
go driving/for a drive, *doraibu o shimasu (suru)*, 198
go in, *hairimasu (hairu)*, 61
golf, *gorufu*, 106
good, *ii*, 79; *yoi*, 98
good at, *jozu(na)*, 176
grandchild, *mago*, 169
grandfather, *ojī-san*, 169; *sofu*, 169
grandmother, *obā-san*, 169; *sobo*, 169
green, *midoriro no*, 191
greengrocer, *yaoya*, 76
group, *gurūpu*, 189
guest, *o-kyaku-san*, 161

hair, *kami*, 193
half, *han*, 30
hand, *te*, 193
hard, *muzukashii*, 100
have, *arimasu (aru)*, 124

have a headache, *atama ga itai*, 176
have a meal, *shokuji o shimasu (suru)*, 100
head, *atama*, 176
healthy, *genki(na)*, 100
hear, *kikimasu (kiku)*, 83
heater, *hītā*, 121
heavy, *omoi*, 191
hello, *moshi moshi*, 88
helpful, *shinsetsu(na)*, 100
here, *kochira*, 61; *koko*, 76
high, *takai*, 100
hiking, *haikingu*, 117
hip, *koshi*, 193
history, *rekishi*, 110
hold a meeting, *kaigi o shimasu (suru)*, 86
holiday, *yasumi*, 76
home, *uchi*, 26
hospital, *byōin*, 74
hot (temperature), *atsui*, 104; (spicy) *karai*, 191
hot spring, *onsen*, 179
hotel, *hoteru*, 91
house, *uchi*, 26, 88
how, *dō*, 103; *dōyatte*, 145; *ikaga*, 95; *nani/nan de*, 62, 63
how long, *donogurai*, 134
how many, *ikutsu*, 46, 76
how much, *donogurai*, 146; *ikura*, 39
husband, *go-shujin*, 88; *shujin*, 169

I, *watashi*, 19
ice cream, *aisukurimu*, 184
important, *daiji(na)*, 191
in, *ni*, 66
inconvenient, *fuben(na)*, 191
inexpensive, *yasui*, 100
in front of, *mae*, 68; *(no) mae ni*, 133
inside, *naka*, 68
interesting, *omoshiroi*, 100
intersection, *kōsaten*, 139
introduce, *shōkai o shimasu (suru)*, 198
is/are (animate), *imasu (iru)*, 66
is/are (inanimate), *arimasu (aru)*, 20, 66

Japanese rice wine, *sake*, *o-sake*, 83
jaw, *ago*, 193
jog, *jogingu o shimasu (suru)*, 92
juice, *jūsu*, 83
just before, *temae*, 142

key, *kagi*, 29
kind, *shinsetsu(na)*, 100
kitchen, *daidokoro*, 66
know, *shirimasu (shiru)*, 170

large, *ōkii*, 48
late, *osoi*, 166
late afternoon, *yūgata*, 147

later, *ato de*, 88
lavatory, *o-tearai*, 69
lawyer, *bengoshi*, 19
leave, *demasu (deru)*, 146
left, *hidari*, 139
left-hand side, *hidari-gawa*, 155
leg, *ashi*, 193
lesson, *jugyō*, 126
letter, *tegami*, 83
library, *toshokan*, 178
light, *karui*, 191
light (electric), *denki*, 121
likable, *suki(na)*, 109
lip, *kuchibiru*, 193
liquor store, *saka-ya*, 76
listen, *kikimasu (kiku)*, 83
live, *sumimasu (sumu)*, 168
lively, *nigiyaka(na)*, 99, 104
living room, *ima*, 66
long, *nagai*, 191
look at, *mimasu (miru)*, 78, 130
look forward to, *tanoshimi ni shite imasu*, 190
lots of, *takusan*, 74
low, *hikui*, 191
lunch, *hiru-gohan*, 80
lunch time, *hiru-yasumi*, 33

mail box, *posuto*, 73
magazine, *zasshi*, 83
make, *tsukurimasu (tsukuru)*, 189
make a phone call, *denwa o shimasu (suru)*, 79, 89
make a reservation, *yoyaku o shimasu (suru)*, 198
man, *otoko, otoko no hito*, 58
many, *takusan*, 74; *ōi*, 191
map, *chizu*, 83
marriage, *kekkon*, 126
marry, *kekkon shimasu (suru)*, 168
meal, *gohan*, 80; *shokuji*, 100
meat, *niku*, 76
meat store, *niku-ya*, 76
medicine, *kusuri*, 76
meet, *aimasu (au)*, 89
meeting, *kaigi*, 36
meeting room, *kaigi-shitsu*, 158
melon, *meron*, 183
menu, *menyū*, 139
milk, *miruku*, 83
minute, *-fun (-pun)*, 32
Monday, *getsu-yōbi*, 35
money, *o-kane*, 126
month(s), *-gatsu*, 33
morning, *asa*, 83
morning (a.m.), *gozen*, 33
mother, *haha, okāsan*, 91
mountain, *yama*, 178

mouth, *kuchi*, 193
movie, *eiga*, 36
much, *ōi*, 191
mug, *koppu*, 117
music, *ongaku*, 83
my, *watashi no*, 26

nail, *tsume*, 193
name, *namae*, 26
narrow, *semai*, 191
near, *chikai*, 98; *(no) chikaku ni/de*, 68
neck, *kubi*, 193
necktie, *nekutai*, 110
nephew, *oi, oigo-san*, 169
never (do) . . . , *zenzen . . . -masen*, 91
new, *atarashii*, 100
news, *nyūsu*, 83
New Year's card, *nengajō*, 91
newspaper, *shimbun*, 29
next, *tsugi*, 138
next to, *tonari*, 73
niece, *mei, meigo-san*, 169
nine, *kyū, ku*, 28; *kokonotsu*, 48
no, *iie*, 20, 23
nobody, *dare mo . . . -masen*, 66
no good, *dame*, 155; *dame(na)*, 191
noisy, *urusai*, 121
noon, *hiru*, 33
no parking, *chūsha kinshi*, 154
nose, *hana*, 193
not at all, *zenzen . . . -masen,,* 104
not good, *yokunai*, 98
nothing, *nani mo*, 69
not often, *amari . . . -masen*, 89
not very, *amari*, 97
not yet, *mada desu*, 143
now, *ima*, 32
nowadays, *saikin*, 190
nowhere, *doko ni mo*, 67
number, *bangō*, 26

ocean, *umi*, 117
often, *yoku*, 89
old, *furui*, 100
older brother, *ani, o-nii-san*, 168, 169
older sister, *ane*, 110; *o-nē-san*, 169
on, *ni*, 61, 145
once, *ichi-do*, 137
one, *ichi*, 28; *hitotsu*, 47
one hundred, *hyaku*, 33, 41
one thousand, *sen*, 41
one time, *ichi-do*, 137
only, *dake*, 130
open, *akemasu (akeru)*, 120; open, *hirakimasu (hiraku)*, 32
other, *hoka*, 189
over there, *asoko*, 70; *achira*, 199

painful, *itai*, 176
parcel, *nimotsu*, 180
parents, *ryōshin, go-ryōshin*, 169
park, *kōen*, 95, 100
park, *tomemasu (tomeru)*, 138, 142, 154
parking lot, *chūshajō*, 155
part, *bun*, 41
party, *pātī*, 36
pen, *pen*, 61, 151
person, *hito*, 32
pharmacy, *kusuri-ya*, 76
photocopy, *kopī, kopī o shimasu (suru)*, 120
photograph, *shashin*, 68
picture, *e*, 83
place, *tokoro*, 189
play golf, *gorufu o shimasu (suru)*, 198
play tennis, *tenisu o shimasu (suru)*, 81, 198
pleasant, *tanoshii*, 191
police box, *kōban*, 76
policeman, *keikan*, 154
polite, *teinei(na)*, 191
politics, *seiji*, 189
postage stamp, *kitte*, 49
post box, *posuto*, 73
postcard, *hagaki*, 68
post office, *yūbinkyoku*, 36
pretty, *kirei(na)*, 95
professor, *sensei*, 91, 189
purple, *murasaki no*, 191
push, *oshimasu (osu)*, 130

quiet, *shizuka(na)*, 97

radio, *rajio*, 42
read, *yomimasu (yomu)*, 79, 83
really, *hontō ni*, 101
receipt, *reshīto*, 42
receive, *moraimasu (morau)*, 108, 109
recently, *saikin*, 190
reception, *uketsuke*, 70
record, *rekōdo*, 83
red, *akai*, 48
reservation, *yoyaku*, 143; make a reservation, *yoyaku o shimasu (suru)*, 198
residence, *o-taku*, 88
rest (period), *yasumi*, 33
restaurant, *resutoran*, 80; *shokudō*, 69, 86
return, *kaerimasu (kaeru)*, 53
ride, *norimasu (noru)*, 145
right, *migi*, 138
room, *heya*, 76; *shitsu*, 158
rude, *shitsurei(na)*, 191

safe, *anzen(na)*, 191
salad, *sarada*, 83
salty, *shiokarai*, 191

sandwich, *sandoitchi*, 83
Saturday, *do-yōbi*, 35
say, *iimasu (iu)*, 137
school, *gakkō*, 29
sea, *umi*, 117
sea mail, *funabin*, 61, 180
secretary, *hisho*, 23
see, *mimasu (miru)*, 78, 130
sell, *urimasu (uru)*, 170
send, *okurimasu (okuru)*, 178
seven, *nana, shichi*, 28; *nanatsu*, 48
shabu-shabu, *shabushabu*, 183
shelf, *tana*, 68
shoes, *kutsu*, 83
shop, *kaimono o shimasu (suru)*, 81
shop, *mise*, 91
shopping, *kaimono*, 83
short, *mijikai*, 191
shoulder, *kata*, 193
show, *misemasu (miseru)*, 39; *oshiemasu (oshieru)*, 90, 91
show case, *kēsu*, 150
shut, *shimemasu (shimeru)*, 121
siblings, *kyōdai*, 126, 169
sisters/brothers, *kyōdai*, 126, 169
sit, *kakemasu (kakeru)*, 61
six, *roku*, 28; *muttsu*, 48
ski, *sukī o shimasu (suru)*, 198
skiing, *sukī*, 114
skillful, *jōzu(na)*, 176
skin, *hifu*, 193
slide, *suraido*, 158
slow, *osoi*, 166
slowly, *yukkuri*, 139
small, *chiisai*, 44
smoke, *tabako o suimasu (suu)*, 155
so, *kara*, 73
society, *shakai*, 189
socks, *kutsushita*, 179
sometimes, *tokidoki*, 86
son, *musuko, musuko-san*, 127, 169; *botchan*, 169
soup, *sūpu*, 83
sour, *suppai*, 191
spa, *onsen*, 179
speak, *iimasu (iu)*, 137
spicy, *karai*, 191
spoon, *supūn*, 117
start, *demasu (deru)*, 146
station, *eki*, 56
stay, *imasu (iru)*, 130
stomach, *onaka*, 178
stop, *tomemasu (tomeru)*, 138, 142, 154
store, *mise*, 91
store clerk, *ten'in*, 39
straight ahead, *massugu*, 142
student, *gakusei*, 23

study, *benkyō o shimasu (suru)*, 80
subway, *chikatetsu*, 57
sukiyaki, *sukiyaki*, 183
summer, *natsu*, 37
summer vacation, *natsu-yasumi*, 37
Sunday, *nichi-yōbi*, 35
superintendent, *kanrinin*, 73
supermarket, *sūpā*, 73
sweater, *sētā*, 171
sweet, *amai*, 191
switchboard operator, *kōkanshu*, 92

table, *tēburu*, 66
take, *torimasu (toru)*, 150
take (get on), *norimasu (noru)*, 145
take (medicine), *nomimasu (nomu)*, 81, 83
take (time), *kakarimasu (kakaru)*, 145, 146
take a photograph, *shashin o torimasu (toru)*, 150
take a trip, *ryokō o shimasu (suru)*, 129
take a walk, *sampo o shimasu (suru)*, 116
talk, *hanashi o shimasu (suru)*, 161
tangerine, *mikan*, 49
tape, *tēpu*, 49
tape recorder, *tēpurekōdā*, 42
tasty, *oishii*, 95
taxi, *takushī*, 61
taxi stand, *takushī-noriba*, 74
tea, *cha, o-cha*, 83
teach, *oshiemasu (oshieru)*, 90, 91
teacher, *sensei*, 91
telephone, *denwa*, 26; *denwa o shimasu (suru)*, 79, 89
telephone number, *denwa-bangō*, 26
telephone operator, *kōkanshu*, 92
television, *terebi*, 42
tell, *oshiemasu (oshieru)*, 90, 91
temple, *o-tera*, 130
ten, *jū*, 28; *to*, 45
tennis, *tenisu*, 83
text, *tekisuto*, 190
Thank you very much, *dōmo arigatō gozaimasu*, 26
thanks, *dōmo*, 142, 159
that, *sono*, 44, 46
that (one), *sore*, 39, 46
that (one) over there, *are*, 40, 46
that (over there), *ano*, 46, 48
that place, *soko*, 76
that place (over there), *asoko*, 70
theater booking agency, *pureigaido*, 79
then, *soshite*, 53
there, *soko*, 76; *sochira*, 199
thing, *koto*, 174
this, *kono*, 46, 47
this (one), *kore*, 26, 39, 46
this direction, *kochira*, 61

this person, *kochira*, 19, 21
this place, *koko*, 76
this side of, *temae*, 142
this way, *kochira*, 61
three, *san*, 28; *mittsu*, 45
throat, *nodo*, 178
Thursday, *moku-yōbi*, 33, 35
ticket, *kippu*, 76
ticket gate, *kaisatsuguchi*, 76
ticket office, *kippu-uriba*, 76
time, *jikan*, 124
-times, *-do*, 137
to, *e*, 53
to, *made*, 145
to, *ni*, 53, 79, 88, 108, 109, 114, 115
tobacco, *tabako*, 155
today, *kyō*, 33
toe, *yubi*, 193
together (with), *issho ni*, 114
toilet, *o-tearai*, 69
tomato, *tomato*, 179
tomorrow, *ashita*, 33
tongue, *shita*, 193
tonight, *komban*, 83
too, *mo*, 39
tooth, *ha*, 178
top, *ue*, 66
town, *machi*, 106, 137
traffic light, *shingō*, 139
train (electric), *densha*, 56
travel, *ryokō o shimasu (suru)*, 129
travel agency, *ryokō-gaisha*, 168
tree, *ki*, 101
trip, *ryokō*, 106
truly, *hontō ni*, 101
Tuesday, *ka-yōbi*, 35
turn, *magarimasu (magaru)*, 138
turn off, *keshimasu (kesu)*, 121
turn on, *tsukemasu (tsukeru)*, 121
TV set, *terebi*, 42
two, *ni*, 28; *futatsu*, 49
type, *taipu o shimasu (suru)*, 198
typing, *taipu*, 89, 138

umbrella, *kasa*, 39, 42
uncle, *oji, oji-san*, 169
under, *shita*, 69
underground, *chika*, 170
underground railway, *chikatetsu*, 57
understand, *wakarimasu (wakaru)*, 73
uninteresting, *tsumaranai*, 98
unkind, *fushinsetsu(na)*, 191
unlikeable, *kirai(na)*, 191
unskillful, *heta(na)*, 191
until, *made*, 32
use, *tsukaimasu (tsukau)*, 150
useless, *dame*, 155

vacation, *yasumi*, 126
various, *iroiro(na)*, 174
vase, *kabin*, 108
vegetable, *yasai*, 100
vegetable store, *yaoya*, 76
vehicle, *kuruma*, 29
very, *totemo*, 95
very much, *dōmo*, 26
very soon, *mō sugu*, 190
video, *bideo*, 121

wait, *machimasu (matsu)*, 92
waitress, *weitoresu*, 139
walk, *sampo*, 116; *arukimasu (aruku)*, 145
warm, *atatakai*, 191
watch, *mimasu (miru)*, 78, 130
watch, *tokei*, 27
water, *mizu*, 42
way of thinking, *kangaekata*, 189
we, *watashi-tachi*, 100
weather, *tenki*, 101
wedding, *kekkon-shiki*, 126
Wednesday, *sui-yōbi*, 35
weekend, *shūmatsu*, 78
welcome party, *kangeikai*, 121
well, *genki(na)*, 100
well known, *yūmei(na)*, 95, 100
what, *nani/nan*, 27, 29
what kind of, *donna*, 96, 100

when, *itsu*, 32, 36
where, *doko*, 48, 80; *dochira*, 119
which, *dono*, 50
which one, *dore*, 44
white, *shiroi*, 191
who, *dare*, 21; *donata*, 21, 23
whose, *dare no*, 29
why, *dōshite*, 73, 76
wide, *hiroi*, 191
wife, *kanai*, 111, 169; *okusan*, 66, 169
window, *mado*, 68
wine, *wain*, 166
with, *to*, 53
woman, *onna, onna no hito*, 32
wonderful, *subarashii*, 152
work, *shigoto*, 36; *shigoto o shimasu (suru)*, 81
write, *kakimasu (kaku)*, 89
wrong, *chigau*, 92

yen, *en*, 39
yellow, *kiiroi, kiiro no*, 191
yes, *ee*, 26; *hai*, 23
yesterday, *kinō*, 33
you, *anata*, 21, 23
young, *wakai*, 191
younger brother, *otōto, otōto-san*, 169
younger sister, *imōto, imōto-san*, 126, 169

zero, *rei*, 28; *zero*, 26, 28

INDEX

KODANSHA INTERNATIONAL DICTIONARIES
Easy-to-use dictionaries designed for non-native learners of Japanese.

ポケット版　ローマ字和英辞典
KODANSHA'S POCKET ROMANIZED JAPANESE-ENGLISH DICTIONARY
Easy-to-use and convenient, an ideal pocket reference for beginning and intermediate students, travelers, and business people.
- 10,000-word vocabulary.   • Numerous example sentences.

Paperback, 480 pages, ISBN 4-7700-1800-2

ローマ字和英辞典
KODANSHA'S ROMANIZED JAPANESE-ENGLISH DICTIONARY
A portable reference written for beginning and intermediate students of Japanese.
- 16,000-word vocabulary.   • No knowledge of *kanji* necessary.

Vinyl binding, 688 pages, ISBN 4-7700-1603-4

ポケット版　教育漢英熟語辞典
KODANSHA'S POCKET KANJI GUIDE
A handy, pocket-sized character dictionary designed for ease of use.
- 1,006 *shin-kyoiku kanji*.   • 10,000 common compounds.
- Stroke order for individual characters.

Paperback, 576 pages, ISBN 4-7700-1801-0

常用漢英熟語辞典
KODANSHA'S COMPACT KANJI GUIDE
A functional character dictionary that is both compact and comprehensive.
- 1,945 essential *joyo kanji*.   • 20,000 common compounds.
- Three indexes for finding *kanji*.

Vinyl binding, 928 pages, ISBN 4-7700-1553-4

日本語学習使い分け辞典
EFFECTIVE JAPANESE USAGE GUIDE
A concise, bilingual dictionary which clarifies the usage of frequently confused Japanese words and phrases.
- Explanations of 708 synonymous terms.   • Numerous example sentences.

Paperback, 768 pages, ISBN 4-7700-1919-X

和英熟語慣用句辞典
A DICTIONARY OF JAPANESE & ENGLISH IDIOMATIC EQUIVALENTS
Over 10,000 Japanese and English idiomatic words and phrases, systematically organized by theme and cross-referenced for ease of use.

Vinyl binding (boxed), 336 pages, ISBN 4-7700-0789-2

Vinyl binding (Standard Edition), 336 pages, ISBN 4-7700-1843-6

ザ・コミュニケーター：ふりがな学習和英辞典
THE JAPANESE COMMUNICATOR
A Basic Japanese–English Speaking Dictionary
A new type of user-friendly dictionary which helps you put new vocabulary to good use. Not just a list of words, it provides detailed explanations of usage and carefully written sample sentences.
- 15,000-word basic vocabulary.   • Extensive cross-referencing.

Vinyl binding, 688 pages, ISBN 4-7700-1937-8

Japanese Language Learning Materials from Kodansha International

ＮＨＫラジオ日本「やさしい日本語」　全４巻
LET'S LEARN JAPANESE　*Nobuko Mizutani, Ph.D.*
Basic Conversation Skills

A four-volume series of easy lessons in practical conversational Japanese from NHK's popular Radio Japan language program. Audio cassettes of the broadcasts are also available for individual or classroom study.

Volume I:	Text	paperback, 136 pages	ISBN 4-7700-1711-1
	Tapes	three audio cassettes, 195 mins.	ISBN 4-7700-1741-3
Volume II:	Text	paperback, 136 pages	ISBN 4-7700-1784-7
	Tapes	three audio cassettes, 195 mins.	ISBN 4-7700-1785-5
Volume III:	Text	paperback, 136 pages	ISBN 4-7700-1786-3
	Tapes	three audio cassettes, 195 mins.	ISBN 4-7700-1787-1
Volume IV:	Text	paperback, 152 pages	ISBN 4-7700-1788-X
	Tapes	three audio cassettes, 195 mins.	ISBN 4-7700-1789-8

日本語をハナス！
HANDY JAPANESE!　*Tom Gally*
Surviving with the Basics

Teaches enough language skills to communicate in everyday situations. Ideal for travelers, business people, and beginning students.

Paperback with audio cassette, 160 pages, ISBN 4-7700-1748-0

日本語で歌おう！
SING JAPANESE!　*Peter Tse*
The Fun Approach to Studying Japanese

Learn to croon popular Japanese standards with this innovative guide to the world of *karaoke*. Includes a 50-min. prerecorded cassette with twelve songs. For beginners and intermediate students.

Paperback with audio cassette, 144 pages, ISBN 4-7700-1866-5

手書き日本語読本
A READER OF HANDWRITTEN JAPANESE　*P. G. O'Neill*

100 pieces of correspondence illustrate the many styles of handwritten Japanese in common use—from clearly written characters to very demanding cursive script.

Paperback, 268 pages, ISBN 4-7700-1663-8

新聞の経済面を読む
READING JAPANESE FINANCIAL NEWSPAPERS
Association for Japanese-Language Teaching

An innovative and comprehensive textbook for business people who need direct access to the financial pages of Japanese newspapers.

Paperback, 388 pages, ISBN 0-87011-956-7

敬語読本
MINIMUM ESSENTIAL POLITENESS　*Agnes M. Niyekawa*
A Guide to the Japanese Honorific Language

Explains how to use polite and honorific Japanese, emphasizing how to avoid unintentional rudeness. Indispensable for business and everyday conversation.

Paperback, 168 pages, ISBN 4-7700-1624-7

Innovative Workbooks for Learning Japanese Kana & Kanji.

ひらがながんばって！
HIRAGANA GAMBATTE!   *Deleece Batt*
An entertaining and effective illustrated workbook for younger learners. Clever mnemonic devices make learning the *hiragana* syllabary fun and easy.
Paperback, 112 pages, ISBN 4-7700-1793-6

カタカナがんばって！
KATAKANA GAMBATTE!   *Deleece Batt*
This new, interactive workbook teaches *katakana* with *manga*-style art and nearly 100 mini-articles on Japanese society and culture.
Paperback, 112 pages, ISBN 4-7700-1881-9

ひらがな
LET'S LEARN HIRAGANA   *Yasuko Kosaka Mitamura*
A well-tested, step-by-step program for individual study of the *hiragana* syllabary.
Paperback, 72 pages, ISBN 0-87011-709-2

カタカナ
LET'S LEARN KATAKANA   *Yasuko Kosaka Mitamura*
The companion volume for learning the *katakana* syllabary used for foreign words and new terms.
Paperback, 88 pages, ISBN 0-87011-719-X

速習かなワークブック
KANA FOR BUSY PEOPLE   *Association for Japanese-Language Teaching*
Through simultaneous use of the eyes, ears and hands, this text and audio cassette tape makes learning *kana* easier for adult beginners.
Paperback with audio cassette, 80 pages, ISBN 4-7700-1616-6

日本のかな
JAPANESE KANA WORKBOOK   *P. G. O'Neill*
A systematic introduction to *hiragana* and *katakana* for beginning students.
Paperback, 128 pages, ISBN 0-87011-039-X

はじめての漢字リーダー
KANJI FROM THE START   *Martin Lam and Kaoru Shimizu*
A basic-level reader which teaches *kanji* reading and writing skills in 12 graded lessons. Includes a grammar glossary and index, and Japanese-English and English-Japanese word lists.
Paperback, 384 pages, ISBN 4-7700-1936-X

常用漢字完全ガイド
THE COMPLETE GUIDE TO EVERYDAY KANJI
Yaeko S. Habein and Gerald B. Mathias
An exhaustive guide to the 1,945 most frequently used Sino-Japanese characters in the Japanese language.
Paperback, 344 pages, ISBN 4-7700-1509-7

KODANSHA NIHONGO FOLKTALES SERIES
やさしい日本語教室シリーズ

Hiroko C. Quackenbush, Series Editor
An innovative series of colorfully illustrated readers for practicing the *hiragana* syllabary. Each story is presented in Japanese, and includes an English translation and notes on usage and culture.

ANIMAL FABLES イソップどうわ

A series of traditional European folk tales told in Japanese offer a fun way to master *hiragana*.
Paperback, 32 pages, ISBN 4-7700-1794-4

CINDERELLA シンデレラ

The familiar story of Cinderella is told in Japanese for those not so familiar with *hiragana*.
Paperback, 32 pages, ISBN 4-7700-1796-0

THE GRATEFUL CRANE つるのおんがえし

A beautiful young girl brings a series of miracles to a poor farmer and his wife.
Paperback, 32 pages, ISBN 4-7700-1761-8

MOMOTARO, THE PEACH BOY ももたろう

An old couple find an amazing baby boy in a giant peach.
Paperback, 32 pages, ISBN 4-7700-1760-X

THE RUNAWAY RICEBALL おむすびころりん

A kindly old farmer finds a kingdom of mice and it leads to adventure.
Paperback, 32 pages, ISBN 4-7700-1762-6

THE STORY OF SNOW WHITE しらゆきひめ

A familiar fairy tale told in Japanese for those not so familiar with *hiragana*.
Paperback, 32 pages, ISBN 4-7700-1795-2

The best-selling language course is now even better!

改訂版　コミュニケーションのための日本語　全3巻

JAPANESE FOR BUSY PEOPLE　Revised Edition

Association for Japanese-Language Teaching (AJALT)

The leading textbook for conversational Japanese has been improved to make it easier than ever to teach and learn to speak Japanese.

- Transition to advancing levels is more gradual.
- English-Japanese glossary added to each volume.
- Short *kanji* lessons introduced in Volume I.
- Clearer explanations of grammar.
- Shorter, easy-to-memorize dialogues.

Volume I

Teaches the basics for communication and provides a foundation for further study.

- Additional appendices for grammar usage.

Text	paperback, 232 pages	ISBN 4-7700-1882-7
Tapes	three 40-min. audio cassettes	ISBN 4-7700-1883-5
Compact Discs	two 60-min. CD's	ISBN 4-7700-1909-2
Workbook	paperback, 182 pages	ISBN 4-7700-1907-6
Workbook Tapes	two 50-min. audio cassettes	ISBN 4-7700-1908-4
Japanese Teacher's Manual	paperback, 160 pages	ISBN 4-7700-1906-8

Volume II & Volume III

Teaches the basic language skills necessary to function in a professional environment.

- Original Volume II has been divided into two separate volumes.
- New, larger type size is easier to read.

Volume II		Volume III	
Text, paperback, 232 pages	ISBN 4-7700-1884-3	Text, paperback, 240 pages	ISBN 4-7700-1886-X
Three 80-min. audio cassettes	ISBN 4-7700-1885-1	Three 80-min. audio cassettes	ISBN 4-7700-1887-8

HIRAGANA

あ	い	う	え	お
か	き	く	け	こ
さ	し	す	せ	そ
た	ち	つ	て	と
な	に	ぬ	ね	の
は	ひ	ふ	へ	ほ
ま	み	む	め	も
や	(い)	ゆ	(え)	よ
ら	り	る	れ	ろ
わ	(い)	(う)	(え)	を
ん				

きゃ	きゅ	きょ
しゃ	しゅ	しょ
ちゃ	ちゅ	ちょ
にゃ	にゅ	にょ
ひゃ	ひゅ	ひょ
みゃ	みゅ	みょ

りゃ	りゅ	りょ

が	ぎ	ぐ	げ	ご
ざ	じ	ず	ぜ	ぞ
だ	ぢ	づ	で	ど
ば	び	ぶ	べ	ぼ
ぱ	ぴ	ぷ	ぺ	ぽ

ぎゃ	ぎゅ	ぎょ
じゃ	じゅ	じょ

びゃ	びゅ	びょ
ぴゃ	ぴゅ	ぴょ